YOU SHOULD *REALLY*
WRITE A B

YOU SHOULD *REALLY*
WRITE A BOOK

How to Write, Sell, and

Market Your Memoir

Regina Brooks *and* Brenda Lane Richardson

ST. MARTIN'S GRIFFIN ☙ NEW YORK

YOU SHOULD *REALLY* WRITE A BOOK: HOW TO WRITE, SELL, AND MARKET YOUR MEMOIR. Copyright © 2012 by Regina Brooks and Brenda Lane Richardson. All rights reserved. Printed in the United States of America. For information, address St. Martin's Press, 175 Fifth Avenue, New York, N.Y. 10010.

www.stmartins.com

Design by Richard Oriolo

Library of Congress Cataloging-in-Publication Data

Brooks, Regina.
    You should *really* write a book : how to write, sell, and market your memoir / Regina Brooks, Brenda Lane Richardson.
        p. cm.
        ISBN 978-0-312-60934-4 (pbk.)
        ISBN 978-1-250-01566-2 (e-book)
    1. Autobiography—Authorship.   2. Authorship—Marketing.
I. Richardson, Brenda Lane.   II. Title.
    CT25.B76 2012
    808'.06692—dc23   2012014629

First Edition: August 2012

10 9 8 7 6 5 4 3 2 1

With love to Tiger, who was born with a writer's heart.

—B.L.R.

For my mother, Nolia M. Brooks

They say we earn our living by what we do, but we make a life with what we give.

Thank you for giving my story *life*—and my life *story*.

—R.B.

CONTENTS

This book could not have been written without Regina Brooks, my agent and friend. I am also enormously grateful to Daniela Rapp, editor for St. Martin's, for her encouragement and passion for this subject. Thanks be to God for my husband, the Reverend Doctor W. Mark Richardson, our sons, H.P. and Mark Jr., our daughter, Carolyn, and our grandson, Tiger. —B.L.R.

To Julie Silver from The Harvard Writers Course (www.harvardwriters.com), thank you for providing a platform. Listening to doctors' stories gave me the spark to write this book. To Jane Friedman, you are my kindling. Thanks for being a sounding board for crafting this idea. To Brenda, thank you for being the fire keeper. With your relentless research, you skillfully gathered all the literary embers needed to bring this book to life. I couldn't have done this without you. To Daniela Rapp, my editor, your enthusiasm and belief in this book provided much-needed fuel. Thank you for your patience and incisive input. This project is all the better because of you. To Adam Janusz, my cover designer, thank you for helping me to see that light comes in so many hues and shines in all directions. And to Katharine Sands, who always reminds me to feed my inner flame.

Thanks to my dad, Robert R. Brooks, my mom, Nolia M. Brooks, and my sister, Vivian A. Hariharan, and to all my friends who are my family. Thanks to the St. Martin's team of professionals: designer Michelle McMillian and publicist Katie Ginda. Finally, to the Serendipity Literary Agency staff; your assistance and teamwork provided space for me to work on this project.—R.L.B.

YOU SHOULD *REALLY*
WRITE A BOOK

INTRODUCTION

•

More Than an Interesting Story

T'S SPRING IN BOSTON AND I AM SITTING WITH A PANEL OF other publishing professionals, listening to an accomplished and elegantly groomed young woman who, hoping to get published, is delivering the final book pitch of the day. She describes a time that left her praying that she would die, and she had tried to, and yet, here she is. Hoping to inspire others with a memoir of prevailing over impossible circumstances, she is one of scores of conferees attending Harvard Medical School's workshop, "Publishing Books, Memoirs, and Other Creative Non-Fiction."

This annual course, attended by participants of various professional backgrounds, including Harvard Medical School grads, surely brings together some of the smartest aspiring writers in the country. I am one of several literary agents among a larger group of publishing professionals invited to help individuals strengthen their writing chops and polish the seventy-second story pitches that they hope to one day see expanded into books.

And what of the young would-be writer? After listening attentively to our advice and encouragement, this young woman, whose personal details have been changed for the purpose of anonymity, returned to the audience, joining other conferees, leaving me deeply moved by her presentation. Despite her arresting presence and the dramatic events in her life, I would not be willing to wager whether her story will ever be transformed into a manuscript that I, or any agent, can sell to an editor for publication.

After fifteen years of listening to pitches and reading thousands of query letters and first chapters, one of the things I know for sure is that just because something interesting happened to someone doesn't mean that she has the makings of a memoir. In today's book business, a good story simply isn't enough.

People may have told you that the events in your life have been so dramatic that you should really write a book. The challenge, though, is not only how to write the story and make it readable, but how to sell and market it, too. While this book does not aim to give you line-by-line writing, editing, or structural advice, it is designed to show you how to turn your dream of writing a published memoir into a reality, from conceiving the story to selling and marketing it.

"Writing," "selling," and "marketing" are the operative words here. Most people assume that it's best to write a memoir first and then consider how to sell and market it. But these days, that's a counterproductive idea. Working through *You Should* Really *Write a Book* can make the difference between producing a manuscript written to appeal to friends and relatives versus one that can convince an agent to invest energy and time on your behalf in trying to sell it to an acquisitions editor for publication.

I'm aware that many memoirists write for the sake of posterity, while others write to reexamine their past and heal from traumatic experiences. A parent or grandparent might write a memoir to pass on familial information. Someone working with a therapist might write a memoir for the purpose of resolving hurtful experiences.

Some may choose to self-publish, or may have no desire to work with an agent or a publishing house. The good news for them is that with the growing popularity of electronic books (e-books) and self-publishing, it has become easier for authors to get their work produced without going through traditional publishers.

The nontraditional route may prove fruitful to some, including Laurel Saville, who chronicled her mother's downward trajectory, from beauty queen to homeless murder victim, in a 2009 self-published memoir.* A year later, when Saville advertised in a *Publishers Weekly* listing of two hundred self-published titles, the magazine selected her book for a capsulized review. Amazon.com then offered to republish the book. Saville reportedly struck a deal with the online bookseller—sans literary agent—and without receiving an advance, as she would have with a traditional publisher. The retitled *Unraveling Anne* (AmazonEncore: 2011) was made available directly to the site's buyers.

Saville is far from the first self-published author to work the nontraditional route via Amazon. By December 2011, thirty authors of various genres had each sold more than 100,000 copies of their books via Amazon's Kindle self-publishing program, with a dozen others selling more than 200,000 copies, according to *The Wall Street Journal*. Sara Burleton began selling her 2010 self-published story, *Why Me?*, as one of Amazon's Kindle offerings. Her coming-of-age story, which recounts the severe physical and mental abuse she suffered at the hands of her mother, became a *New York Times* e-book bestseller. The measure of these publisher-bypassing deals and similar ventures will be watched closely in the marketplace.

Traditionally printed books and electronic versions are often portrayed

*Saville's book was originally entitled *Postmortem* (iUniverse.com: 2009).

as having an adversarial relationship, but as Robert Darnton explains in *The Chronicle of Higher Education*, while the sale of e-books doubled in 2010, "there are indications that the sale of printed books has increased at the same time. The enthusiasm for e-books may have stimulated reading in general, and the market as a whole seems to be expanding." Worldwide, Darnton also points out, one million printed books were expected to be produced in 2011, a figure not including those printed by nontraditional methods.

Nontraditional methods include self-published titles. I often meet and teach authors who have taken this kind of independent route. More than 133,000 self-published titles were released in 2011, up from 51,237 in 2006, according to *The Wall Street Journal*. With a riveting story line captured on *60 Minutes*, Sibel Edmonds might have easily been picked up by a trade publisher for her whistle-blowing face-off with the FBI, but she self-published her book *Classified Woman: The Sibel Edmonds Story*. Some authors also earn money by distributing books on their own. And it is not just Amazon that is offering e-book opportunities. As a *USA Today* article pointed out, an author can digitally format her own manuscript, "set a price, and sell it to readers through a variety of online retailers and devices." The reading audience is vast, and there is room for mavericks. What remains unchanged is that working through literary agents and traditional publishing houses is still considered the gold standard.

If that is your aim, it's important to recognize that there is a world of difference between memoirs and commercial memoirs. *You Should Really Write a Book* is essential reading if you're hoping to create a commercially viable memoir in today's vastly changed publishing industry. This book is written primarily for writers, both novices and established authors with memoirs in progress, who may be looking for a competitive edge after experiencing rejection in the marketplace. Writing coaches, editors, and marketing professionals hoping to encourage authors to bring their ideas to fruition may also want to recommend this work.

The days are long gone when publishing professionals were willing to purchase a manuscript because it's based on a compelling experience or even because it's well written. With eyes focused on the bottom line, today's agents and editors look for authors who not only write well and have memorable story ideas (which are called "hooks" in the industry), but those who bring an established audience along, too. Having an "audience" means that the author has developed a "platform." As the word suggests, a platform is something that elevates you over others, a way of making your voice heard, whether through cyberspace or in the traditional media (or better, a combination of both).

Today's standard for successful book sales is pretty much the same among the big publishing houses. Typically, editors want to be able to show sales of a minimum of ten thousand units. While some books never reach that figure, editors want to at least feel confident that they can move that number. Smaller houses have lower minimums.

You Should Really *Write a Book* will help you conceptualize and strategize campaigns that cause buzz, fueling word of mouth and boosting your chances of attracting attention in the publishing world and beyond. In workshops, I teach writers the importance of extending their content into other sales areas. After all, a memoir might become the basis of a film or inspire a clothing line, which in turn fuels book sales.

GOING VIRTUAL

Many writers are startled to learn that they should build an online fan base before, during, and after writing a memoir. The term "platform" describes the ways you reach out to people—such as a campus radio show, lecture tour, popular blog—and the term also refers to people interested in what you write, as if they allowed you to stand on their shoulders, elevating you as you raise your literary voice. Those people include friends, family, and colleagues, and especially others you've drawn into your orbit by networking.

Platform building doesn't have to be a distraction. A fan base can feed creativity. Working with interested colleagues can be like conversing with a focus group.

At my agency, Serendipity Literary, I depend on social media experts, such as Foladé Bell, to keep me updated on social marketing trends. I asked Foladé to share some of her thoughts about the importance of authors building readerships, and using social media to create community. She began by pointing out that as the publishing landscape changes, authors need to recognize that the people formerly known as the audience have broken the fourth wall. "They now have a voice," said Foladé. "Media is no longer being held by a gatekeeper, and instead is being driven by the best aggregators of information, who share through Twitter, Facebook, LinkedIn, Brazen Careerist, Pinterest, Quora, Instagram, Stumbleupon, etcetera."

Foladé cautions that it's a bad idea to use these tools to air your frustrations with publishers, editors, or your followers. Your brand is about your work and isn't something you want associated with negativity. And while we're on that subject, Foladé concludes, "Keep the social media you participate in for your work separate from your personal networking with family and friends. Of course, you want them to follow what you're doing and recommend your work to others, but your brand is your business and the community that you're building around it should have the focus that a publisher would have in marketing your work."

No matter where you may be in the writing process, if you're not already active on at least one popular platform, this may be the time to get started. At the time of this writing plenty of authors use Facebook. There may be no better reminder of the power of this social networking Web site than *Revolution 2.0: The Power of the*

People Is Greater Than the People in Power: A Memoir (Houghton Mifflin Hartcourt: 2012), by Wael Ghonim. The Egyptian-born author, a relatively unknown Google executive, created the Facebook page "We Are All Khaled Said," to protest the beating death of young man at the hands of Egyptian police. Ghonim's social networking activism helped to launch his country's revolution, sending protesters out in Cairo's Tahrir Square, eventually leading to the resignation of President Hosni Mubarak and the dissolution of the ruling party. There is a wide array of social networking sites available. You'll have to be the judge of where to seek out fans, and this decision may depend on subject matter. For instance, if you are writing about war experiences, you may have specific sites in mind that attract those interested in the military. Or perhaps your subject matter will lend itself to the blogging site Tumblr, Yahoo user groups, bulletin boards, Google+, or e-commerce sites. Novice writers may find that it's best to use only one or two sites, to allow ample time for developing a manuscript.

If you're already an active social networker, you may reconsider what to write, after you determine whether you need a mission statement. My coauthor, Brenda Lane Richardson, and I often recommend writing a paragraph-long mission statement that authors can frame and keep nearby as a guide while writing posts. To begin, list the most important lessons based on your literary subject and, keeping in mind that consumers drive the market, stick to ideas that can help your readers. Here is an example: "Grief can be passed down in families." Or perhaps you prefer a statement of intent, such as: "I want others to know the truth about this insidious disease." When you've finished, if any of your ideas sound repetitive, keep the most salient ones and get rid of the others. Prioritize by identifying the three most important messages.

Combine these into a paragraph that conveys what you want to relay. You might want to frame your mission statement, and keep it within your line of vision as you write.

....

Why does *You Should* Really *Write a Book* focus solely on writing, selling, and marketing memoirs, as opposed to other genres? Well, judging from what I have observed in writing workshops, conferences, and online discussions, people not only want to read memoirs, they also want to learn how to write and sell them, too. In a book dedicated to the continuing fascination with the genre, *Memoir: A History* (Riverhead: 2009), author Ben Yagoda pointed out that the number of autobiographical works published in four years had increased by 400 percent.

Another sign of the memoir's continuing popularity is the success of *Smith Magazine*'s book series of six-word memoirs. From around the world folks continue to log into the magazine's Web site (http://www .smithmag.net/sixwordbook) contributing nanomemoirs, such as Nikki Beland's, "Catholic school backfired. Sin is in!" and nine-year-old Hannah Davies's, "Cursed with cancer. Blessed by friends," as well as newly dumped Zak Nelson's, "I still make coffee for two."*

That there is an audience for commercial memoirs is also evident in the Best Sellers section of *The New York Times Book Review*,** in which listings are based on weekly sales reports from independent and chain bookstores and wholesalers throughout the United States. The number of memoir/autobiographical bestsellers on *The New York Times* lists waxes and wanes. Memoirs have at times comprised half of the titles on the paperback top-20 nonfiction list.

On April 10, 2011, of the top fifteen titles on *The New York Times*

*These six-word samplings are excerpted from *Not Quite What I Was Planning: Six-Word Memoirs, by Writers Famous and Obscure* (Harper Perennial: 2008), Larry Smith and Rachel Fershleiser, editors.
**U.S. publishing professionals often discuss *The New York Times Book Review*. According to 2010 sales figures, in that year the magazine had reached an audience of an estimated 2.7 million consumers who purchased more than 34.5 million books for themselves and others.

hardcover nonfiction listing, four were memoirs, but only one was written by a widely known figure: *Life*, by rock musician Keith Richards, with James Fox. That Richards's book experienced success in the marketplace is not surprising. People of renown have national fan bases and well-oiled marketing machines that provide them with built-in platforms, which help attract the attention needed to sell books. Fortunately for the rest of us, celebrity isn't the sole or most important criteria for selling personal stories. The remaining bestselling hardcover memoir titles on that April 10, 2011, listing included Joshua Foer's *Moonwalking with Einstein*, Gabrielle Hamilton's *Blood, Bones, and Butter*, and Amy Chua's *Battle Hymn of the Tiger Mother*.

Competing with the rich and famous for attention might ordinarily seem like fighting a losing battle, but that's not necessarily so with memoirs. This genre attracts readers drawn to the idea that the protagonist could be the man or woman next door, and they can imagine themselves walking in that person's shoes. With the industry fighting to survive, and editors making tough decisions about what will be published and in what form, the paperback nonfiction list has emerged as a bastion of literary populism.

As for hardcovers, publishers are like Broadway producers who boost ticket sales by casting celebrities in theatrical productions. Book publishers often try the same tactics when it comes to hardcover autobiographical/memoir works. Publishers operate on a thin margin. If a company prices a hardcover at twenty-six dollars, about half that amount goes to a bookseller like Barnes & Noble. The remaining revenue pays for the book's printing, storage, and shipping, as well as copyediting, cover design, typesetting, marketing, and office overhead. And let's not forget the author's percentage, 10 percent on hardcovers; often a higher percentage for celebrities, bestselling writers, and occasional newcomers deemed to have highly promising sales potential. After shelling out money up front, the publisher is left with a profit of a little over three dollars per hardcover unit.

Just in case you're wondering how agents are paid, we generally do not make money on a manuscript until we have sold it to a publisher, and then we get a 15 percent commission on our authors' book earnings, which include advances. An "advance" is the lump sum the publisher pays before a book is published and that the author doesn't have to repay unless the book fares well. Publishers track the author's share of earnings ("royalties") and don't pay the author again unless the advance is "earned out" or repaid to the company. This allows the publisher to recoup the advance. In reality, few authors ever earn their advances back, so publishers usually write off these sums as a loss.

Publishing houses largely profit from authors whose earnings surpass repayment of advances and then continue selling. Keep in mind the nature of business is to earn a profit, and most publishers are not engaged in money-losing enterprises. A survey of the publishing landscape found a 5.6 percent increase in 2010 net revenues, which marked a 4.1 percent increase over 2008.

Why Memoirs from Relative Unknowns Are Often Published as Paperbacks

The rise of the trade paperback was a direct result of the leaner, meaner publishing model. The smaller mass-market paperback has long been produced in volume and can be sold at a relatively low cost. But their larger trade paperback cousins—viewed by consumers as having more cachet—can be sold at a higher price point. Until recent years trade paperbacks were not reviewed as often as the hardcover titles, but that has changed. Reviewers now treat many trade paperbacks as they do hardcovers.

Historically, softcover books have cost publishers less than hardcovers to print, store, and ship. Trade softcover is the realm in which editors are more likely to take a chance on unknown authors, and the reason that the paperback bestsellers territory has developed a more democratic feel. The downside for author and agent is that there's less money to be made here than with hardcovers. Advances are generally smaller, paperbacks sell at half to one third of hardcover prices, and authors earn about 7.5 percent on each paperback sold.

As for the rapidly expanding field of e-books, the terrain is new enough for standards to be in flux. With e-books, publishers don't have to pay for printing, storage, or shipping—although there are additional operating and technical costs. This may prove to be a plus for authors. Agents often ask for royalties of 25 percent or more for their authors. Released concurrently with hardcovers, e-books offer consumers a less costly option and have surged in popularity. As a nod to this trend, *The New York Times* introduced e-book bestseller listings in 2011. E-books are offering new opportunities for authors, some whose older works are finding a new generation of readers. Miklos Nyiszli's story, *Auschwitz: A Doctor's Eyewitness Account*, published in the U.S. in 1960 by Fawcett Crest, was reissued by Skyhorse in 2011 and became an e-book bestseller. E-books are also offering opportunities for newspapers and magazine and information sites to pump up their bottom lines. *The New Yorker, Vanity Fair, The Huffington Post, Politico, The New York Times, Boston Globe,* and ABC News have all published e-books.

Trade paperbacks and e-books may be cheaper to produce, but no matter the form, editors still focus on the bottom line, and are selective in signing authors. Those demonstrating willingness to work at getting their books to the top of the publishing pyramid are more likely to be chosen than those who might, for instance, shy away from the public eye.

While the industry continues to grapple with profound shifts in book reading and buying behaviors, one aspect remains unchanged. In this business, as in most, consumers drive the market. In an era of belt-tightening, cost-conscious book buyers are more likely to take a chance on an untested author if the price is right. And eureka, some relatively unknown authors have struck publishing gold.

Memoir Bestsellers by Previously "Unknown" Authors

The most intriguing aspect of *The New York Times* April 10, 2011, bestseller nonfiction paperback listings is that among the top 20, half were memoirs, and while four were written by people of renown,* the other six authors were relative unknowns. These authors' names and books include Todd Burpo and Lynn Vincent's *Heaven is for Real: A Little Boy's Astounding Story of His Trip to Heaven and Back* (Thomas Nelson: 2010), a boy's account of meeting Jesus and angels, which sold over three million copies. Don Piper and Cecil Murphey's *90 Minutes in Heaven: A True Story of Death and Life* (Revell: 2004), a minister's story of celestial encounters, which remained on the bestsellers list for more than 250 weeks. Greg Mortenson and David Oliver Relin's *Three Cups of Tea* (Penguin: 2007) on an American former nurse building schools for Pakistani and Afghani children, which sold more than four million copies. Elizabeth Gilbert's *Eat, Pray, Love: One Woman's Search for Everything Across Italy, India and Indonesia* (Penguin: 2006) about a yearlong quest, sold more than six million copies. Tucker Max's *I Hope They Serve Beer in Hell* (Citadel: 2006), the tales of a proudly inebriated womanizer, was made into a film. Finally, Ron Hall and Denver Moore, with Lynn Vincent's *Same Kind of Different as Me* (Thomas Nelson: 2006), is the story of the relationship forged between a homeless wanderer and an international arts dealer, which has been optioned for a film.

Brenda Lane Richardson and I refer to Relatively Unknown authors or "RUs" as a way of reminding ourselves of that moment when so many carefully planned efforts of countless writers are foiled. Agents and editors, deluged with submissions, only have a stretch of moments to review work by relatively unknown writers. But people in this business

---

*Those celebrity memoirs include: Jeannette Walls's *The Glass Castle*, Patti Smith's *Just Kids*, and Chelsea Handler's *Are You There, Vodka? It's Me, Chelsea*, and also by Handler, *My Horizontal Life*.

remain a hopeful lot, and even the most overworked publishing professionals begin reading with an unformed question: "*Are you* going to be a writer I should know?" Thus, the term "RU" was incorporated into our nomenclature. It is our hope that Relative Unknowns working through this book will be able to answer with an unqualified "Yes."

It's also important to state what has not been included in *You Should Really Write a Book*. There is no information about how to write a celebrity memoir. This book was not written for politicians, movie stars, supermodels, or rock singers. It was designed for RUs, people generally not widely known or recognized outside their own circles. It is especially for those who do not have household names. Our aim is to level the playing field for those who are not superrich, or famous, or powerful. Written to give you a competitive advantage, this book will teach you to think like publishing professionals, so you will know what they will expect of you.

A MARKETPLACE SURVIVAL TIP

Writing a commercial memoir requires you to hone your craft while simultaneously keeping an eye out for what's happening in the publishing industry. It's easy to get distracted with so much information and news to sift through. With that in mind, I am delighted to direct your attention to Serendipity Literary agency's curated online newspaper, *The Book Addict Daily* (paper.li/serendipitylit/1309637263 [2]), where you can find articles, blog posts, relevant tweets, and updates focused on book publishing. I invite you to engage with us by joining the conversation.

You may also be interested in the Web site for Publishers Marketplace (www.publishersmarketplace.com). This resource offers the lowdown on which manuscripts have sold, within what price range, and the names of the authors, agents, and publishing houses involved. You can subscribe to the site's free daily e-mail newsletter, or another affordable option offering a wider range of selections, including agent contacts and book reviews. (By the way, book reviews can be helpful in your quest to write and sell a commercial memoir. Often penned by experienced writers and editors, book reviews are instructive, offering the dos and don'ts of polished writing.) If you're new to the book business, and scrolling through the site leaves you feeling overwhelmed, try reading a bit daily at first.

You can also subscribe to the longstanding and highly respected (sometimes called the bible of publishing) *Publishers Weekly*, a trade news magazine that targets publishers, librarians, booksellers, and agents. Literary editors keep an eye out for *PW* recommendations—as do purchasing librarians and bookstore buyers. A starred review in one of these pages is highly valued in the industry. For more information and a sampling of the company's free online offerings visit www.publishersweekly.com.

Finally, the biweekly, more cerebral magazine, *The New York Review of Books,* is chock full of articles about books, culture, and current affairs. Information on this thought-provoking publication can be found online at www.nybooks.com.

By familiarizing yourself with publishing culture, you won't seem like a neophyte when you reach out to an agent or editor. By the way, it's best not to refer to your work as a book until just before it becomes one. You may want to refer to your nascent work as a manuscript. If you approach a publishing professional about your "book," you put yourself at risk of sounding presumptuous.

If you're a longtime fan of memoirs you may already know that they are among the most maligned of genres. Critics so often denigrate these books that in January 2011, when Neil Genzlinger at *The New York*

Times wrote a highly critical essay, "The Problem With Memoirs," it seemed like business as usual. Noting the surge of titles in what he calls an, "absurdly bloated genre," Genzlinger called out, "people you've never heard of, writing uninterestingly about the unexceptional, apparently not realizing how commonplace their little wrinkle is or how many other people have already written about it. Memoirs have been disgorged by virtually everyone who has ever had cancer, been anorexic, battled depression, lost weight. By anyone who has ever taught an underprivileged child, adopted an underprivileged child or been an underprivileged child. By anyone who was raised in the '60s, '70s or '80s, not to mention the '50s, '40s or '30s. Owned a dog. Ran a marathon. Found religion. Held a job."

If you're feeling discouraged by Genzlinger's criticism, it might cheer you to know that despite this derision, many of his colleagues at the *Times* have been sitting at computers tapping out their own memoirs. From 2010 through early 2012, *New York Times* current and former journalists wrote at least eleven published memoirs. A list follows.

Former Boston bureau chief Carey Goldberg, with Beth Jones and Pamela Ferdinand, *Three Wishes: A True Story of Good Friends, Crushing Heartbreak, and Astonishing Luck on Our Way to Love and Motherhood* (Little, Brown and Company: 2010), on the bond they formed in their quest for motherhood.

Foreign editor of the magazine, Scott Malcomson, *Generation's End: A Personal Memoir of American Power After 9/11* (Potomac Books: 2010), examines the author's and the country's response to the 9/11 attacks; National Legal Correspondent John Swartz, *Short: Walking Tall When You're Not At All* (Flashpoint: 2010), survival tips for the vertically challenged; Religion Columnist Mark Oppenheimer, *Weisenheimer: A Childhood Subject to Debate* (Free Press: 2010), recounts the exploits of a wordsmith; retired reporter John Darnton, *Almost a Family* (Knopf: 2011), examines the life of his deceased father, who was a *New York Times* correspondent; Culture Reporter David Itzkoff, *Cocaine's Son* (Villard: 2011), reflects on how his life was impacted by his father's addiction;

Health Columnist Jane Gross, *A Bittersweet Season: Caring for Our Aging Parents—and Ourselves* (Knopf: 2011), shares the lessons she learned in caring for her aging mother; in former sports columnist Robert Lipsyte's *An Accidental Sportswriter* (Ecco: 2011), a formerly wimpy kid grapples with jock culture's influence on business, politics, and family life; in blogger Lou Ureneck's *Cabin: Two Brothers, a Dream, and Five Acres in Maine* (Viking: 2011), the author reconnects with his sense of self and family by undertaking a rural building project; Executive Editor Jill Abramson, *The Puppy Diaries: Raising a Dog Named Scout* (Times Books: 2011), which is based on an online column, describes the author's unabashed love for a four-footed companion. Finally, there is also *House of Stone: A Memoir of Home, Family, and a Lost Middle East* (Houghton Mifflin: 2012), by the publication's acclaimed Mideast correspondent Anthony Shadid, who died on February 16, 2012, while on assignment in Syria.

That print journalists are contributing to this literary form would not surprise anyone who understands those working in this field. Journalists live or die professionally by the quality of their writing and research, and because they practice it regularly, it becomes second nature, a principal manner for expressing themselves.

Memoir writing exists between the borders of reportage and fiction. Please note, however, that memoir writing is neither of the two. Journalists are expected to report facts, while fiction writers create imagined situations. Facts and truth, subjects of great import, will be explored later in this work. Let it suffice to say for now that the subject of objective versus subjective truth has tripped up many a memoirist. Lee Gutkind, a professor at Arizona State University, explained in an interview on National Public Radio that truth is subjective in personal experience; it's a matter of how you recall your own life. Gutkind said, "It's *your* story, that's what a memoir is . . . It's your own personal truth, and is not necessarily factually accurate, and not necessarily the truth that other people have possessed."

Memoirists hail from many backgrounds. They work as executive assistants, teachers, financial executives, mechanics, and homemakers. What they share is a love of the written word. Some also work in such various writing fields as advertising copyeditors, book editors, writing teachers or students, poets, novelists, dramatists, and creators of TV shows and films. While leading workshops and seminars around the U.S. and beyond, I find that about 15–20 percent of the aspirants I speak with started off as print journalists.

I singled out print journalists intentionally. From my vantage point, television journalists don't seem to write as many memoirs as their print colleagues, perhaps because brevity is their watchword. Skilled at writing concise accounts for the purpose of enhancing visual images, some television journalists may not be eager to transition into lengthier narrative works. Of course, that is not by any means true for all television journalists, as some have written bestselling memoirs.*

Criteria for Choosing Memoirs to Discuss in This Book

With the splintering of audiences, consumers might view even some top-tier journalists as Relative Unknowns. But national TV and radio anchors and commentators, as well as some elite journalists at major newspapers and magazines aren't regarded as unknowns in the publishing industry. They're considered to have stronger platforms than their rank-and-file counterparts. That's certainly true of *New York Times* journalists.

You may notice that we often refer to *The New York Times* in this work. While we read books voraciously and discuss news stories and essays from various periodicals, as well as what's available strictly online, and on television and public radio, we pay particular attention to

---

*Memoirs by TV journalists include: former MSNBC.com gossip columnist Jeannette Walls's *The Glass Castle* (Scribner: 2005); former NBC anchor Tom Brokaw's *A Long Way From Home: Growing Up in the American Heartland* (Random House: 2002); Noticiero Univision news anchor Jorge Ramos's *No Borders: A Journalist's Search for Home* (Harper: 2003); and former CBS anchor Dan Rather's *The Camera Never Blinks: Adventures of a TV Journalist* (William Morrow: 1977).

the *Times* because it holds great significance in the publishing industry, for reasons that are geographical, historical, and cultural.

Since the nineteenth century, Manhattan has been the center of the U.S. publishing community. Despite a growing number of exceptions, most agents and publishers work in the New York metropolitan area. While *The New York Times* has grown into a national paper, it remains a cultural habit in the publishing community. Just as people around the world learn English, the "national language," for those hoping to sell and market books in the U.S., it's a good idea to read the *Times* as a lens through which you can view the publishing marketplace. That helps explain why the words "*New York Times* bestseller" or "*New York Times* bestselling author" on book jackets are considered to be honorifics.

One measure of the paper's gravitational force is made clear in a 2009 academic study, "Positive Effects of Negative Publicity." Researchers found that a positive review in *The New York Times* increases a book's sales between 32 and 52 percent. In contrast, a negative *New York Times* review of books written by established authors led to an estimated 15 percent decrease in sales. What surprised many is that negative reviews of relatively unknown authors had the opposite effect, increasing sales by 45 percent.

Fortunately for high-status journalists, including those writing for the *Times*, and for readers who enjoy their subsequent memoirs, their books are usually reviewed in the paper's literary supplement, with all the benefits that conveys. Additionally, when these journalists submit proposals or manuscripts, agents and editors are more likely to begin reading their works with the presumption that they are excellent writers. Since this book aims to level the playing field for RUs, it would be a mistake to include as role models those positioned to enjoy extra advantages. We therefore limited analytical discussions to memoirs written by those who begin without the benefit of high-wattage platforms.

Readers from all backgrounds can learn from *You Should Really Write a Book*. Even the most experienced writers come to realize that creating, selling, and marketing a memoir is more challenging than it appears.

The literary struggle for memoirists is learning to write imaginatively, while adhering to journalism's basic tenants, including developing areas of expertise. If you aren't writing daily, we hope you'll begin to do so. The following information can get you thinking about what to write.

HONING YOUR CRAFT

If you're trying to figure out what to include or omit in your story, learn the difference between a commercial memoir and an autobiography. It is especially important for RUs to understand the difference between the two, because if you tell a publishing professional that you're writing an autobiography, you risk being dismissed as a neophyte.

Before we explain the difference between the two, let's eliminate further confusion by getting the word "biography" out of the way. Authors of biographies write about the lives of others. In *Steve Jobs* (Simon & Schuster: 2011), Walter Isaacson offers insight into the life of the Apple entrepreneur, including his struggle with pancreatic cancer, which ultimately killed him.

What people seem to find most challenging is the difference between memoir and autobiography. Memoir is a genre unto itself, but it is related to autobiography. The two are kissing cousins that folks mistake as twins. Even those expected to know better have difficulty telling the difference. For instance, notice the subtitle of the bestselling *American Sniper: The Autobiography of the Most Lethal Sniper in U.S. Military History,* by Chris Kyle, with Scott McEwan and Jim DeFelice (William Morrow: 2012). Despite its subtitle, the story fits well within the boundaries of memoir form. While there are some childhood photos and childhood reminiscences, most of the story covers Kyle's experiences during his Iraq deployments and when he is home between tours.

Contributing to the confusion, the prefix "auto" means "self," and in both memoir and autobiography the author is writing about himself. Both are written from a first-person point of view. It becomes easier to tell the two apart if you contrast how the authors of each genre might describe their work. An autobiographer might say, "I'm writing about my entire life." A memoirist might say, "I'm writing about a period of my life."

Here's something else that might clear up the confusion. In autobiography, the author writes about herself as the main character, focusing much of the drama on herself. It is not unusual for memoirs however, to have more than one main character. *Life, On the Line: A Chef's Story of Chasing Greatness, Facing Death, and Redefining the Way We Eat* (Gotham: 2011) is told by Chef Grant Achatz and his business partner, Nick Kokonas.

When it comes to autobiography, think celebrity. If it's announced that someone is writing an autobiography, that's a signal that this person has spent serious mileage time in the spotlight. An autobiography is comprehensive and the story follows the trajectory of a life.

Editors almost universally insist that they will only publish an autobiography by someone whose "entire" life is of interest to many, usually someone with super-celebrity wattage. In the bestselling autobiography *Bossypants* (Reagan Arthur: 2011), Tina Fey writes of her humble roots in Pennsylvania and takes us through her career as a comedienne, actress, writer, and producer.

Published memoirs are often shorter in length than autobiographies (although there are exceptions) and have narrower parameters. They focus on areas of expertise and related events, as well as meaningful themes or periods in the author's life. In a memoir, if a writer tells of incidents outside the narrative framework, weaving into the story bits and pieces from other periods of his life, it's usually for the sake of putting into context incidents related to the book's specific theme and finite time period. A memoir is comprised of scenes that build upon one another and lead to a pivotal moment.

Gordon Warnock, senior literary agent for Andrea Hurst & Associates, weighed in via e-mail on the differences between the two genres. "Commercial memoir is not autobiography or chronicle. It is not a listing of every event that happened in your life from birth until the present. Commercial memoir should take one specific event or theme in your life, unpack it and present it in a continuous, cohesive narrative, much like a novel. It needs the same elements of tension, story arc, and character development to create an enjoyable reading experience."

Some memoirists use main titles to signal a time period. Let's consider for instance, adolescence, which is a popular focus in this genre. Acclaimed author Esmeralda Santiago chose the title *Almost a Woman* (Vintage: 1999) in her exploration of her adolescent life in the States, with roots in Puerto Rico. Former financial executive Jen Lancaster's comedic memoir subtitles suggest adolescent phases of her life: *Pretty in Plaid: A Life, A Witch, and a Wardrobe, or, the Wonder Years Before the Condescending, Egomaniacal, Self-Centered Smart-Ass Phase* (NAL: 2009).

....

Part II of this work includes six chapters on major memoir categories. No matter your subgenre, each chapter imparts information that can help you write, sell, and market your memoir, so it is to your advantage to read this book in its entirety.

Regularly occurring features throughout chapters three through seven include:

- **$$$ANALYSES:** This feature examines the three components necessary for success, including a hook, competent writing, and a platform. In this feature, each component is symbolized by dollar signs. Some bestsellers only have one of three components, but very few succeed without at least two.

- **TAKE THIS PERSONALLY:** Another continuing feature, this offers personal advice that a psychologically astute agent might offer a client. In these sections, the information is aimed at helping authors avoid self-defeating behaviors.

- **A MARKETPLACE SURVIVAL TIP:** This section offers information that will allow you to communicate effectively with those in the marketplace.

- **HONING YOUR CRAFT:** This section is designed to get you writing competently.

- **GOING VIRTUAL:** This includes social networking and marketing ideas.

Part III is comprised of two short chapters, offering collaboration advice for those working with ghostwriters or coauthors, and tips for contacting agents.

Brenda Lane Richardson and I look forward to hearing about your progress. It is no coincidence that I am collaborating with an award-winning journalist and author of ten books, who is also a New York University–trained social worker, specializing in memoir writing as a therapeutic modality. We are full and equal partners in the creation of this book, and enjoy sharing our experiences and knowledge about writing, publishing, and marketing matters. Thanks to Brenda's therapeutic specialization you will be encouraged to consider the emotional ramifications of unearthing what might be troubling memories. You can find her blog memoirhealing at our Web site www.youshouldreallywriteabook.co. We hope you'll find our work supportive of your efforts.

PART ONE

A GENRE UNTO ITSELF

One

Learning from Memoir's History

AS YOU ENVISION FANS AROUND THE WORLD READING AND discussing your work, a sign that you've made it to the top in today's highly competitive world of publishing, it might be tempting to skip this chapter about the history of the memoir. In focusing on your future, you might wonder why you should read about the past, especially as far back as A.D. 400. It might seem that someone putting a quill to parchment more than 1,600 years ago has nothing to do with selling a memoir that you're writing now. We beg to differ.

Reading about how memoirs were sold in the past has a great deal to do with the commercial viability of your manuscript today. There's actually truth to the maxim that you can't know where you're going if you don't know where you've been. It's important to look back at the early history of personal writing because events way back then set the stage for what's going to be required for your memoir to succeed today. So we want to take you back, all the way back.

Saint Augustine: One of the First Memoirists

During the late fourth and early fifth centuries, Augustine of Hippo, a Catholic bishop and theologian from Algeria, raised more than a few eyebrows when he wrote that his early life had been ruled by lust. In a series of books aptly entitled *Confessions*, he detailed his moral transgressions, including petty theft as a youngster, and later, having sex outside of marriage—lots of it and often, including with a mistress, with whom he had a child.

All of that came to an end, Augustine explained, when, while meditating in a garden, he heard the voice of a child urging him to read. Opening the Bible, Augustine's heart was opened to God. Today, Augustine—who was later named a saint—is considered one of the most important figures in the ancient Western church, and is credited with practically inventing the genre of autobiography. Initially, the term "memoir" was not widely used in publishing. Autobiographies were the antecedents to memoirs.

Confessions, written long before the invention of the printing press and at a time of widespread illiteracy, was recognized early on as being of such great spiritual and intellectual importance that scribes produced hand-written copies, which is one reason it is still around today to be read and discussed by leading scholars.

With a *mea culpa* to the saint, we plan to measure *Confessions* with the same yardstick that you will find throughout Part II, to help explain how and why some memoirs sell. Of course in the fifth century, the word "sell" when referring to books had a different meaning. There were no Amazon .com rankings, bestsellers lists, or Nielsen BookScan reports that detail how many copies of each book are selling in individual markets such as Los Angeles or Rhode Island. Sales activity back in the days of *Confessions* refers to what transpired to convince people that this was a work they wanted to read and discuss. In other words, we're interested in what generated the buzz that elevated this Algerian bishop's book above others.

What made *Confessions* a hit back then is connected to the same elements significant for selling a book today. We will describe these elements by prefacing the information with a dollar sign ($) to help alert you to what to look for in your own work if you're hoping editors will acquire your manuscript. Most bestselling memoirs have at least two out of three of the following elements: (1) $trong writing, (2) $trong hook, and (3) $trong platform. Beginning with the first element, let's examine Saint Augustine's narrative, using a rubric of 1–10 points per category.

$Writing Chops

Saint Augustine's early training was in rhetoric, at the time a major field of study. Trained in communication, he knew how to write and speak persuasively. In *Confessions* you feel St. Augustine's moments of sadness, his longings, and sense of loss and joy. Saint Augustine's work is still read widely and discussed by theologians, clerics, and lay people. Many continue to marvel that his story reflects their own interior lives, and that it was written with a touch of humor. This is the man who famously prayed, "Give me chastity and continence—but not yet." In other words, the man could write. His score on this count is 10 out of 10.

$Narrative Hook

The best way to understand a narrative hook is to consider how hooks are used as tools in everyday life. We use hooks to keep things in easy reach: an oven mat, keys, or a towel. Similarly, a narrative hook implies accessibility. Picture an acquisitions editor meeting with your literary agent. What would you want your agent to say right off the bat? What would make your story sound accessible in a few words? Hopefully it would be something that intrigues the editor and is considered memorable. It should come to mind easily and telegraph your story's appeal. Like a news report, a hook should be of interest to a great number of people.

A good narrative hook can be one sentence or a phrase that grabs a reader's interest, and explains the plot succinctly. Imagine that the hook to *Confessions* might have been, "From sinner to saint . . ." Crass, admittedly, but our guess is that even back in ancient societies there were folks like Nicole "Snooki" Polizzi and Mike "The Situation" Sorrentino (we sure hope so). As Stendhal pointed out in *Memoirs of an Egotist*, published posthumously in 1892, "Great success is not possible without a certain degree of shamelessness. . . ."

Although good timing isn't always necessary when trying to hook a reader, it can be helpful. But don't wait for the right time; make the time right. To understand the importance of timing, imagine using a real hook and trying to grab someone. It would make your job easier if someone was moving past just as you reached out.

GOING VIRTUAL

Given that by 2012 the newspaper industry was half as big as it had been seven years earlier, you might be tempted to believe that newspapers are history, but *au contraire*. While an estimated one-third of U.S. newsrooms have disappeared, other companies are continuing to cover their markets—in print and/or online—with fewer reporters while continuing to look for content (written by various writers, and that could mean you). Community newspapers and those with national footprints seem to be holding ground. And there are also more online news organizations, as well as newspaper editions using bloggers to keep the public informed on local stories. So in your effort to build a platform, don't ignore old media in favor of new. It can be beneficial to incorporate both in your plans. To that end, keep an eye on newspaper Web sites, because that's precisely what editors at understaffed organizations are doing: trolling the sites of established media, and searching for content and story ideas. Getting stories, essays, letters, reviews, or your blog into a newspaper can help you build an audience, especially if the publication will include your online contact information at the end of the piece.

Author Susan Gregory Thomas used newspapers to great effect in the marketing of her memoir *In Spite of Everything* (Random House: 2011). Three weeks before the book's publication, she was one of several people interviewed in a *New York Times* feature, "How Divorce Lost Its Cachet." The story and Gregory Thomas's book examined trends that suggest a reluctance to divorce among college-educated Generation Xers, in response to growing up in the shadow of the high rate of marital failures of their baby boomer parents. The feature story also ran on the paper's popular Web site, which has more than 34.5 million unique monthly visitors. Three days before the release of Thomas's memoir, one of her essays, "The Divorce Generation," ran in the paper with the largest U.S. weekly circulation, *The Wall Street Journal*. A week later, her book ranked an impressive 1,345 at Amazon. This ranking does not reflect sales on the site or in other retail outlets, but indicates the frequency by which a title is searched on Amazon.

Susan Gregory Thomas has written for a number of publications and surely has contacts in the media. Following are some suggestions for those hoping to replicate her success:

- Read local and national newspapers, print and/or online to keep up with stories, that might intersect with your work, providing the opening you need for writing a feature, or to interest an editor in developing a story around your topic.

- Identify which staffers cover topics that intersect with your interests. As you develop an expertise, write to these journalists and their editors, submitting stories or essays on your chosen subject, including interviews with experts.

The idea is to interest a journalist in a topic that might be the subject of an essay or feature, written by a staffer or perhaps by you (this might lead eventually to a review of your book, once it is published).

- Contacting a journalist is more effective with traditional mail. Journalists receive little snail mail. Busy with deadlines, they are unlikely to open mail with computer-generated labels and metered postage. Send a typed letter, no longer than two-thirds of a page, in a hand-addressed envelope with a postage stamp.

- Identify bloggers who cover your topic and offer to guest blog.

- Attempting to get into *The New York Times* is always worth a try, especially when the Sunday print edition has 1.35 million readers, and when so many publishing professionals relax over this paper.

- Pay particular attention to feature pages and Op-Ed sections of several major newspapers. You can find a listing by Googling "U.S. newspaper circulation."

- Market your book by weighing in on subjects you're knowledgeable about in the Letters to the Editor sections, or Op-Ed pages. A number of Web sites offer advice for crafting these pieces. If your Op-Ed piece touches upon issues in the news, that is a hook with a competitive edge.

Magazine features also have clout in the publishing industry. If you have honed your skills as a writer and have newspaper features to submit along with a feature story idea, submit your pieces to magazines. In April 2012 in *Vogue*, Dara-Lynn Weiss wrote of her efforts to get her seven-year-old daughter to slim down and created a firestorm, with some accusing her of fat-shaming her child. She also attracted a publisher's eye, and signed with Random House. Elif Batuman's highly lauded *The Possessed: Adventures with Russian Books and the People Who Read Them* (Granta: 2011) began as articles by the author that ran in *Harper's* and *The New Yorker*.

- If you are new to feature writing, don't rule out local city newspapers, as well as smaller regional papers in your pursuit of credentials. Free local publications can help you establish credibility. If an editor has run even one of your stories, the media is more likely to take you seriously. So start small, if necessary, and then move up. Later, when you query agents, include clips or links to some of your online features.

- Finally, consider attending a conference to meet journalists with your interests. For instance, if you're writing a religious memoir, visit the Religion Writers Web site: www.religionwriters.com.

Saint Augustine had timing in his favor. *Confessions* had no other real competition. In addition to it being among the first autobiographical works, it was all the more unique because it was written in the form of prayers. In offering the world an interior view of his life, Saint Augustine's candor strengthened his narrative hook. Consider today's clerics and the public faces they present to the world. Unless mired in scandal, they don't often talk about struggles in their lives. Imagine how shocking it must have been for a fifth-century bishop to discuss his lusty memories. If Barnes & Noble had been operating, readers would have lined up through the streets waiting to buy copies. Saint Augustine scores another 10-pointer, this time in the narrative hook category.

$Platform Strength

As discussed, a strong platform describes the ways in which a writer is visible or connected to a community of potential or actual readers. Back in his day, Saint Augustine raised his voice above others in his community, while remaining part of it. As a Christian bishop and a great communicator he had one of the highest platforms of his time—a pulpit. In that particular era of the Holy Roman Empire, church controversies stirred great passion, as they do today. What's more, Saint Augustine was said to have preached in the language of the common folks. Can Saint Augustine get a 10-pointer on his platform? Yes, he can, bringing him to a full 30 points overall. That heavenly score adds up to the makings of a bestseller. Compelling writing, strong hook, and prominent platform. Saint Augustine would have been a literary agent's dream.

We won't use the same yardstick to evaluate the bestselling writing potential of Benjamin Franklin, the founding father credited with writing the first autobiographical book in the United States. This has little to do with the fact that he took nineteen years to write *The Autobiography of Benjamin Franklin* and that he died before completing it, which would give any agent nightmares. No, Franklin gets little room on these pages because he was already an international celebrity by the time he started writing his autobiography. Since he emerged from the box with a built-in platform, he was decidedly not an RU.

Escaped slave Frederick Douglass was not an RU for long. After a cadre of abolitionists spread word about his book, *Narrative of the Life of Frederick Douglass, an American Slave*, which was published in 1845, he embarked on a speaking tour, and his book became highly controversial. After being asked to address a crowd of abolitionists, he stepped on a stage, found his voice, and learned the power of personal history. Unflinchingly honest, his work was viewed as so moving that racist critics fought back with the claim that it could not have been written by a black man. Douglass's *Narrative* sold 5,000 copies in four months; by 1847, 11,000 copies had been sold—a major achievement at a time of widespread illiteracy. The book continues to inspire and sell.

Two Noted Memoirists, Two Different Levels of Recognition

The success of the RUs is a fairly recent trend. Frank B. Gilbreth Jr. and Ernestine Gilbreth Carey's *Cheaper by the Dozen* (HarperCollins: 1948), the story of two efficiency experts raising a brood of twelve children in Montclair, New Jersey, did become a bestseller that was adapted into a film. However, from the 1950s to 1980s stars of television and the big screen wrote most of the autobiographical bestsellers, with occasional contributions from those in the corporate and political world. One notable exception was the publication of *Below Stairs* (Peter Davies: 1968), by Margaret Powell, whose memoir of post–World War I domestic service in England inspired the popular TV series *Upstairs Downstairs*, and *Downton Abbey*. The book has since been republished with a new subtitle as *Below Stairs: The Classic Kitchen Maid's Memoir That Inspired Upstairs, Downstairs and Downton Abbey* (St. Martin's: 2012).

The late sixties marked the publication of the memoir *Stop-Time*, by Frank Conroy. This haunting, beautifully written coming-of-age tale details the author's journey from boyhood to adolescence. If you're scratching your head, wondering why you've never heard of this fine author, you are helping to make the point. *Stop-Time* earned kudos within the literary world, and it was nominated for a National Book Award. At the time Conroy was already a familiar name in literary circles.

So why didn't his memoir catch fire in the larger world? It's our guess that this has to do with the weakness, at the time, of the author's narrative hook and platform. You can figure out if a book has a weak hook if even an admiring reader finds it difficult to explain in a few sentences why "others" would find it interesting. It's difficult to describe what makes *Stop-Time* unique; its hook remains elusive.

Please don't mistake these words as criticism of Conroy. It is an honor for an author to be respected by critics and fellow writers, but that kind of praise doesn't necessarily send readers rushing to buy books. One of the tasks of *You Should* Really *Write a Book* is to offer information on how to sell and market memoirs, which requires us to speak candidly. Conroy most likely sold *Stop-Time* because of the prestige associated with his name. Unsurprisingly, his editor was probably an admirer of his work and of the man, so the book may have been published even if it appeared unlikely that the company would profit from it. (The book has surely yielded profits. *Stop-Time* continues to sell and is often included on recommended reading lists.) These kinds of admiration deals occur infrequently in today's bottom line–driven market.

By the time Conroy's novel *Body & Soul* (Houghton Mifflin Harcourt: 1993) was published, he had served as the director of the literature program at the National Endowment of the Arts and had begun directing the influential Iowa Writers' Workshop at the University of Iowa, both of which heightened his platform. His novel was a bestseller and brought him the recognition he deserved. Conroy died in 2005, at the age of sixty-nine.

In contrast, only two years following the publication of Conroy's memoir, Maya Angelou emerged onto the literary landscape with *I Know Why the Caged Bird Sings* (Random House: 1969), the first of six of her autobiographical works. As with Conroy's coming-of-age tale, reviews for *Caged Bird* were nothing short of wonderful, but Angelou also enjoyed relatively early commercial success. For two years *Caged Bird* remained a *New York Times* bestseller, and it continues to have a life of its own as new generations embrace its theme about the healing power of literature. The book is studied in high school and college classrooms, and the story was made into a TV movie.

Maya Angelou—who has since been awarded honorary doctoral degrees, and is often referred to as Dr. Angelou—remains a literary celebrity. Lauded on the *Oprah Winfrey Show,* she has appeared in films, and she read one of her poems, "On the Pulse of Morning," at President Bill Clinton's 1993 inauguration.

It is difficult to imagine that Angelou might have once been considered Relatively Unknown, but that is the truth of it. Her story makes a good case that the best-known memoirists bring more than excellent writing to the table. In addition to powerful writing, *Caged Bird*'s hook can be described in a few words: a girl who is raped and struck mute speaks again after being introduced to great works of literature. The book's time frame couldn't have been better selected. Angelou came of age in the 1960s, a time when the reading world seemed to be holding its breath waiting to hear from excellent black authors.

The mainstream reading public had already signaled an interest in the "Black experience," making bestsellers out of autobiographical and semi-autobiographical works describing life at the intersection of poverty and racism. These titles include James Baldwin's *Go Tell It on the Mountain* (Knopf: 1953); Malcolm X and Alex Haley's *The Autobiography of Malcolm X* (Grove Press: 1965); and Claude Brown's *Manchild in the Promised Land* (Macmillan: 1965). Another author, Piri Thomas, debuted in the same year as Angelou. The son of a Puerto Rican mother and Cuban father, Thomas described a world of violent crime and poverty in Spanish Harlem in *Down These Mean Streets* (Knopf: 1967). While these five authors have since died, millions of copies of their books have been sold and remain staples on recommended reading lists.

What many of those authors, including Angelou, did not have back then was a strong platform. As you will see in Part II, RUs with two out of three (and only occasionally even one) of the essential elements can sometimes attract publishers. If an editor views a manuscript as well written, with a strong narrative hook, she might help an appealing author build a platform.

In that respect, the decision to publish *Caged Bird* would seem to rank in the no-brainer hall of fame. Angelou's stage presence was probably apparent from early on. A former dancer accustomed to appearing in public, she has a magisterial presence, and in a voice of the finest timbre, speaks in expressively precise diction. Random House editor Robert Loomis reportedly heard from a colleague about her speaking and story-telling gifts. He must have recognized upon meeting her that she would stand at a microphone and breathe life into her story.

Angelou was among a small cadre of RU autobiographical successes in the early 1970s, along with another woman who had come of age in a different world.

The seventies was the era when sex came out of the dark and from under the sheets. First Lady Betty Ford unsettled many when she told an interviewer that she had sex with her husband "as often as possible." It was also a time when readers, unhinged from the old verities, looked for advice from bestsellers that included *The Sensuous Man*, *The Joy of Sex*, and *Your Erroneous Zones**. It wasn't unusual for readers to cover those books with brown-paper wrappers or tuck them away in their bedrooms.

It was a different world from today, when eyebrows are hardly raised over the launch of Hollywood madam Heidi Fleiss's reality TV show "Prostitutes to Parrots." Imagine the response, though, in the early seventies, when former call girl and madam Xaviera Hollander burst onto the scene with *The Happy Hooker: My Own Story* (Harper: 1971). Putting a face on the sexual revolution, this memoir soared to the top, eventually selling twenty million copies.

Although written with coauthors, the quality of the *Happy Hooker*'s prose wasn't Shakespearean, but who cared? Self-assured and conventionally good-looking, Hollander had the strongest possible narrative hook. Rather than skulking about in shame, as might have been expected, she seemed proud. In fact, the secret of her publishing success

---

*The Sensuous Man (Dell: 1971), by "M," *The Joy of Sex* (Simon & Schuster: 1972), by Alex Comfort, and *Your Erroneous Zones* (Funk & Wagnalls: 1976), by Wayne W. Dyer.

was signaled in the title—she claimed to be a *Happy Hooker*. The book was made into a film.

Forty years later, Hollander still understands the importance of a strong platform. For decades she wrote "Call Me Madam," an advice column for *Penthouse*. She has also penned other books, as well as plays, and her Web site promotes a "Happy House" bed-and-breakfast inn in Amsterdam, as well as workshops on how to become a better lover.

A MARKETPLACE SURVIVAL TIP

Titles are important for selling memoirs, helping you to build a brand, a distinctive name that identifies your interests. Like effective commercials, titles grab attention and are memorable. *The Happy Hooker* works because readers wonder what a woman in this profession is happy about. Great titles make people stop and think. James McBride's bestselling *The Color of Water: A Black Man's Tribute to His White Mother* (Riverhead: 1996) poses contradictions between the title and subtitle. Water is colorless, but the first thing some people notice about a white mother and her black son is their color.

There are also successful memoirs with forgettable titles. Jung Chang's *Wild Swans: Three Daughters of China* (Simon & Schuster: 1991), the story of three generations of the author's family, might have been a forgettable title had it not sold more than ten million copies. Success helped make the *Wild Swans* title memorable for millions of fans.

If you haven't thought of a showstopper title, don't be discouraged. Use a temporary working title that encapsulates your plot, such as *Farm Family: A Memoir,* followed by the words "working title" in smaller font. Folks in the publishing industry understand that this means that your intellectual property is under development.

With some subgenres, such as addiction and transformation memoirs, consider including some reference to the subject or theme. For example, Elizabeth Weil's main title, *No Cheating, No Dying,* offered little clue to her subject, but the subtitle explained her point, *I Had a Good Marriage. Then I Tried to Make It Better* (Scribner: 2012). Both the main and subtitle can be informative, as with Claire Dederer's *Poser: My Life in Twenty-three Yoga Poses* (Farrar, Straus and Giroux: 2010). The merits of this tactic are also clear. People search out books looking for inspiration, help, and information around a particular subject, and your title may help them find your work.

As for coming up with a strong title, try, try, and try again, but if at first or second or third try you don't succeed, give it a break. An editor or agent may also enjoy coming up with a title for you. It's probably wise to resist becoming attached to a title, since it might be changed, even more than once, through the publication process. With the 2006 hardcover publication for Greg Mortenson's *Three Cups of Tea,* the subtitle was *One Man's Mission to Fight Terrorism and Build Nations . . . One School at a Time.* An estimated twenty thousand copies of the Viking Penguin book sold subsequently. With the 2007 release of the paperback it was republished with the more positive subtitle *One Man's Mission to Promote Peace . . . One School at a Time.* The improved subtitle, price, and marketing helped this paperback remain a bestseller for four years.

Finally, since editors often devise winning titles by brainstorming, you can do the same, polling relatives and friends. Or load manuscript excerpts onto an MP-3 player or cell phone. Listening to your own words will help you tap into a new level of creativity.

A Memoirist Entitles His Book for "Mom"

In 1996, a retired Manhattan schoolteacher who had been working for decades on a memoir about growing up in Ireland electrified the publishing world with a book he named for his mother as he considered her grief-filled life. Frank McCourt's *Angela's Ashes* is breathtakingly lyrical, and by turns tragic and laugh-out-loud funny. The book won the 1997 Pulitzer Prize, sold more than four million copies, and inspired a 1999 film.

Angela's Ashes covers two decades in McCourt's life, as he grew up in the home of a good-natured but harmfully neglectful drunken father. The funereal tone of the title fit the narrative. Angela gave birth to seven children but lost three, including a young daughter and a set of twins, to what were probably preventable causes. *Angela's Ashes* is an ode to the memory of a mother who never emerged from the grief over the loss of her children and her own wasted life. That her son, Frank McCourt, made something of his own life, which is clear from the power of his prose, offers hope to those who have feared they will never recover from childhood neglect caused by a parent's alcoholism.

It's important to note that beyond the strength of his writing and his story's narrative hook, McCourt was a showman in his own right. For decades, he worked as a high school writing teacher, a job that is difficult to survive spiritually unless one learns to engage an audience with humor and knowledge. He was also raised in a family of raconteurs. At one point, McCourt and his brother Malachy performed in a series of autobiographical sketches. Fueled by Frank McCourt's success, Malachy and another brother, Alphie, wrote memoirs of their own.*

In a 2009 interview, a friend, Mary Breasted, suggested that McCourt's *raconteur* skills propelled his impressive sales. "He had this amazing storyteller's talent. He could speak for an hour without notes."

---

*Malachy McCourt is the author of *A Monk Swimming* (Picador USA: 1998) and *Singing My Him Song* (HarperCollins: 2000). Alphie McCourt is the author of *A Long Stone's Throw* (Sterling & Ross: 2008).

McCourt wrote two sequels to *Angela's Ashes*. By his 2009 death, ten million copies of his books were in print.

The "Age of Oprah" Helps to Ignite a Memoir Market

Oprah Winfrey's network talk show may have ended in 2011, but not before it drove shifts in behaviors. In the years leading up to Winfrey's show, TV journalist Barbara Walters primed the pump by prying tears and confessionals from the rich and famous. Winfrey hit it big, in part because she included in her lineup the guy and girl next door. She also distinguished herself from competitors by sharing on air her personal history of childhood sexual abuse. Through the years, as Winfrey reached ever-larger audiences, her show and others helped normalize and popularize therapy and self-help books. This was also a time when President Bill Clinton was portrayed as interested in the "pain" of others. Still, it was Oprah Winfrey in particular who instigated a cultural shift, whetting appetites for the personal stories of ordinary people.

TAKE THIS PERSONALLY

Writing a memoir often puts authors in touch with unexpressed emotions. Like new patients working with therapists, inexperienced memoirists often feel the need to tell everything, a phenomenon known as "flooding." When this occurs in therapy, a clinician is trained to encourage the client to dwell on individual experiences, so they can be processed. For the sake of writing a commercially viable manuscript, if you refrain from leaping from one memory to another, you will be less likely to skim over what might be your story's high points. Too many subplots make a story seem unwieldy.

Marion Roach Smith, a writing teacher, encourages literary restraint. The author of *The Memoir Project: A Thoroughly Non-Standardized Text for Writing & Life* (Grand Central: 2011), Smith advised in a

National Public Radio interview that rather than cramming memories into a story, focus on relating the narrative to broader themes. She uses as an example a decision she made while writing the memoir *Another Name for Madness* (Houghton Mifflin: 1985), which depicts her mother's struggle with Alzheimer's. Although she wrote about her mother's alcoholism, she omitted references to her mother's infidelity, convinced they would move the story in the wrong direction. Instead she focused on the devastation of Alzheimer's.

Delving into hurtful experiences should also be undertaken with consideration about personal consequences. In 1920, author Virginia Woolf, during a gathering of writers, read aloud from an essay about having been molested. Her inclination to discuss this troubling experience is understandable, but talking about trauma without adequate support can lead to anxiety and depression. Woolf may have felt shame when men in the group appeared bored and uncomfortable. She wrote in a diary that her confession left her feeling "most unpleasantly discomfited . . . What possessed me to lay bare my soul?" Personal writing may be therapeutic, but it's not a substitute for therapy. Like Woolf, you may find it helpful to keep a journal or work with a clinician to process your reactions.

During the 1990s, as people became convinced that intimacy among strangers could be therapeutic, thanks in part to a changed landscape in daytime talk TV, interest in autobiographical works energized the publishing industry. Among personal stories, memoirs became the books of choice, allowing RU authors to offer personal views of specific periods of their lives, as opposed to more expansive autobiographies.

Surely there will always be memoirists that rise to prominence who might be described as poor writers, or whose stories contain no easily discernible plot and who have not built platforms, but their numbers are dwindling. As demonstrated on these pages, memoirists have long combined strength of writing, charisma, and marketing skills to fuel book sales. What has changed is the greater reliance by publishers on the writer's successful use of social networking.

It seems fitting, then, that a memoir of multiple themes, including a boy's grief over his absent father, would be the first of its kind to help launch a national political career. Young law school graduate Barack Obama's memoir *Dreams from My Father: A Story of Race and Inheritance* (Times Books: 1995) earned modest sales before it was republished in 2004, and became a megabestseller.

By then, Obama had claimed a platform of his own. Two weeks earlier he had delivered a powerful keynote address at the Democratic National Convention. Four years later, his campaign managers had mastered the art of networking. This, along with a multiplicity of factors, helped him become the forty-fourth president of the United States.

HONING YOUR CRAFT

In reading memoirs, look for the authors' approaches to issues that you might be grappling with in your writing. Suggested titles of various subgenres follow.

1. *Why Be Happy When You Could Be Normal*, by Jeanette Winterson (Grove: 2012)

2. *Wild: From Lost to Found on the Pacific Coast Trail*, by Cheryl Strayed (Knopf: 2012)

3. *Immortal Bird: A Family Memoir*, by Doron Weber (Simon & Schuster: 2012)

4. *Blood, Bones & Butter: The Inadvertent Education of a Reluctant Chef*, by Gabrielle Hamilton (Random House: 2011)

5. *The Boy in the Moon: A Father's Journey to Understand His Extraordinary Son,* by Ian Brown (St. Martin's: 2011)

6. *Maman's Homesick Pie: A Persian Heart in an American Kitchen, by* Donia Bijan (Algonquin: 2011)

7. *Ghosts by Daylight: Love, War, and Redemption,* by Janine di Giovanni (Knopf/Doubleday: 2011)

8. *House of Prayer No. 2: A Writer's Journey Home,* by Mark Richard (Nan A. Talese: 2011)

9. *The Possessed: Adventures with Russian Books and the People Who Read Them,* by Elif Batuman (Granta: 2011)

10. *Mighty Be Our Powers: How Sisterhood, Prayer, and Sex Changed a Nation at War,* by Leymah Gbowee (Beast: 2011)

11. *I Wore the Ocean in the Shape of a Girl,* by Kelle Groom (Free Press: 2011)

12. *The Memory Palace,* by Mira Bartok (Free Press: 2011)

13. *Moonwalking with Einstein: The Art and Science of Remembering Everything,* by Joshua Foer (Penguin: 2011)

14. *SEAL Team Six: Memoirs of an Elite Navy SEAL Sniper,* by Howard E. Wasdin and Stephen Templin (St. Martin's: 2011)

15. *The Hare with Amber Eyes: A Family's Century of Art and Loss,* by Edmund de Waal (Farrar, Straus and Giroux: 2010)

16. *What's Left of Us,* by Richard Farrell (Citadel: 2009)

17. *Beautiful Boy: A Father's Journey Through His Son's Addiction,* by David Sheff (Houghton Mifflin: 2008)

18. *A Long Way Gone: Memoirs of a Boy Soldier,* by Ishmael Beah (Farrar, Straus and Giroux: 2007)

19. *Take This Bread: A Radical Conversion*, by Sara Miles (Ballantine: 2007)

20. *Man in the White Sharkskin Suit: My Family's Exodus from Old Cairo to the New World*, by Lucette Lagnado (Ecco: 2007)

21. *Fun Home: A Family Tragicomic*, by Alison Bechdel (Houghton Mifflin Harcourt: 2006)

22. *The Tender Bar*, by J. R. Moehringer (Hyperion: 2005)

23. *Daughter of Heaven: A Memoir with Earthly Recipes*, by Leslie Li (Arcade: 2005)

24. *Four Corners: A Journey to the Heart of Papua New Guinea*, by Kira Salak (National Geographic: 2004)

25. *Waiting for Snow in Havana: Confessions of a Cuban Boy*, by Carlos Eire (Free Press: 2003)

26. *Persepolis: The Story of a Childhood*, by Marjane Satrapi (Pantheon: 2003)

27. *Walking the Bible: A Journey by Land Through the Five Books of Moses*, by Bruce Feiler (William Morrow: 2001)

28. *The Pianist: The Extraordinary True Story of One Man's Survival in Warsaw*, by Wladsylaw Szpilman (Picador: 1999)

29. *Tender at the Bone: Growing Up at the Table*, by Ruth Reichl (Random House: 1998)

30. *Slow Motion: A Memoir of a Life Rescued by Tragedy*, by Dani Shapiro (Random House: 1998)

31. *An American Requiem: God, My Father, and the War That Came Between Us*, by James Carroll (Houghton Mifflin: 1996)

32. *The Color of Water: A Black Man's Tribute to His White Mother,* by James McBride (Riverhead: 1996)

33. *Angela's Ashes,* by Frank McCourt (Scribner: 1996)

34. *Under the Tuscan Sun: At Home in Italy,* by Frances Mayes (Chronicle: 1996)

35. *The Liar's Club,* by Mary Karr (Viking: 1995)

36. *When I Was Puerto Rican,* by Esmeralda Santiago (Da Capo: 1993)

37. *My Own Country: A Doctor's Story,* by Abraham Verghese (Simon & Schuster: 1994)

38. *This Boy's Life,* by Tobias Wolff (Atlantic Monthly Press: 1989)

39. *The Road from Coorain,* by Jill Ker Conway (Knopf: 1989)

40. *I Know Why the Caged Bird Sings,* by Maya Angelou (Random House: 1969)

Two

Your Role as a Memoirist

IN THE PRECEDING CHAPTER WE LOOKED AT THE ORIGINS OF the memoir and hypothesized about the reasons for the genre's rise in popularity. We noted that in terms of how these books were sold even hundreds of years ago, although methods changed, the factors that paved the way to success—quality writing, a unique idea, and the need for a strong platform—have remained much the same. In this chapter, as we reflect on what memoirs have evolved into, you will be encouraged to reflect upon your role of writing in a genre that fulfills one of the most basic of human needs.

You'll know what this means if you recall how you felt the last time you moved to a new neighborhood (or started a new job or enrolled in a new school) and found that you felt out of sorts until you reached a point of familiarity and acceptance. The owner of the local deli might have begun nodding at you in recognition; or a neighbor stopped to converse, and you felt yourself relaxing as you were incorporated into the community.

Social biologists have long suggested that humans crave to be in relationships with others. Forming relationships is a survival mechanism, and communication is the key to making them work. Before we had books to discuss, as far back as the Mesolithic period, thousands of years ago, there were rock paintings depicting groups of humans, a pictorial message, perhaps for the purpose of saying simply, "We were here together."

In the 1930s and '40s, much of the industrialized world united around the radio. In the United States, President Franklin Roosevelt addressed Americans with fireside chats, offering reassurance and information to a nation gripped by economic fear. With the advent of television, a community of viewers laughed, watching shows such as *I Love Lucy*, and recognized themselves in *Leave It to Beaver*. Then, in the blink of an eye, it seemed, television *impresario* Ed Sullivan was introducing the long-haired Beatles.

Our society has since undergone unprecedented social change. Divorce, employment, and immigration have separated many and sent millions into the anonymity of cities. Today, our global village is in flux, but the community of the World Wide Web serves as, what was for generations before, neighbors talking over the back fence.

Although our world has expanded greatly, our need for relationships with those who share our values has remained steady. The ways in which we seek relationships are as traditional as attending places of worship and as modern as joining the blogosphere. Still, there are books and book discussions, as we travel the narratives of one another's lives. The popularity of books about real people reflects our reading choices. Of the ten bestselling nonfiction books in 2011, seven were memoirs, autobiographies, or biographies. Memoirs, in particular, allow us to feel in relationship with the author, making it seem as if he or she is seated right beside us, speaking to us directly. Readers can feel as close an attachment to memoir protagonists as they do to their own relatives and friends.

As the author-in-residence, you are a version of the ancient rock painter, of the voice that comforts, fires up, entertains, warns, and educates. In decades past, as an author, you might have sat alone, demanding uninterrupted isolation. Today, in our wired world, you can engage with others, reaching out in the spirit of community.

GOING VIRTUAL

Social media offers a number of opportunities for creating new relationships. You may want to start your own writer's blog eventually, after you have figured out a unique niche. A blog helped Steve Dublanica become a published memoirist. A former seminarian and laid-off psychiatric worker, he started the blog WaiterRant.net to share hysterical and sometimes lurid tales about behind-the-scenes events at a restaurant. The popularity of the blog led to the publication of his memoir *Waiter Rant: Thanks for the Tip— Confessions of a Cynical Waiter* (Ecco: 2008).

Notice that Dublanica carved out a unique niche (aka narrative hook). He's not a blogging chef or restaurant or food critic. He started a blog from the point of view of a waiter (and a fed-up one at that), something he knew a lot about.

With your own blog in mind, start surfing the Web and find out what's already out there. Hone your skills and search for an audience by writing guest entries at various sites. When you find a few that you admire and that catch your attention, search the archives and read earlier postings. If reading and participating in blogs is new to you, it is best to invest time getting familiar with the scene before sharing your thoughts. You will want to make a good impression with others. That requires being knowledgeable and engaging before inviting others to continue conversing with you on your blog.

To join an online community of memoir writers, consider the National Association of Memoir Writers (NAMW) at www.namw.org.

According to the Web site, NAMW ". . . is a membership organization for memoir writers from all over the world . . . to connect, learn, and become inspired about writing true stories based on real life. Our goal is to help memoir writers feel empowered with purpose and energy to begin and develop their life stories into a publishable memoir, whether in essay form, a book, a family legacy, or to create a blog." Hopefully, you will reach the point of writing your own blog. According to advice offered at authormedia.com, Web sites with built-in blogs get 55 percent more traffic than Web sites with no blogs.

In considering memoir writing through the prism of relationships, it's important to alert you to two deadly sins. From the standpoint of trying to engage readers, these "sinful" behaviors are every bit as offensive as going on a first date and talking ad nauseam about your ex, or texting at the movies.

Two Behaviors to Resist at All Cost

1. SELF-PITY

Invite folks to a pity party, and you will be a lonely host. If you want to avoid sounding sorry for yourself, consider whether you have resolved most of the issues you're writing about. If you have not, you may want to concentrate on writing strictly for the sake of healing, with plans to undertake a more commercial endeavor later. It's up to you to decide whether you have triumphed over these difficult circumstances.

Some people have accused one of the richest men in the world of exhibiting self-pity. He is a founder of Microsoft—Did you have to reread that sentence? How could anybody accuse Microsoft founder Bill Gates of sounding self-pitying? That's the point. It's *not* Gates, but Paul Allen, the *other* founder of Microsoft. Although well known within the technology industry, Allen is not widely recognized beyond.

Allen is brilliant and a visionary, deserving of widespread recognition. Yet, to some readers, his book, *Idea Man: A Memoir by the Cofounder of Microsoft* (Portfolio/Penguin: 2011) feels like a cry for recognition and sympathy. On CBS's *60 Minutes*, Allen agreed with the description of Gates as a tough taskmaster who engaged in verbal attacks, yelling, and screaming. Allen recalled feeling marginalized at work.

Allen, who left Microsoft in 1983, does a disservice to himself in portraying his former partner as a bully, because it makes Allen sound like a victim. It's a matter of how images are conveyed. Think of the difference between the words "victim" and "adversary." One is perceived as weak; the other is assumed to be equally as worthy.

While it's never a good idea to try to rewrite someone else's book, it's difficult not to imagine how much fun *Idea Man* might have been, had Allen made light of being largely unrecognized. How about a Letterman-type list of the ten best things about being an unknown zillionaire? Nine months after publication, about fifteen thousand hardcover units of *Idea Man* had been sold. That doesn't qualify as a disaster, but it is instructive. The problem with self-pity is that readers may feel sorry for you, but won't respect you in the morning.

2. VENGEANCE

If you want to sell your memoir, don't write to air old grievances. Sourcebook's trade editorial manager Peter Lynch explained that he loses interest in manuscripts if the author's motives feel too personal. "If your goal in publishing a memoir about your custody battle is to let the world know how terrible your ex is, that is of little interest. But if your goal is to show how a parent's love is complicated and sometimes requires tough decisions, that's a universal theme."

In memoir writing, attempts to retaliate will backfire, causing you to portray yourself, the protagonist, in the most flattering light, while your antagonist comes off as one-dimensional and malevolent. Hissable villains only work in dated cartoons. Readers will turn against you when they sense you are trying to manipulate them onto your side.

This antivengeance advice also pertains to your parents. If you catch yourself blaming them for your problems, it may be a good time to do genogram work. This therapeutic system allows you to trace familial behaviors, beliefs, and patterns. It can help you better understand your parents and yourself. Instructions for constructing genograms by hand or with software can be found at various sites on the Internet. You may also choose to seek out a clinician who utilizes the genogram in therapeutic practice.

Other efforts at healing, which might include working with a therapist or supportive group, may also help you feel more forgiving, which is a self-enhancing process—and facilitative to the writing process. The word "forgiveness" is by no means a suggestion that you forget what happened to you. By its very nature, memoir writing is about remembering. However, if you hope to sell your manuscript, you have to work through the issues you're writing about, so readers will be more likely to trust you.

Speaking of relationships with parents, you may have noticed that some critics find it "amazing" when an author writes of loving or forgiving the most flawed mothers and fathers. In truth, it's not unusual to find even adults who were removed from abusive homes longing for their parents. The bond between parent and child is often enduring. How else could humankind survive? Please don't misinterpret this as a suggestion that you should manufacture emotions, which wouldn't be healthy for you or your writing. The truth is, though, if you present a parent as the embodiment of evil, it will be a disservice to you and your work.

If writing about a major character makes you furious, you may want to complete a first draft of your manuscript as an exercise in anger relief, with plans to rewrite before sharing it with professionals. If you do rewrite, describe the other persons' behaviors in the most objective way possible, and then trust readers to draw their own conclusions.

Another approach to dealing with burdensome emotions is to compose letters that you don't plan to send, but that are addressed to the person that hurt you (whether living or dead). The trick with these letters is to let your feelings rip, get those angry emotions out and onto the page as you describe to that person what he or she did and how it made you feel. No one is hurt in this exercise, but your writing will benefit. When finished, you can tear the letters into shreds. Therapeutic support can also assist you in gaining distance.

With neither self-pity nor vengeance impeding your opportunity for engaging readers, let's flip the coin. What follows are three memoir-enhancing suggestions.

Three Behaviors That Enhance Your Chances of Writing a Memoir That Sells

1. FEED YOUR PASSION

Dreaming is one of the few remaining delicious pastimes open to the public that's absolutely free. There is no better way to remain passionate than to dream big. Some writing guides discourage authors from aiming for the bestsellers list. You won't hear that from us. That's like telling a hardworking high school student to forget about applying for Harvard. We wouldn't dare talk down to you in that manner. Surely you realize that while many aim for the top, only a few make the cut. At the same time, passion can act as a fuel. It may make all the difference in the quality of your writing—and in forming a relationship with readers.

It can keep you moving ahead, doing much of what is recommended here in your determination to get your book to market.

You will not, however, want to give free rein to passion, especially if it comes off sounding like bombast. Brooke Warner, former executive editor for Seal Press, and now operating Warner Coaching Inc., to help aspiring writers get published, says she is turned off by author displays of grandiosity, boasting, or grandstanding. When she hears from authors that their manuscripts are the "greatest" or "amazing" she becomes wary. "I want the quality of the manuscript to speak for itself," she says.

Trust us when we say that you don't want to turn off editors, the guardians of publishing houses' purse strings. If editors perceive you as having poor social skills, they're likely to keep their purses shut.

2. DEMONSTRATE SELF-AWARENESS

Have you ever dated someone and not allowed yourself to get close because you couldn't figure out the other person's intentions—or where the relationship was headed? Readers are pretty much the same way. That doesn't mean that they're looking for something formulaic—quite the opposite—but they will see right through you (and probably quit reading) if you present yourself without clarity.

Successful memoirists often offer candid, uncompromising views of their own behaviors. A book that comes to mind is Nathan McCall's bestselling *Makes Me Wanna Holler: A Young Black Man in America* (Vintage: 1995). McCall—at the time a reporter for *The Washington Post*, and more recently on faculty at Emory University—describes his angry youth as a hustler in a Portsmouth Virginia working-class neighborhood. He offers as vivid examples gang rape and a prison term for armed robbery.

Why would a respected journalist write this book? McCall doesn't simply tell what happened. He reflects on his experiences, and offers insight about self-hatred and generational alienation. It appears that his purpose was to call the nation's attention to youngsters trapped in bleak neighborhoods, like the one he left behind. His success also challenges them to question their choices and offers them reason to be hopeful.

There are different levels of offering uncompromising views of yourself. Knowing your audience can make all the difference in what you'll write, so on occasion being self-serving might actually work. Notice the difference between McCall's honest but painful self-exposure, as opposed to using self-criticism in a cynical way, designed to tease prurient readers.

In Tucker Max's *I Hope They Sell Beer in Hell* (Citadel: 2009), the author doesn't try to rehabilitate his image. In fact, in the introduction to this comedic memoir, which originated with a highly popular blog launched in 2002, this is how Max describes himself: "I get excessively drunk at inappropriate times, disregard social norms, indulge every whim, ignore the consequences of my actions, mock idiots and posers, sleep with more women than is safe or reasonable, and just generally act like a raging dickhead."

Max's book received more than six hundred reviews on Amazon .com, many highly critical. One described Max as "shallow," another as an "abusive pig." What would Max's intentions have been? His disingenuous and cynical form of self-criticism is clearly boasting. In appropriating the *clichés* of crude male-buddy comedies and celebrating vulgarity and bravado, he is addressing an audience that laughs at frat-boy jokes. His message assures readers that people can defy bourgeois propriety and still achieve conventional success. Max's motivations seem clearly extrinsic. He wanted to make money, and counted on his gauche behavior attracting negative attention, which it did.

After a modest hardcover launch, with sales of twenty thousand units, *I Hope They Sell Beer in Hell* has sold more than one million copies in paperback and remained on the *New York Times* bestseller list for more than three years. The book was made into a film. The author's next book, *Assholes Finish First* (Gallery: 2010), was another bestseller, as was *Hilarity Ensues* (Blue Heeler: 2012), which he self-published.

Max's work has attracted heated criticism. In a 2009 speaking engagement at Ohio State University, a feminist campus group, Women and Allies Rising in Resistance, picketed against him for promoting "a culture of rape." Later that year, at a screening of the *I Hope They Sell Beer in Hell* film, The Women's Center of North Carolina State University staged a similar demonstration. Max told a *New York Times* interviewer, "I don't go out looking for trouble . . . It just happens to me because of who I am."

Yet we can't help but wonder *who* he is. It is true that Max's relationship with his readers seems oddly familiar. We've all known men or women who've dated someone like him, and when challenged, shrugged their shoulders, as if saying, at least I know who he is. But *do* readers know Max? That may be an aspect of the book's conceit. Max graduated with honors from the University of Chicago, then attended Duke Law School, where he was a scholarship student. He almost sounds like a guy you'd want to take home to Mom. You've got to wonder whether he's laughing as hard at his readers as they are at his book.

While McCall and Max both found reading audiences with different approaches of self-awareness, few authors come close to offering the level of revelation achieved by Margaux Fragoso, the author of *Tiger, Tiger* (Farrar, Straus and Giroux: 2011). Her memoir chronicles her fifteen-year relationship with Peter Curran, the pedophile who sexually abused her and later committed suicide. Raised by a mentally ill mother, Fragoso was seven, and her abuser fifty-one, when they met. This book serves as a warning to those who wonder how these situations occur. Dealing the most difficult hand of all, Fragoso describes the emotional hunger a needy child feels when finally encountering an adult who claims to love her.

In reviewing *Tiger, Tiger* Kathryn Harrison praised Fragoso's ability to render both her own and the pedophile's, "points of view convincingly, as different—opposed—as they are." Harrison's praise continued: "Written without self-pity, rancor, or even judgment, *Tiger, Tiger* forces readers to experience Curran simultaneously as the object of a little girl's love and fascination and as a calculating sex offender who cultivates her dependence on him while contriving to separate her from anyone who might prevent his molesting her." While the story may not sit comfortably with many, Fragoso's admirers get to know these characters because of her high level of self-understanding.

Tiger, Tiger was a critical rather than a commercial success. Fragoso's gut-wrenching subject matter makes the book an unlikely bestseller. So on March 27, 2011, it must have given Fragoso some measure of satisfaction to see her name on a *New York Times* E-Book Best Sellers list— *Tiger, Tiger* ranked twenty-fourth out of twenty-five titles. Far from momentous, it might seem, unless you noticed that she was listed one rung above a longtime favorite that had dominated bestseller lists for years: the light and somewhat humorous, *Eat, Pray, Love.*

TAKE THIS PERSONALLY

Every once in a while the publishing industry goes gaga over an author. In 2011, the toast of literary New York was Jon-Jon Gouilan, and it wasn't hard to see why. With striking good looks—the result of a combination of nose jobs, a childhood diet of nonfat, dry-curd cottage cheese and vegetable protein, plus countless hours at the gym—he is a tattooed and tantalizingly androgynous protagonist, which helps explain the memorable title and the author's back cover photo for *The Man in the Gray Flannel Skirt* (Random House: 2011). Gouilan also appears to be keenly intelligent. After earning an undergraduate degree from Columbia, he completed a law degree at New York University. His book is filled with *bon mots*. It's no wonder that a *New York Observer* journalist wrote, "Is there anyone more likeable than Jon-Jon Gouilan?" In the months leading up to his book's publication, he was a media sensation. Yet despite this attention and a reported $700,000 book advance, the reasons for his local celebrity may have worked against him.

The relationship between author and reader relies on the author providing crucial insight, but there can be no relationship if the author is unknowable. *The Man in the Gray Flannel Skirt* remains a cipher even to himself. For instance, why take up law, only to turn his back on the profession when he realizes that a bejeweled, lip-glossed, skirted man might not be welcome in this arena? Deep insights elude him and readers. Rather than readers understanding *why* Gouilan is as he is, his book explains *who* he is. Dan Kois wrote in a National Public Radio review that Gouilan had missed the most important job of a memoirist: "To create empathy, to help the reader feel what it's like to *be* the person he is."

There must be therapeutic transaction in memoirs, a give and take that allows the reader to nod in acknowledgment and perhaps grow. Gouilan does describe his memoir as a "deep and painful stab at self-analysis." This intent undergirds the efforts of many fledgling memoirists. Here's a warning, though: Few people are willing to sit through their own therapy, let alone a stranger's.

There are signs that the inaccessibility that drew the literati to Gouilan led readers to resist him. According to the *New York Post*, a month after release, *The Man in the Gray Flannel Skirt* had only sold 957 hardcover copies, out of an estimated 200,000 that would have to sell for the publisher to realize a profit. His is a cautionary tale for all who take this business to heart. A book is far more than its cover.

Self-revelation can be achieved in more than obvious ways. Fueled by a sense of outrage, some literary provocateurs reveal themselves to readers by disguising themselves in public. In so doing, they lead the way to spirited discourse through understated but poignant commentary.

In *Self-Made Man: One Woman's Journey into Manhood and Back Again* (Thorndike: 2006), Norah Vincent became a media celebrity, after disclosing that she had disguised herself and lived as a man for eighteen months. In addition to visiting a lap dance club, Catholic monastery, and participating in a men's therapy group, she worked as a door-to-door salesman. Her exploits and insights about the differences between the sexes make for a riveting story.

In *Nothing to Lose But Your Life: An 18-Hour Journey with Murad* (Bloomsbury USA: 2012), Palestinian architect Suad Amiry disguised herself as a man and crossed the Israeli border illegally to seek work. Traveling with Murad, a Palestinian laborer, she learned firsthand about difficulties of life for ordinary Palestinians.

Finally, an adjunct professor of English disguised his name from readers and tackled conceptions about the need for most people to receive higher education. *In the Basement of the Ivory Tower: Confessions of an Accidental Academic* (Viking: 2011) tells the story of Professor X introducing college-level work to high school graduates whom he views as unprepared for intellectual challenges and unable to learn. He pointed out that while there were 1.5 million college students in the United States in 1940, by 2006 there were 20.5 million. The future bodes poorly for many students and our nation, Professor X suggests. Statistics help make his point.

A MARKETPLACE SURVIVAL TIP

There is an adage that writers should write what they know, but some memoirists think they *know* when they don't. They may consider research unnecessary because, "I'm just telling my story." This misassumption has turned off many a publishing professional. Every story requires research, even if most of it won't show up in your manuscript. Your head should be so full of information that you're like a film editor starting with 500,000 feet of footage, knowing only 26,000 of it will end up as finished product.

Marc Resnick of St. Martin's Press and the editor of the 2011 bestseller *SEAL Team Six: Memoirs of an Elite Navy SEAL Sniper*, explains that one of the attributes that drew him in was author Howard Wasdin's erudition. "Knowledge is one of the most important strengths an author can bring to the table," Resnick explained.

So let your research be guided by the Latin words *sapere aude*: dare to know.

Like Wasdin, if you have already spent years studying your subject, your knowledge will serve you well. For the rest with general interest, let research be your guide. If you find an interesting fact in Wikipedia, try to follow the citations to a referenced publication. Too much effort? Your response could signal a lack of passion. Why would you want to write a story to feel matter-of-fact, as opposed to one that is factually based?

As is the case with film biopics and documentaries, one reason for the memoir's surge in popularity is that it offers opportunities to learn about subjects that might otherwise seem dull, were they not offered within the context of entertaining personal narratives.

Consider how cyberspace has whetted the public appetite for learning. Around the world, people are downloading podcasts hoping to become better informed, and online learning has changed the notion of educational outreach. In just one of many examples, Stanford University offered a no-credit, free-of-charge artificial intelligence online technology course in 2011, and 160,000 students from 160 countries registered. While your target reading audience probably isn't looking for information that requires an understanding of linear algebra and probability theory, critics and readers will be looking to learn about a specific subculture through your story. Despite its humor, Rhoda Janzen's bestselling *Mennonite in a Little Black Dress* (Henry Holt: 2009) includes an appendix to help understand the religion; Joshua Cody's acclaimed and lesser known [*sic*] (W. W. Norton: 2011), a cancer survival story, was described by a *New York Times* critic as "striated with fragments of culture, all of them made meaningful."

Your knowledge will help you to build trust with readers—those you acquire in building a platform, as well as those who buy your book—so keep an eye out for venues in which aspiring writers can read selections from works in progress. Audience members that you interest sufficiently may give you contact information and you can offer yours. To attract venue managers who might be interested in your research, contact local men and women's clubs, local Ys, or public library branches. Remember also that your knowledge can help convince editors that you are qualified to write essays for newspaper Op-Ed sections. Links to authors' Web sites are generally included in online editions.

When writing to a literary agent to describe your platform, you will want to include places where you have been interviewed or where you were involved in public speaking or teaching, and/or a description of your blog, with statistics about your Web traffic.

When you're sending a fact-supported query letter to an agent, statistics can be essential. The agent will repeat numbers to the editor; the editor will recite them in acquisitions meetings to make the case that the subject is worth the company's investment. If the book is published, that same editor will use the statistics to convince company sales people that this is an exciting subject and that your title is one they will want to talk up to book buyers. These statistics and your knowledge will also help interest the media in reviewing your book or interviewing you.

If you're writing about a rare subject, use that to attract interest. Heather Sellers's *You Don't Look Like Anyone I Know* (Riverhead: 2010) familiarizes readers with prosopagnosia, a condition most people can't even pronounce, let alone understand. Although Sellers can see faces, this unusual neurological condition renders her unable to read their features cohesively, leaving her unable to recognize people, even family members. Her story seems like one in a million, which is also a good selling point.

In upcoming chapters that delve into the writing, selling, and marketing of particular subgenres, you will have plenty of opportunities to continue considering your purpose for writing a memoir. For now, in offering suggestions about the reader/author relationship, it is important to mention the memoirist's greatest responsibility of all.

3. TELL THE TRUTH

If there was ever evidence that many memoir readers feel they're in a relationship with their favorite authors, it can be found in their reactions after they've learned that they have been lied to. Their responses are similar to those of lovers who discover that someone they've trusted has cheated on them. They feel angry, betrayed, and disgusted.

Consider what occurred in 2005, after revelations that Oprah Book Club memoirist James Frey, the author of *A Million Little Pieces* (Anchor: 2005), had distorted and exaggerated details of his drug addiction and recovery. In publicly taking Frey to task on her TV show for lying, Winfrey offered the kind of girlfriend moment that had made her a force to be reckoned with. The nation's everywoman scolded Frey publicly for taking us down a tumultuous road and leaving us stranded. We understood her anger. We'd been there. We had shown him the love, but he wasn't that into us.

Only in retrospect did we wonder why we'd ever trusted that bad boy in the first place. Surely there were others more worthy, like the he-who-will-not fail-us type, Greg Mortenson, the former nurse and author of *Three Cups of Tea*. His inspirational memoir tells of a failed attempt to climb a mountain in one of the most remote areas in Pakistan, and then stumbling into a mountain village, where he resolves to repay the kindness he is shown by building a school—which he does subsequently, and not just one, many of them in remote regions of Pakistan and Afghanistan.

Taking his story to heart, readers interpreted his message as a charge to make the best of the challenges they encountered along their own unexpected paths. President Obama contributed $100,000 of his Nobel Peace Prize winnings to Mortenson's charity. The book became recommended reading for U.S. military troops in the area.

All this goodwill heightened a collective sense of stunned disbelief in 2011, when a *60 Minutes* segment charged Mortenson of bordering on dishonesty pertaining to events in his book. One of Mortenson's earliest donors, bestselling author Jon Krakauer, wrote the exposé *Three Cups of Deceit: How Greg Mortenson, Humanitarian Hero, Lost His Way* (Anchor: 2011). Among other key aspects challenged in Mortenson's story was the scene in which he gets lost and then stumbles upon that remote village. Reportedly, his guides had led him there. Mortenson's dates in the story were also said to be off. More seriously, he was accused of misrepresenting the number of schools founded by his organization and of mismanaging his charity's finances. The author denied the charges, but admitted that he had compressed some of the events in the book. After an investigation was conducted by the Montana Attorney General, where the Central Asia Institute is headquartered, Mortensen was ordered to repay $1 million to the organization, and he was required to step down from his leadership role.

Other memoirists have been accused of creating stories out of blatant lies. Herman Rosenblat, a Jewish Holocaust survivor, wrote *Angel at the Fence*, which was scheduled for a 2009 publication. Despite rave advance reviews and sales of film rights, plans for the book were cancelled when Rosenblat was accused of fabricating key elements. Brenda and I call fake narratives "fauxmoirs."

A few memoirists who have been accused of exaggerating or lying have been exonerated to some extent. Dave Pelzer, the author of *A Child Called "It": One Child's Courage to Survive* (HCI: 1995), had his credibility challenged by journalists and family members over details of the horrifying childhood abuse he described at the hands of his mother. Pelzer wrote about being starved, stabbed, forced to swallow ammonia, and eat excrement from a sibling's diaper. While the incidents were not entirely verifiable, social services did remove him from his family home, and a former teacher familiar with his situation asserted that Pelzer's was the third-worst case of child abuse on record in the state of California. Additionally, one of his brothers wrote a memoir validating his version of events,* while a second brother denied that their mother had been abusive.

Augusten Burroughs, author of the tragically hilarious *Running with Scissors* (Picador: 2002), which spawned a film, was also accused of taking liberties with facts. The family of the psychiatrist depicted in the story sued for defamation, and settlements were reached. Two of Burroughs's family members also sought to tell their own sides of the story. His brother** wrote a memoir, as did their mother.† All three agreed that painful events had occurred, but their different perspectives served as reminders that emotional memories are in the eyes of the beholders.

So what is a memoirist to do in a genre that uses a creative approach to

---

*Richard B. Pelzer is the author of *A Brother's Journey: Surviving a Childhood of Abuse* (Grand Central: 2005).

**John Elder Robison is the author of *Be Different: Adventures of a Free-Range Aspergian with Practical Advice for Aspergians, Misfits, Families & Teachers* (Crown Archetype: 2011).

† Margaret Robison, *The Long Journey Home* (Spiegel & Grau: 2011).

telling a true story? How can someone know whether his take on a situation is truthful, while relying on emotional memories to recall conversations, sensations, even traumatic events that occurred years, often decades ago? Unlike Ishmael Beah, author of the page-turning *A Long Way Gone: Memoirs of a Boy Soldier* (Farrar, Straus and Giroux: 2007), not many people claim to have a photographic memory and the ability to recall most events. It's likely that Beah stopped making that claim after he was accused of getting dates and other particulars wrong in his bestselling story.

In fairness, it must be noted that even Tolstoy's masterpiece *War and Peace* was found by at least one scholar to mislead readers in the depiction of Russia's war against France. Even if that's true, some might argue, *War and Peace* is fiction, not memoir.

The difference, writes Judith Barrington, a highly regarded writing teacher and the author of *Writing the Memoir: From Truth to Art* (Eighth Mountain Press: 1997), is that while imagination plays a role in both kinds of writing, fiction is, *"circumscribed by what the reader will believe,"* while, "the application of it [the imagination] in memoir *is circumscribed by the facts."* Like many writing teachers and publishing professionals, Barrington points out that it is common practice for memoirists to use composite characters, reorder events chronologically, and compress time periods.

Since this is a common practice in memoirs, and yet news of literary sleights of hand draws condemnation, it raises the question as to whether the bar is set too high. Author and culture critic Touré Neblett addressed the slipperiness of truth, writing in *The New York Times*, ". . . all autobiographies are, in part, lies. They rely on memory, which is notoriously fallible, and are shaped by self-image. They don't really tell us who you are but whom you want the world to see you as."

Be that as it may, readers expect and deserve the truth, and it is they who drive the market. How many more scandals have to occur before readers begin filing for divorce—uh, we mean, stop purchasing books in this genre? Time will surely tell, but in the meantime, some suggestions follow as to how interested parties can bring about change.

What Publishing Professionals Can Do:

When scandals occur, editors often play the Good Wife, standing by their authors in the face of accusations, agreeing to review the facts, and sometimes bailing out if evidence proves to be irrefutable. That's fine, and who can blame them? Let's put an end to the collective throwing up of hands, however, when publishers issue statements that they share the fans' disappointment, because they, too, have been hoodwinked.

Some publishing houses are already taking a more active role in the vetting process, and have begun to seek verification from authors. Not all have changed their policies, though, and from a business standpoint you have to wonder why. It has long been common practice at respected news organizations to ask even highly credentialed reporters for documentation. And why wouldn't they? It seems to make a lot of sense, when you consider that most tax accountants require documentation when they prepare individual tax returns. They don't want to be seen as responsible for falsifications. In book publishing, documentation review should be *de rigueur*. Copy editors might be the ones to handle this task. These hardworking and widely knowledgeable professionals enter the life of a manuscript after it has been sold to a publishing house. Copy editors are often an author's last line of defense from being made to look foolish by mistakes missed by the author, agent, and acquisitions editor.

New authors are sometimes taken aback when their manuscripts are returned with questions and challenges. A copy editor might write, "You mention this has to do with X, but I checked a source and found that . . ." Over the years, thousands of authors have thanked their lucky stars for copy editors, the unsung heroes of publishing.

It would seem worth it for publishing houses to pay copy editors to check data. Some author experiences are impossible to document, but a great deal can be. If someone claims that he was a certain age when fighting in a war, it doesn't take much effort to verify historical facts. These renewed efforts won't catch everything, but when an acquisitions editor says she stands behind her author, she can speak with conviction.

What Memoirists Can Do:

As for the role of the memoirist in this regard, when and if necessary, include a disclaimer, even if it means risking the loss of potential readers. Increasingly, authors are doing just that. In Susanna Sonnenberg's memoir, *Her Last Death* (Scribner: 2008), about her traumatic childhood with a glamorous addicted mother and narcissistic father, the author wrote: "I have conflated or changed some events and dialogue, and created occasional composites." A *Publishers Weekly* writer criticized the author as having diluted the story's power by blurring nonfiction. Criticism such as this failed to dim the author's prospects. The book became a bestseller and attracted many positive reviews. Sonnenberg should be commended for her honesty.

In *The Memory Palace* (Free Press: 2011), Mira Bartok makes her quest for the truth a major theme. In an author's note, she writes that she has, ". . . reconstructed various conversations and condensed certain moments from my life. . . . I have tried my best to follow my own memory's capricious and meandering path along the way."

Other authors make narrative distinctions between unforgettable moments and those that exist only as broad outlines. In *The Boys of My Youth* (Little, Brown: 1998), a collection of autobiographical sketches, Jo Ann Beard offers both strange and foggy bursts of memories, and up-close experiences so deeply felt that at one point readers can imagine riding on her handlebars.

Mary McCarthy, the author of *Memories of a Catholic Girlhood* (Mariner: 1972), went a step further in communicating her approach to truth telling. McCarthy, now deceased, was a well-known critic and political activist. She wrote interchapter notes explaining which details were inferred or invented and admitted that it was impossible to recollect every detail of every event and conversation. Admittedly, she had an established fan base when her book was published, but her work continues to attract readers.

Should your book become subject to challenge, learn from the mistakes of countless politicians. Get the truth out, and get it out early. It will probably come out anyway, and this way, at least, you can retain a modicum of control.

Finally, since this chapter examines the relationship between the reader and memoirist, it's crucial to challenge you, the memoirist, to examine your relationship with yourself. Telling the truth is a way of maintaining readers' trust in you and the genre, but just as important, it's also about honoring your life with a story well told.

As author Walter Mosley suggested in a *New York Times* essay about his childhood home, our truths are self-contained and are the essence of who we become and remain. He wrote, "This is my memory of home. The boundaries have become smaller as I have aged. The passions have receded and the sun shines less brightly. But none of that matters because the primitive heart that remembers is, in a way, eternal."

Trust that your truths will lead you to your own unique story. The distortion that Greg Mortenson may have created about stumbling upon a path that ultimately led to his future of building schools, may have been as much a loss for him (and of his coauthor) as it was for readers. We will always be left to wonder how this point might have been told truthfully while still retaining its power. Here's what may have actually occurred: Guides from an entirely different culture led him through dangerous mountain ranges. Now, that's a point of vulnerability that might well have been explored. The kind of cross-cultural trust necessary in this situation could be far more dramatic than getting lost.

As an example of the power of truth, there is Tobias Wolff's intense and celebrated memoir, *This Boy's Life*. In writing about his emotionally bruising childhood, Wolff might have attracted more attention had he depicted his stepfather as even more of a monster—beating him senseless, for instance. Instead, this writer depicts a battle of wills between the man and boy, which intensifies the drama, especially because, as it turns out, this brute meets his match. Wolff's darkly brilliant book, which was made into a film, remains a classic. This author's work and his enduring career are reminders that memoirists owe truth telling to their readers, to their craft, and just as important, to themselves. Telling the truth is a literary act of self-love.

HONING YOUR CRAFT

If you aren't writing, here are some tips to get you going.

- **Schedule time on your calendar to write, and protect and use that time.**

- **Turn off your phone and Internet.**

- **Record your earliest memory and make conjectures about why you retained this memory and what it might suggest about your life.**

- **Study photos of yourself taken during the time period about which you plan to write. Write what comes to mind.**

- **Write a chronology of your life in bullet points. Read through it aloud. Choose a period that resonates with you, and then write about that.**

- **No matter how little you may write during your designated time period, try not to get distracted with chores or by anything else.**

- **If you do get distracted, go back and record on your calendar how much time you spent writing. In subsequent efforts, lengthen your writing time.**

- When stuck, print what you've written and continue by writing by hand—your earliest form of writing—to trick your brain into releasing memories.

- If you're still resisting, it may be that the youthful aspect of your personality might need soothing, so give in. Climb into bed, or a comfortable chair or sofa and turn on a movie, TV show, or favorite music, keeping the volume low, while you attempt to write. Give yourself permission to watch the movie or show, or enjoy the music. After a while, you may become engaged in writing, and forget about the entertainment.

- Speak lovingly and encouragingly to yourself. Turn self-defeating thoughts into something positive, allowing your imagination to flower.

- Remember the mind/body connection. When you nurture your body (eating well, exercising, etc.) you're nurturing your mind, and expanding and strengthening your creative possibilities.

- Finally, self-visualization has proved beneficial to some top athletes, and can help you, too. If you still aren't writing, picture yourself writing your memoir. Make that vision specific: imagine the words that you will be writing. Take yourself to where you want to be imaginatively.

PART TWO

MAJOR MEMOIR CATEGORIES

Three

Coming-of-Age Memoirs

IT HAS BEEN SAID THAT THE ONLY GOOD THING THAT EVER came from having bad parents is that they make good memoirs. That's an interesting saying; unfortunately, it is a widespread notion that leads too many writers to turn out boilerplate coming-of-age memoirs, the subgenre that covers the passage of time from childhood to adulthood.

The good news is that many agents would love to get their hands on a coming-of-age story that sends editors into a bidding frenzy. And not just because bidding wars can translate into big advances, which would then ensure that a publisher would work especially hard to promote the book once it's sent to the market.

A coming-of-age manuscript that attracts attention would signal the arrival of something unique. Reading through stacks of submissions I feel tremendous sympathy for those who have suffered, but at the same time, I find that unique coming-of-age story lines are few and far between. Too many of these manuscripts boil down to true-life horror stories, mind-numbingly similar narratives of dysfunctional parents.

The first time I heard that story line I was so captivated by the dramatic course of events that I practically sat on the edge of my seat. That would have been when I was a girl in church, listening to a reading from Genesis 22, as Abraham stretched forth his hand and took the knife to slay his son.

The next time I read that story line I found it highly disturbing in *Mommie Dearest* (William Morrow: 1978), written by Christina Crawford, the adopted daughter of film legend Joan Crawford. The author accused her Academy Award–winning mother of abuse. This exposé became a bestseller and made it to the big screen. Best of all, the book put the subject of child abuse on the cultural map.

A more recent book that follows the template is *Whateverland: Learning to Live Here* (Wiley: 2011). Authors Alexis Stewart and Jennifer Koppelman Hutt captured much attention with their dual memoir, and not simply because the two host a television show. Stewart's mom happens to be Martha Stewart. Although Alexis Stewart claims that the book was intended to be humorous, it does seem to ensure that the lifestyle guru who raised her will not be honored with a Mother of the Year award.

So many complicated childhoods have been turned into books that the only way to beat what's already out there is to tell your own story in a way that separates it from the pack. Here are suggestions to help you accomplish that.

1. Do Some Voice Training

Think of how frustrating it can be when you answer the phone and someone starts talking without stopping to identify herself, assuming that you recognize her from the sound of her voice, but you don't. Or how about a text message wishing you a happy holiday, but the person doesn't include his name. That's the kind of frustration readers experience when an author hasn't developed a distinctive writing style, aka "writer's voice."

From the perspective of the reader/author relationship, checking out a writer's voice is like speed dating, when potential partners spend just a few minutes interviewing one another to see whether there's any interest. Even before readers reach the end of the first page, they may decide it's time to move on, and away from your story.

A writer's voice isn't necessarily made distinctive with fancy words or accents or inflections. *Riding in Cars with Boys: Confessions of a Bad Girl Who Makes Good* (William Morrow: 1990), is told in the no-nonsense voice of Beverly Donofrio's narrator. The voice fits the character, and with use of humor, insight, and doses of inspiration, the author spins what might have been a run-of-the mill story of teenage sex, drinking, and early pregnancy into a page-turner. This bestseller was made into a film.

Your writer's voice should sound like you, reveal your personality, perhaps a sense of humor, and, if you are writing as your younger self, reflect through the use of idioms and phrases the time and place about which you are writing. A successful memoirist can wipe bored looks right off the faces of the most jaded agents. Think of Scottish singer Susan Boyle and how she wowed Simon Cowell in the famous YouTube video clip of *Britain's Got Talent*. Boyle sang "I Dreamed a Dream," from *Les Misérables*. Folks had heard the song many times before, but Boyle's voice and earnest manner got everyone excited.

In writing *The Liars' Club* (Viking: 1995), Mary Karr pulled off a literary version of Boyle's feat. Karr created a young narrator from East Texas who speaks so authentically that my coauthor, Brenda Lane Richardson, one of Karr's ardent fans, claims she wanted to grab that girl by the hand and promise to take her home and feed her, if she would just keep talking. Listening to the audio version or reading the book aloud is an excellent way to do some voice training. In the scene that follows, Karr is a child, riding in a car that her mother is driving over a bridge:

> Not surprisingly, this was the scene of a suicide every year or so. Jilted suitors and bankrupt oilmen favored it. Those who jumped from the highest point of the bridge broke every bone in their bodies. I remember Mother reading this fact out loud from the paper one time, then saying that women tended to gas themselves or take sleeping pills—things that didn't mess them up on the outside so much. She liked to quote James Dean about leaving a beautiful corpse.
>
> Anyway, it was this bridge that the car bumped onto with Mother singing the very scariest part of "Mack the Knife." She sang it very whispery, like a lullaby:
>
> *"When the shark bites with his teeth, dear,*
> *Scarlet billows start to spread . . ."*
>
> The car tipped way back when we mounted the bridge. It felt sort of like the long climb a roller coaster will start before its deep fall. Mother's singing immediately got drowned out by the steel webbing under the tires that made the whole car shimmy. At the same time—impossibly enough—we seemed to be going faster.

Karr's voice retains its youthfulness—with the use of words and phrases such as "anyway," and slang such as "mess up." She parrots grown-up hyperbole, such as "broke every bone in their bodies." Like a musical instrument, her voice plays varying notes. There is one note that she uses when telling of "Mother" offering tidbits from the paper, calmly discussing a womanly approach to suicide. Karr strikes a different chord when depicting her mother's scary rendition of a familiar song. Notice the syntax, the way in which she conveys her experience. For instance, the car bumps onto the bridge, rather than rolls. And lullabies are generally expected to be reassuring, but not from this mother. The rhythm of Karr's sentences change as she transitions from women gassing themselves to the shimmying of the car.

Through the strength of her voice, Karr takes us for a ride—not by depicting her mother as a venomous harridan, but by convincing us that this intelligent, observant woman is very human and yet very dangerous. She has prepared her daughter quite conversationally for this moment, when they might man up and join the bankrupt oilmen who don't care about dying pretty, so anxious are they to plunge into the waters.

HONING YOUR CRAFT

Mary Karr and several other notable memoirists studied poetry before narrative writing, and their literary voices are all the better for it. Too many writers dismiss poetry as inscrutable code language for the elite. That's unfortunate, because there's a world of poetry—from haiku to sonnets to free verse to lyrics—that soundly refutes that charge. If you doubt this, read works by U.S. Poet Laureate Philip Levine. When it was announced in 2011 that this former laborer had been appointed the nation's top poet, sales of his books soared, a rarity for poetry. Here are some other ideas for honing your voice with poetry.

- Read Rita Dove's *Thomas and Beulah* (Carnegie-Mellon University Press: 1986), a collection of interrelated poems loosely based on the life of her grandparents. Dove is a former U.S. Poet Laureate, and a Pulitzer Prize recipient.

- Watch folks recite their favorite poems by visiting www .favoritepoem.org/videos.html.

- Visit the poetryfoundation.org to find poems and browse through archived issues of *Poetry* magazine, dating back to 1912.

- View discussions of poetry by visiting pbs.org/newshour. Under "Teacher Resources," if you enter "poetry" into the search engine you'll find interviews with contemporary poets, some reading their works aloud. There are also writing lessons that include subjects such as "Rap as Lyrical Poetry."

- Support the organization whose name honors the connection between narrative writers and poets. The nonprofit literary organization Poets & Writers is well known for its bimonthly magazine. You can find news about workshops and informational pieces about writing, social networking and marketing on the organization's Web site: www.pw.org/magazine.

- If there's a child in your life, read aloud infectious selections by poets such as Marilyn Nelson's *A Little Bitty Man and Other Poems for the Very Young* (Candlewick: 2011), Shel Silverstein's *Where the Sidewalk Ends* (HarperCollins: 1974), Eloise Juan Felipe Herrera's *Cinnamon Girl: Letters Found Inside a Cereal Box* (HarperCollins: 2005).

- Browse through poetry collections at a bookstore or a public library. When you find something that resonates, notice the poet's economy of words, figurative language, and images that remain most vivid to you. Consider copying favorite poems and carrying them in your pocket calendar for quick moments of inspiration.

Learning to speak in your own distinct writer's voice is like a child learning to use language. It doesn't happen overnight, but as you continue to read and study exceptional poets, and just as important, practice your own writing, you will notice how vital voice is for turning a ho-hum story into one that hums.

Writers often confuse the literary term "voice" with the technique of "tone." A writer's voice should change in tone, depending upon the characters' emotions and attitudes. Carlos Eire does an excellent job of setting tone in his deeply moving first memoir, *Waiting for Snow in Havana: Confessions of a Cuban Boy* (Free Press: 2004).

The scene that follows mentions Eire's father, an aristocratic Cuban judge who's convinced that he is a reincarnation of Louis XVI. There's also mention of the family's maid, Caridad, an unabashed thief. The scene occurs shortly before the Cuban revolution. The boy's father has banned the maid from playing Cuban music in the main part of the house, because it disturbs his memories of concerts at Versailles. Eire writes:

> Caridad loved to taunt me when my parents weren't around. "Pretty soon you're going to lose all this. Pretty soon you'll be sweeping my floor." . . . With menacing smirks, she threatened that if I ever told my parents about her taunts, she would put a curse on me.
>
> "I know all sorts of curses. Changó listens to me; I offer him the best cigars, and plenty of firewater. I'll hex you and your whole family. Changó and I will set a whole army of devils upon you."
>
> My father had warned me about the evil powers of Changó and the African gods. He spoke to me of men struck dead in the prime of life, of housewives driven mad with love for their gardeners, of children horribly disfigured. So I kept quiet. But

I think she put a curse on me anyway, and my whole family, for not allowing her to steal and taunt and until that day, "pretty soon," when she could take over the house. Her devils swooped down on all of us, with the same speed as the rebels that swept across the whole island on that day.

Eire has set a disquieting tone, preparing us for the coming storm. Throughout the book, the narrator employs an irrepressible and likable schoolboy's voice, but it is the tone that conveys the author's feelings toward particular subjects. Caridad's threats are clearly meant to frighten him, but her obstinacy in the face of powerlessness gives her an air of nobility. The rebels may not have yet arrived but she is already in rebellion.

The boy is feeling unsettled. That he's unsure about whom to trust is clear from his choice of memories. For instance, it feels as if it's no coincidence that the father feels a connection to King Louis XVI of France, a monarch beheaded by insurrectionists during the French Revolution. The father implies that the only way a housewife could desire a lowly gardener is if an evil god possesses her mind. The father's words, filtered through the narrator, give us a sense of the father's exaggerated self-importance, and subtly allow us to see what the adult author implies—that this man, and others like him, have an unjustified claim to power, and may indeed need to be overthrown. Finally, using dramatic foreshadowing, the author recalls the day when Caridad's warnings are realized. A *New Yorker* review described Eire's tone as "urgent," and "vividly personal."

2. Universalize Your Story

The themes of Eire's childhood make his story universal. Writers hoping for wide readership will want to universalize a story. This is a way of telling a story with a theme in which, despite differences—such as nationality, race, gender, faith, etc.—it connects with the shared beliefs, assumptions, longings, and fears of many others.

Let's consider the larger picture that unfolds in *Waiting for Snow in Havana*. Shortly after the start of Fidel Castro's revolution, Eire was one of fourteen thousand children sent from the island country to Miami, one of many youngsters separated from their parents. Without his family and all that was familiar, Eire felt he had lost everything. Some of his readers—including many schoolchildren assigned to read *Waiting for Snow*—empathize with Eire's experience in their own family immigration stories. However, his story may also resonate with readers who have not lived through similar circumstances. Most people understand loss, an overarching theme of his book.

Here's a different example of themes connected with universal desires. Many people would agree that there is great value in a simple, self-sufficient life. Yearning for uncomplicated, rural life was the theme of a memoir written by nineteenth-century naturalist Henry David Thoreau. His autobiographical work, *Walden* (Ticknor and Fields: 1854), challenged overconsumption and convinced a great many of the joys of pastoral life. Today, you won't have to look far to find urban dwellers holding fast to the ideal that their lives would improve if they could develop a deep connection with the earth.

Employing a melancholic tone, author Melissa Coleman challenges that notion in her bestselling coming-of-age memoir, *This Life Is in Your Hands: One Dream, Sixty Acres, and a Family Undone* (HarperCollins: 2011). In 1968, Coleman's parents moved to a remote, sixty-acre stretch of land near the coast of Maine, where they became homesteaders.

This story contrasts idealism and reality, the beauty of a bucolic setting versus a family's grueling life. Despite the bountifulness of the land, their existence was often defined by what they did not have: insurance, running water, and electricity. Their lives were shaped by scarcity, including the confines of a one-room house, and eating a diet based solely on vegetables that they raised, which led to vitamin deficiencies.

What's more, the rural setting may have bolstered the family's sense of feeling safer than they might have in a metropolitan area, but the story suggests that there is no place on earth where people can be protected from emotional devastation. In fact, Coleman's three-year-old sister drowned in a pond, her mother struggled with depression, and her parents subsequently divorced. In reviewing the book, an NPR critic wrote: "This is a story of paradise lost; of why the earth both gives and takes away."

A MARKETPLACE SURVIVAL TIP

Be prepared for agents or editors to ask about your theme. Your ability to identify a theme indicates your level of progress. Don't panic if you haven't identified one. It can take a few rewrites before you know where you're going. And "going" is an important word when it pertains to this subject. A manuscript without a theme is like riding in a car that has no steering wheel. Without it, your manuscript will feel directionless, lacking in purpose and guidance. Although the theme may not be stated in your story, your readers should be able to discern it.

If someone in the business asks, "What's your book about?" you might want to mention the theme, and if time allows, embellish upon that by offering details of the plot (a short summation of the story).

If you haven't figured out your theme, here's a question that might prompt a quick response: If you found out that you only had a few minutes to live, based upon your story, what basic lesson or truth would you want to share with your loved ones? Write down some responses and see what you come up with. Some people have answered, "Love makes life worth living," and, "Faith will sustain you." The theme in the first response suggests the importance of love; the second, the importance of faith.

Here's another way of identifying your theme. Based upon your memoir, what quality do you most value? Some might say happiness. This is one of the broad subjects at the heart of many themes. Chris Gardner's *The Pursuit of Happyness*, written in collaboration with Quincy Troupe (Amistad: 2006), was a highly popular memoir that was made into an Academy Award–nominated film. With its theme spelled out in the title, the author—a former homeless man turned successful financial executive—suggested that people had to look inward to their own gifts to find happiness.

Remember that a theme doesn't have to be long and complex or philosophically deep. It can be about the fragility of life or perseverance or overexposure.

Another way to understand the concept of a theme is to think of a children's story that teaches a moral. The story of "Beauty and the Beast" taught us that appearances are often deceptive. The theme would be the nature of beauty, or the importance of interior beauty.

If a theme remains elusive, consider characters, setting, and events. What ideas tie your story elements together? You can also sum up the book's subject: "It's about a boy who never wants to grow up and leave home, but needs to." A thematic interpretation of that would be "Fear of adulthood." It's a universal theme, best known from *Peter Pan*.

3. Understand Why Readers Love Coming-of-Age Stories

On the most simplistic level, a wide swath of people identify with coming-of-age stories because everyone had a childhood. Many people looking back upon their own lives feel they can put their pasts into perspective when reading about those of others.

Readers also have a particular empathy for the narrators of these books since practically all of us can recall being young and at the mercy of adults. While the narrators of various other subgenres may happen to be in a fix because they put themselves wherever they are—such as freezing to death on a mountaintop, or financially ruined at the poker table—the narrators in coming-of-age stories seem simply to have had the bad luck of being born into distressing circumstances. Mind you, there has to be distress—it's what is known as conflict, and without it there can be no story.

TAKE THIS PERSONALLY

For those raised in disruptive situations, portraying conflict can be one of the most difficult aspects of memoir writing. But you might be surprised at the number of conflict-avoiding manuscripts that agents receive. The problem with this is that conflict isn't optional in a commercial memoir. One conflict should to lead to another and these build suspense. Conflict can exist between characters or opposing forces.

If you're having trouble figuring out the importance of conflict in a story, take a field trip to a movie theater to watch a critically acclaimed film or stay home to watch Netflix. You might watch a TV show, such as *Friday Night Lights*, or the film *The Descendants*, starring George Clooney. Make a mental list as one conflict after another is presented, and note how they draw you into the story. In *The Descendants*, one of the main characters, a woman in an irreversible coma, starts out simply as a body on a respirator. As the story develops, conflicts swirl around her and those who know her, and in the process, breathe life into a character that once seemed as stiff and remote as, well, a corpse. In including *The Descendants* in a list of 2011 best films, *Chicago Sun-Times* critic Roger Ebert said of the film's protagonists, "We come to understand how they think, and care about what they decide about the substantial moral problems underlying the plot." As in this story and others that move us, conflict can bring characters vibrantly alive, without forcing a writer to rely on what can be ruinous sentimentality.

Conflict can be presented as a clash of cultures. The title of Ben Fong-Torres's *The Rice Room: Growing Up Chinese-American from Number Two Son to Rock 'n' Roll* (Hyperion: 1994) addresses familial tension. The author was one of the first editors of *Rolling Stone*. His character was portrayed in the film *Almost Famous*. Fong-Torres's story underscores the conflict of growing up with two identities, traditional Chinese and American. Stephanie Elizondo Griest's *Mexican Enough: My Life between the Borderlines* (Washington Square: 2008), offers a cultural schism with a twist. The offspring of a white father and Mexican mother, the author travels to Mexico in search of her maternal roots and arrives during a period of major social upheaval.

Sometimes conflict can occur between parents, which usually means a child gets squeezed between them. In Robert Leleux's gleeful *Memoirs of a Beautiful Boy* (St. Martin's: 2008), the story of a gay boy in Texas, the author wasn't caught in the middle, not one bit. On one side there was the father, insisting his son spend time at a live cattle auction. Standing firmly on the other side were the author and his be-wigged, mink coat–wearing mama, worried that they'd be late for their hair and nail appointments.

Remember, too, that conflict in these stories doesn't have to center around parents. Alison Smith, the author of *Name All the Animals* (Scribner: 2004), hails from a close-knit Catholic family. When she is fifteen and her eighteen-year-old brother is killed in a car accident, she and her parents suffer terribly. The story is Smith's, though. It is not about her parents' failures so much as it is about her emergence from her brother's shadow.

Conflict is both external and internal in the highly lauded graphic coming-of-age story, *Stitches* (W. W Norton: 2009), by award-winning children's book illustrator David Small. Raised in a home where his unhappy parents didn't communicate their feelings or pretty much anything, Small was subjected to numerous X-rays for minor sinus infections by his radiologist father. When he developed cancer, his father operated on him, without explanation. Small awoke to discover that a vocal cord had been removed, and that his throat had been slashed and stitched back together. The conflicts for Small are whether to fight to get his voice back and whether to speak up about his childhood horrors.

As a memoirist who may have experienced trauma in your own life, you, too, will have to decide whether to speak or remain silent. While writing about conflict may prove challenging, it may help to know that it will keep readers turning pages. They will become invested in your story and want to know how things turned out for you.

....

Conflict can also be found in fairy tales. The theories of child psychologist Bruno Bettelheim concerning fairy tales and the conflicts they present may help you understand why readers feel drawn to coming-of-age stories.

Remember the wicked stepmother who mistreated Cinderella? How about the weak and negligent father who allowed Hansel and Gretel to get lost in the woods? Bettelheim's groundbreaking work, *The Uses of Enchantment: The Meaning and Importance of Fairy Tales* (Knopf: 1976), explains that these kinds of stories can, "help a child clarify his emotions, be attuned to his anxieties and aspirations; give full recognition to his difficulties, while at the same time suggesting solutions to the problems that perturb him." In the end, Bettelheim explains, these stories can strengthen a child's confidence in himself and his future.

You may want to reflect further on Bettelheim's theory, pertaining to the ways in which coming-of-age stories can meet similar therapeutic needs in adults, as you read about the two memoirs discussed below.

The title of Mira Bartók's *The Memory Palace* sounds as if it's straight out of a fairy tale, but the story is anything but. Early on, the author returns to Cleveland to visit the mother from whom she has been estranged for more than fifteen years. The mother, a pianist who suffered from schizophrenia and later in life became homeless, raised Bartók and her sister. Their alcoholic father abandoned them in childhood.

Despite their misfortunes, Bartók, an artist and writer of children's books, and her sister, an English professor and writer, become accomplished in their fields. A social worker kept Bartók updated on her mother's whereabouts and needs, so she could send her necessities, as well as gifts and letters. After her mother became violent, Bartók maintained an unpublished phone number and address.

When Bartók returns to see her dying mother, she finds that her own diminished circumstances have brought them closer together. A few years earlier Bartók had been brought low by a car accident in which she suffered traumatic brain injury. Unable to work, she'd had to get by on disability checks as her self-confidence eroded.

At her dying mother's bedside, her own struggle with long- and short-term impaired memory elicits an empathetic response. In one of her mother's diaries Bartók finds the entry, "I am a refugee. I'm looking for my children and the key to my home." Readers understand that the search has ended. The women have found one another. The intense love is re-experienced in their final days together.

Sorting through her mother's storage unit, she finds objects that remind her of times past, memories that comprise much of the book, and for which Bartók imagines an elaborate palace for storing those she wants to retain.

While reading the plot of *The Memory Palace*, you may have noticed that it contains many of the elements of a fairy tale: distracted, weak, or absent parents; innocent children endowed with interior gifts; hardship and a reunion. Bartók's setting sometimes even feels as if borrowed from the Brothers Grimm. Returning to the family home, she finds a "wilderness of brambles and frozen weeds." Finally, she has filled the pages of this book with lovely drawings; many as lushly designed as if for a fairy tale.

Similarities between coming-of-age stories and fairy tales are not unique to Bartók's story. Young memoir protagonists often survive plights reminiscent of heroines such as "Cinderella" or "Jack and the Beanstalk." In *Who Do You Think You Are?* (Touchstone: 2008), Alyse Myers spends the first decade of her life as a treasured daddy's girl. After his untimely death, she becomes the target of her mother's cruelty. Like the beleaguered heroines of fairy-tale lore, Myers's early suffering makes her eventual triumphs—admission to a gifted high school, a sound marriage, and an executive position at *The New York Times*—feel all the more inspiring.

It's interesting to note that Bettelheim suggested that children need symbolic solutions, to help them realize that they, too, can overcome life's challenges. Coming-of-age stories such as *The Memory Palace* and *Who Do You Think You Are?* expand the imaginative reach of adults, allowing them to consider a fuller range of possibilities. Although the two genres share similar elements, commercial success for coming-of-age memoirs requires that they must also be substantially different from fairy tales.

Consider how fairy tales often end with wistful and sentimental images of how the world might be (happily ever after), while coming-of-age stories are grounded in frank recognition of realities. Children's stories include demonized, caricatured characters, while adult stories should offer multidimensional individuals. In some cases, coming-of-age authors might offer an adult perspective that softens a cruel character's image. That happens in *Who Do You Think You Are?* Myers later learns that her father had actually been a philanderer, and her mother a morphine addict.

Of course, in real-life stories, rehabilitating a "villain" may sometimes prove impossible. The unrelenting cruelty of the father in Barbara Robinette Moss's memoir, *Change Me into Zeus's Daughter* (Scribner: 2000), makes him an entirely unsympathetic character. Although he softens toward the end of the book, readers can't help but feel relieved when he dies. *Change Me into Zeus's Daughter* works on so many other levels that it serves as a reminder that if you write well (sometimes) readers will follow.

Villains don't have to be people. In Bartók's book, the "villain" is the overburdened and underfunded mental health system, which fails to provide adequately for people like her mother. In the real world some things that are broken are never mended. But something seemingly magical can happen in these stories. That Bartók and Myers have become gifted memoirists, still capable of experiencing heartfelt love, reminds us that the possibility of healing is a reality.

4. Devise a Unique Way of Telling Your Story

Do you find that the narrative hooks of many coming-of-age stories seem similar to yours? If so, view this as an opportunity to devise something different. Following are suggestions and questions to help you energize your manuscript.

- ◆ **BRING THE SETTING OF YOUR CHILDHOOD TO LIFE: If you were raised in a geographical environment that shaped the events of your life, how might that place figure into a coming-of-age memoir? How has this place shaped you? What descriptions of the climate, geography, architecture, and foods might you include? What makes this area unique? What aspects of the regional culture might be of interest to readers? How might the setting affect the mood of your story? What is distinctive or historic about where you lived? What was happening in this setting during your youth that may have impacted you?**

To see how some published authors have worked place into story, consider Kim Barnes. Born to an Idaho family of loggers, she clearly had her childhood terrain in mind when writing *In the Wilderness: Coming of Age in an Unknown Country* (Doubleday: 1996). As mechanization weakened the logging business, her father turned to religious fundamentalism for strength. Barnes was harshly punished in adolescence when she failed to adhere to the church's strict tenets and was later sent away. In adulthood, she incorporated both love of her parents and the land, and her faith, into her self-image. Her book was a finalist for the Pulitzer Prize.

Another memoir that develops fully the character of the land is *The Road from Coorain* (Knopf: 1989), by Jill Ker Conway. The story of this author's extraordinary life portrays her solitary childhood on the parched Australian plains. Conway might have been defeated by the loss of her beloved brother and father, and her mother's subsequent descent into depression. Instead, like the hardy land from which she hails, she seems to grow in character. She eventually became the president of Smith College and a professor at the Massachusetts Institute of Technology. This bestseller was made into a PBS *Masterpiece Theatre* presentation.

Place may also create a mood that mirrors personality. In Laura M. Flynn's *Swallow the Ocean* (Counterpoint: 2008), the San Francisco of the '60s and '70s—with its threat of earthquakes and the repercussions of the countercultural movement—seems an apt setting for the story's emotionally unstable mother, a paranoid schizophrenic. Flynn's readers may feel that they are holding their breath, waiting for the next unpredictable occurrence.

♦ **IF YOU WERE RAISED IN A CULTURE THAT MAY BE OF INTEREST TO OTHERS, WRITE ABOUT IT.** Offer details about the country/ethnicity in which you and/or your parents were raised. Look up facts about that country or ethnicity that might interest readers. What was the belief system of that country/ethnicity? If your grandparents, parents, or you immigrated to another country, explain why they (or you) left. If you were born as the first-generation family member in a newly immigrated country, describe conflicts that existed between generations. If there was an immigration experience, how did you and your family handle feelings of separation and loss? Did your family speak a different language from those in your neighborhood? If so, describe your thoughts about that language. How did people outside your culture/ethnicity react to you? How did you handle differences? What were some of the greatest benefits and drawbacks of being raised in this country/ethnicity?

A coming-of-age story about growing up in a different culture does not have to be grief-filled. The setting of Firoozeh Dumas's *Funny in Farsi: A Memoir of Growing Up Iranian in America* (Random House: 2004) is humorous and inspirational, and serves as a reminder that people are much the same everywhere—for good or ill.

Rick Bragg depicts northeast Alabama's pinewoods and cotton fields in *All Over but the Shoutin'* (Vintage: 1997). The son of an abusive alcoholic, Bragg seems destined to work at the local mills—with luck—or go to prison. With a gift for writing, he grew up to be a *New York Times* journalist who won a Pulitzer Prize.

5. Tell Your Story Through an Exploration of a Relative's Past

What stories did you grow up hearing about your parents or another intriguing relative? How did that person shape you? Are there mysteries about that individual that you uncovered, which helped you better understand him or her? What lessons can you derive from this person's past that made a difference in your life?

First-time author Ariel Sabar's memoir is fueled by his quest to understand his father, and ultimately himself. *My Father's Paradise: A Son's Search for His Jewish Past in Kurdish Iraq* (Algonquin: 2008) won the

National Book Critics Circle Award, and other honors. Sabar's father was a UCLA professor with a passion for Aramaic, his native language, while the youthful Sabar aspired to be a rock-and-roll drummer. The birth of a son heightened the author's interest in his father's heritage.

In *Pig Candy: Taking My Father South, Taking My Father Home* (Free Press: 2008), acclaimed author Lise Funderburg accompanies her difficult father to his family farm in Georgia. The mixed-race author uses her father's complex family history to explore the land mine of American racism. Author JJ Lee, a journalist who writes about menswear, explored his father's sometimes tortured life by tailoring one of his old suits for himself in *The Measure of a Man: The Story of a Father, a Son, and a Suit* (McClelland & Stewart: 2011). The book was a finalist for the Charles Taylor Prize for Literary Non-Fiction.

◆ **IF YOU ARE AN ARTIST OR KNOW ONE WITH WHOM YOU CAN COLLABORATE, CONSIDER WORKING ON A GRAPHIC MEMOIR.** If you imagined your life in pictures, what would you portray? How would you describe the tone in your childhood home? How might it have been unusual from what most people experienced? Who would you identify as the major two or three characters (besides yourself)? What were these characters like? How did they look? Did they have favorite sayings? Was there some expression that you often saw on the faces of any of these characters? What theme would you convey to universalize this story?

For those hoping to learn to create graphic memoirs there are several instructional books. Although we found none specific to memoirs, much of the advice is applicable. These guides include Barbara Slate's *You Can Do a Graphic Novel* (Alpha: 2010). Slate's book is written for a younger audience, but it is also popular with adults. Also consider Nat Gertler and Steve Lieber's *The Complete Idiot's Guide to Creating a Graphic Novel*

(Alpha: 2009) and Will Eisner's *Graphic Storytelling and Visual Narrative* (W. W. Norton: 2008).

Marjane Satrapi's *The Complete Persepolis* (Pantheon: 2007) is a gripping coming-of-age graphic memoir that tells of growing up in revolutionary Iran. Satrapi's drawings and text capture universal adolescent struggles. Her book was adapted into an animated film.

Another example of a graphic story is *Fun Home: A Family Tragicomic* (Houghton Mifflin Harcourt: 2006), by Alison Bechdel, the artist of the syndicated comic strip *Dykes to Watch Out For*. In *Fun Home*, the characters grapple with issues of homosexuality. When Brenda Lane Richardson speaks about graphic memoirs, she recommends this book as an example of how the best stories offer universal themes. After all, many people struggle to feel at home in their own homes and in their bodies.

> ◆ **IF YOUR LIFE INTERSECTS WITH A SIGNIFICANT PERIOD OF HISTORY, SHARE WHAT YOU'VE LEARNED.** History is always unfolding, so don't discount what may have been happening around you and how it may have intersected with your life. Make a list of some of the big events unfolding during your younger years that people were discussing at home, school, or at your religious institution. The events of 9/11 may have changed your life or colored your world. What about the economic recession? How might you weave interesting cultural background into this story? And you are never too old to look back and share vital reminiscences.

Harry Bernstein was in his nineties when he began writing about how anti-Semitism impacted his childhood. A trade magazine editor during his professional life, his first memoir was *The Invisible Wall: A Love Story That Broke Barriers* (Ballantine: 2007). The book portrayed his childhood in pre–World War II England, where "an invisible wall" kept Christians and Jews apart. Bernstein died in 2011 at the age of 101.

Another mature writer, Marjorie Hart, eighty-two, a cellist and retired professor, penned *Summer at Tiffany* (William Morrow: 2007), about her experiences in 1945. The story is set in wartime Manhattan, when Hart and her best friend were hired as pages at Tiffany's, becoming the first female employees to work the sales floor of this prestigious store. Her memoir became a *New York Times* bestseller.

> ◆ **DON'T LIMIT YOUR STORY'S IMPACT: While it's important to not share *every* detail of the minutiae of your experiences, you don't want to limit the power of your story. A book can be about more than one thing, such as a place, historical period, and a central character, and carefully selected details can be realized. Your narrative may dovetail with an important historical time period; the setting may play an important role, and a parent or other relative may take center stage.**

Fully realized details bring to life Alexandra Fuller's highly lauded *Don't Let's Go to the Dogs Tonight* (Random House: 2003), and *Cocktail Hour Under the Tree of Forgetfulness* (Penguin: 2011). The author chronicles her childhood of growing up in Africa in the 1970s, during the Rhodesian War, in a hostile and dangerous environment. In *Cocktail Hour* her mother, Nicola Fuller, is the character that the author yearns to understand. According to *The New Yorker*, this story is driven by the question of, "what it means to come from somewhere, and to care about where you come from as much as her mother, Nicola does."

Another memoir that takes advantage of an historical time period and locale, with depictions of comedic conflict is Mark Salzman's *Lost in Place: Growing Up Absurd in Surbubia* (Vintage: 1996), a coming-of-age story set in the 1970s.

- ◆ **IF AN ISSUE MOVES YOU, USE IT TO EXPAND ON YOUR STORY.**
  Is there a message or idea or way of life that fires you up? Some
  people are passionate about animal rights, vegetarianism, politics, or
  sports, or have had experiences that made a great impact on them—
  living in a foreign country, falling in love for the first time. What
  affected you deeply? How did one of these or others shape your
  childhood or adolescence? What makes you angry, and what do you
  consider unjust? Do you see any of this impacting your life directly?

Wes Moore expanded his coming-of-age story with issues of social injustice. The idiom "There but for the grace of God," propels his memoir, *The Other Wes Moore: One Name, Two Fates* (Spiegel & Grau: 2010). A Rhodes scholar and former aide to Secretary of State Condoleezza Rice, Wes Moore learns that another African American man of the same name, also raised in Baltimore, is an accused cop killer. After the other Wes Moore is convicted and sentenced to life in a penitentiary, the two meet during prison visits. Both young men realize that during their troubled adolescence, each could have moved in different directions and wound up in the shoes of the other.

An $$$Analysis of this bestselling memoir may prove to be instructive.

$Writing Chops

The Other Wes Moore received a coveted starred review from *Publishers Weekly*, with the reviewer praising the author for writing "with subtlety and insight," and describing this work as "a moving exploration of roads not taken." *The Other Wes Moore* also received a starred review from *Booklist*, a publication of the American Library Association geared toward libraries and booksellers.

Perhaps because the author wants to avoid sounding judgmental, he does not offer much insight as to the other Wes Moore's motivations, which is a shortcoming in this work. Moore tells his story in straightforward and unembellished prose. His research strengths are apparent. The story makes a compelling argument for the need for social intervention in the lives of at-risk adolescents. Moore makes good use of dramatic ironies, writing, "While I was on my way to study at Oxford, my namesake was on his way to do life in prison." Moore scores 7.5 points in the writing category.

$Narrative Hook

Everyone seems to have an opinion on the subject of social equality. Some would insist that everyone has an equal chance to succeed in this country, while others would point out that some people are born with the deck stacked against them. Wes Moore's story of two intelligent young black men, born in the same city, without fathers, and heading in opposite directions is an attention-getter that courts a fair share of controversy. The subtitle spells out the narrative hook: one name, two fates. This dual memoir lands squarely in the memorable narrative hook range, earning a full 10 points.

$Platform Strength

Moore's publishers must have been aware that an estimated 74 percent of people in the U.S. have highly favorable opinions of the American military. Readers may feel predisposed to admire Moore, and that would probably be so even if he were not a veteran. His military involvement certainly burnishes his heroic image and conveys resoluteness. A former paratrooper and captain in the U.S. Army, he served a combat tour of duty in Afghanistan. He comes across as an exemplary figure, knowledgeable but not arrogant, serene and yet commanding. A White House Fellow from 2006 to 2007, where he served as a Special Assistant to Condoleezza Rice, his experience serves him well in interviews. Whether speaking to a crowd or being interviewed by a journalist, he appears unflappable, and projects warmth and passion.

Like many of today's most successful of authors, Moore has the support of a nonprofit group that reflects his interests. As a board member of the Iraq Afghanistan Veterans of America (IAVA), he helps to bring attention to the needs of this group, and his profile and book is available on the IAVA Web site (http://iava.org/blog/wes-moore-afghanistan -veteran-inspirational-leader-and-iava-board-member-releases-critically -ac). The site features a video clip that describes *The Other Wes Moore*. He earns a full 10 points for his writing platform. This bestselling book garners a total score of 27.5.

GOING VIRTUAL

Moore's success is a reminder that a picture is worth a thousand words. Videos of Moore and his book can be seen on sites for Amazon, Random House, YouTube, and IAVA. Mira Bartók, whose memoir was discussed earlier, can be found on Amazon, YouTube, Simon & Schuster, and thememorypalace.com. Robert Leleux offers an animated version of *Memoirs of a Beautiful Boy* on YouTube, and includes a choice of videos.

You may want to view author videos so you can learn from the more successful efforts. Publishing houses produce some of these videos, but that is not always the case. An increasing number are homemade. There are also a number of film/TV and animation students who are looking for ways to build their portfolios. You can contact your local schools and universities to work with students to produce for you. There are also professional companies like Turnhere.com. Many authors use talk show formats shot with webcams and upload them onto YouTube.

You don't have to wait for your book to be published to star in your own video, but you should be knowledgeable. Once you are conversant about the theme, plot, conflicts, facts, and statistics that undergird your book, consider having a friend or colleague interview you on camera. These interviews can be helpful when you're contacting agents so you can display your range of knowledge and the level of comfort you exhibit on camera. The best aspect about starting early is that practice makes perfect. If you're not yet comfortable in front of a camera, you have time to improve.

Don't feel obliged to produce a one-on-one interview. Get creative with the anagram S.M.I.L.E., which can (but doesn't have to) stand for Surprising, Memorable, Inspiring, Loving, or Entertaining. Using the letter L, for example, perhaps your loving idea involves a romantic notion, and you want to have some fun with this theme. You might enjoy writing your own soap opera around the theme of your coming-of-age memoir and convince a friend or relative to star in it with you. And there are lots of ways to present an episodic soap experience. When you're happy with the results you might post your video or photos on sharing sites, such as Pinterest. If you're advanced in the video arena, consider starting a vlog—a blog with videos that emphasizes images over words. If you're lucky enough to have a video that goes viral, learn how to cash in on your good fortune at: www.nytimes.com/2011/10/27/technology/personaltech/cashing-in-on-your-hit-youtube-video.html.

Four

Addiction and
Compulsion Memoirs

ADDICTION TO DRUGS AND ALCOHOL IS SAID TO AFFECT more than 13 percent of the U.S. population, but even more people seem to be affected than that figure implies. Think of all the celebrities who've reportedly battled with alcohol or drugs. A listing of just a few include Amy Winehouse, Lindsay Lohan, Charlie Sheen, Robert Downey Jr., Michael Jackson, Kate Moss, Keith Richards, Whitney Houston, Britney Spears, and Kiefer Sutherland. Addictions have also impacted the lives of a pantheon of authors: Aldous Huxley, William Faulkner, John Cheever, Ernest Hemmingway, F. Scott Fitzgerald, James Baldwin, and Stephen King.

Nor are addictions new. The use of buzz-creating substances may date back to prehistoric times, which means that some hunter-gathers were probably looking for something stronger than wheatgrass. Today, staggering numbers of us have been raised or abandoned by alcoholics or addicts; or brought up hearing about addicted relatives who wreaked havoc; or need only to look in a mirror to see an addict in close proximity.

I don't know why, but it came as a surprise when one of the rising stars in the literary agent community wrote about his addiction to crack cocaine. Bill Clegg, preppy looking and Connecticut-born, founded a Manhattan agency with a partner, where they garnered big advances for their A-list authors; their subsequent books were often short-listed for literary prizes.

Clegg's meteoric descent, including the loss of his agency, his clients, and his boyfriend of many years, were chronicled in his memoir, *Portrait of an Addict as a Young Man* (Little, Brown: 2010). In searing prose that serves as a reminder that many successful agents know how to write, Clegg describes a scene in a hotel, where he lit up and got high, keeping a watchful eye on the cocaine crumbs that fell from his pipe, knowing he would soon be on his knees scrounging: "... sometimes for hours— hunched over carpets, rugs, linoleum, tile—sifting desperately through lint and cat litter and dirt, fingering the floor, like a madman, for crumbs. As I pack those lazy crumb-scattering hits in the beginning, I will, each time, think of the floor like a retirement account. Little bits neglected into a place where I will seek them out later."

The good news for Clegg, his friends, and supporters is that he went through rehab and is working again. If the way his book was embraced by the literary community is any indication, there's good reason to believe that publishers are still looking for addiction memoirs, especially those featuring strong writing. Clegg's book has been praised as "vividly rendered," "brutally specific and oddly poetic." Clegg's agent is said to have distributed 130 pages of his manuscript to publishers, and by week's end it had sold for about $350,000, an advance considered impressive for a first-time author.

As we have pointed out, not even good writing is sufficient to attract a publisher's attention. Clegg clearly had other factors working in his favor, and in this case, it was a strong narrative hook—himself. This author is not only a book agent, but he is the antithesis of the crack addict stereotype. Think of the NBC *Dateline* crime reports featuring wealthy or middle-class criminals or victims of crime. Many TV producers view these stories as having a strong hook because their subjects are considered outside the demographic of those expected to be caught up in these situations.

The same standard is applied for RU protagonists in commercially successful addiction memoirs: these characters could be called counterintuitive—very different from what we expect them to be. They are individuals with whom readers identify, because they view their own addiction struggles through the prism of these narratives. Keep in mind that over the years, addictions have taken on new permutations, expanding to include psychological dependencies and behaviors that include pornography, sex, eating, gambling, work, exercise, hoarding, Internet use, and various types of body abuse.

What Readers Look for in Addiction Memoirs

Some early bestsellers set expectations for what readers look for in addiction memoirs. *Go Ask Alice* (Simon Pulse: 1971) is what many believe to be a fictional diary, written by an adult author hoping to warn teenage readers of the dangers of drug abuse. This book about an addicted teenager caused a sensation, became suggested reading in some schools, and was made into an ABC-TV movie.

Seven years later, *The Basketball Diaries* (Penguin: 1978) was also viewed as a cautionary tale. Written by author and musician Jim Carroll, it is based on diaries he kept as a teenager and depicts, in part, his heroin dependency. The book was made into a film. The author died in 2009 at the age of sixty.

Both the protagonists in *Basketball* and *Alice* hit rock bottom. In *Alice*, the protagonist, the daughter of a college professor, is at times homeless and a prostitute. Carroll, a gifted musician, turns to crime and prostitution. Their humiliating downfalls set the tone for the addiction sub-genre, and shaped readers' expectations.

1. ADDICTION PROTAGONISTS ARE EXPECTED TO BE HIGHLY IMPERFECT

Addiction memoirs are among the only subgenres that are not expected to have an admirable protagonist. Despite a wealth of evidence suggesting that genetic factors account for as much as 40–60 percent in the risk for addiction, the public—and by that we mean readers—often perceive addicts as weak-willed, or lacking in discipline and fortitude. In this reader/author relationship, there tends to be less judgment. While readers are both titillated and jaded about celebrity addictions, they seem to reserve a greater quotient of empathy for folks who are more like them or the addicts that they love.

2. ADDICTION PROTAGONISTS ARE EXPECTED TO EXPERIENCE A HARROWING DESCENT

What readers do seem to demand in addiction memoirs is a very steep descent. If the protagonist is going to hit rock bottom, that person must seem so mentally enslaved that he goes right up to the precipice, arms outstretched and hands circling while he teeters over the edge. Writing in *The New York Times*, David Carr, the author of the riveting drug memoir *Night of the Gun* (Simon & Schuster: 2008), explained that this "genre is built on . . . carnal imperatives. People want to drive slowly by and see the blood and abasement. Once they get a good, hard look, they can thank their lucky stars they aren't the ones upside down in a ditch with the wheels spinning above them."

This need of readers to look over the cliff contributed to the success of James Frey's now discredited *A Million Little Pieces*. It is therefore telling that Frey claims to have tried unsuccessfully to sell his manuscript as fiction. Rebranded as a memoir, this semi-fictional tale of a middle-class youth's debauchery—getting arrested several times, being wanted in three states, assaulting a cop, serving jail time—gave readers what they wanted: a protagonist who had actually screwed up more than they or loved ones had, and lived to tell about it. This is what is known as inspiration in an addiction memoir.

As a literary agent, Clegg led a more interesting life than some people, but he was not among the rich and famous. To feed his habit, he blew $70,000 in savings and was unable to continue living in a comfortable Fifth Avenue apartment. He had attained a sufficiently high level of success, and because he was not the kind of person people generally picture when they think of "crack addicts," his descent seemed startling.

3. REDEMPTION IS NECESSARY—AND IS BEST SPELLED OUT IN THE DETAILS

A good many readers struggling with addictions have turned to treatment programs, and or joined the worldwide movement of 12-Step self-help groups. They may have also tried other means of recovery, including going to rehab, working with therapists, and dealing with the depression, shame, guilt, fear, anxiety, and a host of other troubling emotions and problems, including broken relationships. These same people often turn to addiction memoirs for hope and relief. As for those who love addicts, these books can help them cope, and/or feel more compassionate and patient.

Many an addict has read an addiction memoir and sought recovery. In fact, Caroline Knapp, the author of one of the most successful addiction memoirs, *Drinking: A Love Story* (Dial Press: 1996), explained that she sobered up after being inspired by the popular addiction memoir, *A Drinking Life* (Little, Brown: 1994), by Pete Hamill. The circle of admiration was continued as Pulitzer Prize–winning critic Gail Caldwell wrote of her friendship with Knapp in the memoir *Let's Take the Long Way Home* (Random House: 2010). The two writers had much in common, including that both had quit drinking at the age of thirty-three.

What Has Changed Since the Early Publication of Addiction Memoirs

Today's readers are savvy about recovery because they have either experienced it or seen the process on talk shows or reality TV. So consider *Portrait of an Addict*, which seemed poised for astronomical sales. The media paid a great deal of attention to the quality of Clegg's writing, the story, and the author. Just before publication, an excerpt of *Portrait* and photos of Clegg ran in *New York Magazine*, with circulation of 405,000 and a Web site with 8.5 million unique visitors monthly.* Additionally, a three-page feature, complete with color photos of the author, ran in *The New York Times* "Sunday Styles" section. That was followed by David Carr's review of the book in the *New York Times* literary supplement. There were many flattering reviews, including one in *Vogue*. Like a pinball, reviews of the book ricocheted around the Internet.

Despite brisk sales in Los Angeles, however, *Portrait* did not become a national bestseller. Many reviews were positive, and several critics mentioned Clegg's remarkable comeback.

He had lost a great deal of weight from his drug use, and was now described as fit and tanned again. The filmmaker-lover who left him has returned. Clegg purchased a new apartment. He landed a job at a top literary agency, where he has a roster of former and new clients (including Nick Flynn, whose memoir, *Another Bullshit Night in Suck City*, is recognized in this chapter).

*March 2011 figures.

But it appears that readers of this subgenre want to know the details of recovery. It is a word that implies restoration, a raising-up after a fall. Recovery can be a form of redemption. When it comes to recovery in addiction memoirs, the devil is in the details. The decision to hold back on the details of Clegg's post-recovery struggles may help explain why *Portrait* didn't attract a larger audience. In this Internet age, potential readers don't have to necessarily read a book—they might read an online discussion or review and object to a particular facet of the work.

The years during which Clegg may have clawed his way back to the top were most likely arduous. From a financial standpoint, it made sense for him to reserve details about his struggle for long-term abstinence. His publisher reportedly contracted with him for a second book, with the working title *90 Days*, to explore his post-rehab experience.

Through no fault of his own, positive comeback stories may have made Clegg's return to life seem all too easy, and perhaps to some inauthentic. To outsiders, "authenticity" may sound like sitcom fodder, but for recovering addicts thumbing through dog-eared copies of favorite addiction memoirs, it is no laughing matter. In fact it is something serious enough to lead them not to invest in a book.

HONING YOUR CRAFT

Bill Clegg has said that his journal, which would become the basis for his memoir, was written to help him recall his experiences. People who've been under the influence often forget what happened when they were high. After recovery, anxiety and depression can cause faulty recall. And addicts often get in such chaotic situations that they want to forget many of their horrific experiences. That can be a problem for those writing addiction memoirs. If you haven't kept a journal and you are finding it difficult to remember details, here are a few methods that might help.

- It almost goes without saying that if you have any photos from that period, studying them may be a painful although effective starting point.

- You may want to turn to people you trust who can offer details about the period that you're writing about. David Carr used this method in researching *Night of the Gun*. If someone shares memories, record the conversations, so you can replay the sessions later and reflect on them.

- Try the "memory palace" technique. It's obviously not necessary to live in a palace. Visualize a place where you spent time during the period you're trying to remember. Instructions follow:

1. Get comfortable, and sit in a quiet place where you are free from interruption.

2. Picture where you lived during a specific period. This might be a residence, or a location on a street, at a shelter, a school, or treatment program, someplace emotionally significant.

3. Visualize yourself moving through your "palace." As you "see" familiar objects, or distinctive features, record memories and feelings that come up.

4. After several attempts, if you're unable to remember details, tape together several sheets of paper, and sketch a rectangle to represent your "palace." Draw rectangles for rooms, and embellish each room with drawings or words, to represent furniture and other objects that come to mind.

5. When you've finished sketching, imagine walking through this mental real estate.

6. Dictate or jot down any incidents that come to mind.

If this technique fails to jog your memory initially, keep trying, and remember that the quality of your artwork doesn't matter. This technique can bring up abundant emotions, and you may want to consider seeking clinical support.

In comparison, the following memory-retrieval exercise can feel like a game.

1. Gather a stack of illustrated magazines.

2. Cut out at least twenty-five interesting pictures.

3. Glue or tape each image on separate sheets of paper of the same size.

4. Turn the sheets over to the blank sides and fan them out before you.

5. Look at each picture and consider whether you associate anything with the image.

6. Remind yourself that there are no wrong associations.

7. Question each picture's symbolic importance. Your thoughts might run along these lines: "Why did I choose a yacht? I've hated swimming since . . ." Record the first memories and responses that come to mind. Get the picture? Now get started, and good luck on your memory retrieval. In this game there are no losers.

....

Getting Familiar with What's Available in the Addiction Memoir Market

Among addiction memoirs, alcohol and drug stories attract the largest audiences. Readers tend to gravitate toward subjects that match their own experiences. That doesn't mean that most people reading memoirs about alcohol or drugs are substance abusers or active or recovered addicts. This subject may interest people because the problems caused by these substances are widespread.

Addiction memoirs tend to follow a similar trajectory of fall and redemption through recovery. New authors are challenged to find narrative hooks to attract readers. Given the importance of a compelling backstory, it's important to get familiar with what's already available. This can help you sharpen your focus as you write, and when making a pitch to a publishing professional. An editor is unlikely to buy a manuscript that's similar to a profitable title the house already owns, or even one owned by a major competitor. You'll notice that the listing below includes titles by well-known authors. A number of them were RUs before their addiction stories launched their careers.

Memoirs Focusing on Alcoholism

Diary of an Alcoholic Housewife, by Brenda Wilhelmson (Hazeldon: 2011). A middle-class wife and mother of two vows after numerous drinking episodes and late-night parties to fight for a new life.

Lit, by Mary Karr (HarperCollins: 2009). Karr painfully lets fans in on the sad truth: the little girl from *The Liars' Club* followed in her parents' path and became an alcoholic.

From Binge to Blackout: A Mother and Son Struggle with Teen Drinking, by Chris and Toren Volkmann (NAL: 2006). Mother and son take turns telling a story in which Toren went from model college graduate to down-and-out alcoholic.

Smashed: Story of a Drunken Girlhood, by Koren Zailckas (Viking: 2005). The author began getting drunk early in her teenage years. Most frightening of all are the grim statistics suggesting that the author's behavior is far from unique.

Dry, by Augusten Burroughs (St. Martin's: 2003). Those who laughed at *Running with Scissors* will find that Burroughs has not lost his dark wit. This story recounts the author's inability to resist Dewar's and details his struggle to remain sober.

Drinking: A Love Story, by Caroline Knapp (Dial Press: 1996). A daughter of privilege and an Ivy League graduate, Knapp struggled with alcohol for twenty years. This book helped many readers understand the meaning of functional alcoholics.

GOING VIRTUAL

We hope you're participating on blogs. The best addiction blogs offer comfort and wisdom. Rachael Brownell honed her considerable skills on online parenting blogs, and wrote for the parenting site Babble.com. She now blogs at imperfectparent.com (under Rugrat Reprieve) and RachaelBrownell.com. Admitting her imperfections seems to have been inspiring. She is the author of *Mommy Doesn't Drink Here Anymore: Getting Through the First Year of Sobriety* (Conari Press: 2009). As is clear from the subtitle, much of this book deals with recovery. Given her Web presence, it's no small wonder that her book was discussed on parenting sites. Her focus helped her hone an online identity.

Now the question for you is: Who are you, and where will your writing make the most impact on the Web? (Remember that long before you start your own site, participation in other blogs is recommended.)

If you want to start a blog to build an audience for an addiction memoir, it's important to get appropriately comfortable with writing about incidents you may have kept secret. Here are three steps for moving in that direction.

1. **Participate in a recovery group.** There's nothing like sharing a room with a mix of strangers to become more vulnerable and wiser. Sitting alongside someone, such as a disheveled woman in a housedress, and listening to her hard-won insights can leave you humbled.

2. **Read addiction memoirs.** Some behaviors are so shocking that you'll realize that no matter how low an addiction may have brought you, someone out there survived worse. It would be difficult to top former Princeton University writing professor Michael Ryan's revelations in *Secret Life* (Pantheon: 1995). He revealed that his sexual addiction led him to couple with numerous partners, including Topsy, the family dog. Ryan was hardly the first author to reveal sexual intimacies. Eighteenth-century philosopher Jean-Jacques Rousseau shocked readers with his frank descriptions of masturbation and masochism. Don't get trapped into believing you have to compete with the outrageous behaviors of others. The success of your story will not be based solely on the severity of the addiction or any extreme situations associated with it.

3. **Find a soundtrack and get dancing.** Modulate your mood with music. In a study on the palliative effect of music, scientists at the University of Utah found that subjects experienced relief from pain and anxiety when they focused on melodies, according to a study published in the December 2011 *Journal of Pain*. Jennette Fulda, who chronicled her unhealthy relationship with food in *Half-Assed: A Weight-Loss Memoir* (Seal Press: 2008), started a blog that allowed her readers to follow along with her weight loss. She introduced her next memoir, *Chocolate & Vicodin: My Quest for Relief from the Headache That*

Wouldn't Go Away (Gallery: 2011) with some of her favorite music, at JennetteFulda.com. Her musical blog introduction was no half-assed idea.

How about you? How will you use your experience, expertise and creativity to get through to that audience that is just waiting to hear from you? Remember to S.M.I.L.E. (Surprising, Memorable, Inspiring, Loving, or Entertaining—as discussed in the preceding chapter.) If you chose the "E," you might also think of eating, and perhaps ask yourself what you might give your readers in that regard.

Once you're ready to start your blog, you might enjoy these books:

ProBlogger: Secrets for Blogging Your Way to a Six-Figure Income, by Darren Rowse (Wiley: 2010); *Blogging for Dummies*, by Susannah Gardner (For Dummies: 2012); *The Social Media Bible: Tactics, Tools, and Strategies for Business Success*, by Lon Safko (Wiley: 2010); and *The Zen of Social Media Marketing: An Easier Way to Build Credibility, Generate Buzz, and Increase Revenue*, by Shama Kabani (BenBella: 2010).

For published authors wanting to market their books, there is the platform Odyl, which uses Facebook as a center point and offers content, traces metrics, handles giveaways, and imports blog posts and tour dates along with Twitter and other feeds. Odyl cofounder and CEO Mike Taylor told *Publishers Weekly* that Odyl can help authors attract potential readers, and bring attention for those without high name recognition. He said, "What Facebook has really changed is that you can put yourself at the crossroads and get all your friends to share the information with their friends. Without a proper social media push, authors may just as well be passing out copies of a book from their front steps on a rainy day."

Memoirs of Drug Addiction

Pill Head: The Secret Life of a Painkiller Addict, by Joshua Lyon (Hyperion: 2009). Lyon, a journalist investigating the easy availability of drugs such as Valium, Xanax, and Vicodin, devoured these painkillers and then quickly ordered more.

Beautiful Boy: A Father's Journey Through His Son's Addiction, by David Sheff (Houghton Mifflin: 2008). A supportive parent, Sheff realized that his son had become a methamphetamine addict. This son, Nic Sheff, wrote his memoir, *Tweak: Growing Up on Methamphetamines* (Atheneum: 2008), describing his addiction struggles. The books were published concurrently, and the underlying message was that if this could happen to them, it could happen in any family. The books became bestsellers.

Leaving Dirty Jersey: A Crystal Meth Memoir, by James Salant (Simon Spotlight: 2007). The parents of an eighteen-year-old drop him off at a drug recovery clinic to kick a heroin habit. He hits the streets, gets addicted to crystal meth, and becomes a petty criminal. Choosing between madness and sanity, he fights to remain drug free.

The Lost Years: Surviving a Mother and Daughter's Worst Nightmare, by Kristina Wandzilak and Constance Curry (Jeffers: 2006). This dual narrative recounts Wandzilak's spiral into drugs, prostitution, rape, and homelessness. Her mom tries to rescue her while protecting her other children. Tough love helps Kristina recover.

Permanent Midnight, by Jerry Stahl (Warner: 1995). A top TV scriptwriter, Stahl moves between lunching with stars to the mean streets to score heroin, coke, or crack. Addiction costs him practically everything, then he struggles with the misery of sobriety.

Writing about family life is especially fraught when the situation is complicated by addictions. I usually advise authors to tell their truths as they recall them, and once the manuscript is completed, if it was written for publication, that's the time to show it to people who have been mentioned. Some are likely to be hurt and angry, and may accuse you of lying. All you can do is write your story with integrity and know that people interpret past events from their perspectives.

In *The Lost Child: A Mother's Story* (Bloomsbury USA: 2009), highly praised British author and journalist Julie Myerson described how her son's addiction to marijuana caused problems that led to him being kicked out of their home at seventeen. The son agreed that specific incidents had occurred, but he accused his mother of exaggerating his behavior and exploiting him. Myerson explained that she had shown her son a copy of the manuscript in its early stages, and that she had paid him for allowing her to include some of his poems. Although he threatened to try and block publication of the book, it was released. In protest, he changed his surname. Myerson was criticized in England for writing about her son's troubles, and a public debate ensued over whether there are moral limits to writing about one's own children.

In these situations, it is always important for memoirists to discuss the unacknowledged anger that can exist between parents and children. Addicts are often involved in bizarre and harmful behaviors, and as a matter of fact, that helps give these books juice. Still, that fact doesn't make private revelations any less painful. When it's the child who is addicted, it makes the parents seem flawed, and a natural response in writing a book is to try to tilt the scales.

Dani Shapiro, the author of the acclaimed *Slow Motion* (Harper Perennial: 2010), wondered in a *New York Times* essay how children might later be affected by a parent's memoir revelations. At twenty-three, Shapiro was abusing drugs and alcohol, and sleeping with her best friend's stepdad, when she received word that her Orthodox Jewish parents had been involved in a terrible car crash. This marked the start of her transformation and became the basis for her riveting memoir. Now a mother, she is concerned about her twelve-year-old learning of her past life as depicted in *Slow Motion*. In a *New York Times* essay entitled "The Me My Child Mustn't Know," she explains, "In my attempt to find the Emersonian thread of the universal in my story, I laid myself bare in the most unflattering light." While adding that she was proud of *Slow Motion*, she wondered whether she would have written it if she'd been a mother at the time. She added, "After all, one can't write with abandon if one is worrying about the consequences. And to have children is to always, always worry about the consequences."

Her concerns bring us full circle to the issue of a parent writing about a child. While a memoirist might not worry about how unborn children might one day be impacted by revelations, the line seems clearer when it comes to writing about a child's drug use. If you're a parent and your manuscript includes damaging information about your child, if he or she isn't participating in the project, think long and hard about disclosing this information, and then think again. Is it really worth it?

....

At least one mother-daughter team used pseudonyms for their addiction memoir:

Come Back: A Mother and Daughter's Journey Through Hell and Back, by Claire and Mia Fontaine (HarperCollins: 2006). A fifteen-year-old victim of incest by her biological father runs away and becomes a cocaine addict. Her mother and stepfather send her overseas to turn her life around, but the daughter is not the only one to change. Her mother and stepfather own up to their roles in the girl's disease, and forgive her behavior.

Body Mistreatment Memoirs

The Voice in My Head, by Emma Forrest (Other Press: 2011). Forrest, now a screenwriter, recalls events of a decade earlier when she became bulimic, cut herself with razors, and had an abusive boyfriend. This book is set apart by her sessions with an unnamed and talented therapist.

Designated Fat Girl, by Jennifer Joyner (Skirt: 2010). A TV reporter's food addiction causes her to balloon to over three hundred pounds, and she loses her job. Gastric bypass surgery left her in pain with a partially collapsed lung.

I'm With Fatty: Losing Fifty Pounds in Fifty Miserable Weeks, by Edward Ugel (Weinstein Books: 2010). After a fifty-pound weight gain leads to sleep apnea and the author considers wearing a face mask to bed so his wife can sleep, he becomes determined to lose weight. His struggle is the basis for a witty and inspirational book.

Hungry: A Young Model's Story of Appetite, Ambition, and the Ultimate Embrace of Curves, by Crystal Renn, with Marjorie Ingall (Simon & Schuster: 2009). A plus-size model who has experienced success, Renn writes of valuing personal authenticity over addiction to thinness. By 2011, exercise and a healthier diet turned her into a not-so-plus-size supermodel.

Purge: Rehab Diaries, by Nicole Johns (Seal Press: 2009). This story recounts the author's experiences in a rehab facility, where she was being treated for the often overlooked "Eating Disorder Not Otherwise Specified" (EDNOS).

Wasted: A Memoir of Anorexia and Bulimia, by Marya Hornbacher (HarperCollins: 1997). In this story of the author's long battle with eating disorders, she shows the ugly side of a dangerous eating addiction. Her story sold more than a million copies.

A MARKETPLACE SURVIVAL TIP

If you have a history of addiction, or have been raised by an addict, there are certain behaviors and situations to consider that might affect you emotionally, as well as impact your ability to sell and market your book.

Consider how shame might affect your behavior. An unconscious belief that you're "damaged" could send you into a tailspin during the writing and marketing of your manuscript. It's hard for anyone to resist taking negative criticism personally, and you may feel particular discomfort after receiving rejection letters. Shame might lead you to ignore criticism, and cause you to miss an opportunity to turn your book into something spectacular.

Shame can affect the memoirist in another way. Embarrassment over the past may lead you to sugarcoat your experiences. Crafting prose with an eye on defending the actions of someone, such as an abusive parent, may rob your story of integrity, strength, and energy. Some writers may fail to realize they're sugarcoating because they distract themselves with an interesting backstory, while downplaying the consequences of the addiction. As a result, those reading your manuscript may feel the story lacks clarity.

Many recovered addicts also continue to struggle with narcissistic behavior, which is a cover for fear. A child that has been hurt might think unconsciously, "The only way I'll survive is to concentrate solely on my own needs." This might be an effective survival strategy for a child, but in adulthood it might lead you to believe that you're always right and that everybody else has a problem. If events trigger your "inner saboteur," it may sometimes seem that the closer you get to success, the harder you work to keep yourself from experiencing it (perhaps acting impulsively, blowing up, overspending, procrastinating, etc.).

If working with an agent, you may behave as if you are this person's only client and make rash demands. You might complain to an editor about the publicity department not getting you booked for more interviews, or that staff doesn't get back to you fast enough. You can see why this would be self-sabotaging. Such behavior could cause editorial staff to ignore your book.

Finally, addicts or those raised by them also struggle with boundary issues. If you work with an editor, it is best not to confide in that person or ask personal questions. Refrain from discussing your moods ("I feel down today"). Treat work with an editor or agent as a business relationship, which it is. If you do say something you regret, apologize and move on.

Here's how to emotionally prepare for the rigors ahead:

- Make maintaining sobriety your primary goal.

- Read Allen Berger's *12 Smart Things to Do When the Booze and Drugs Are Gone* (Hazelden: 2010).

- Consider starting an emotional support group for memoirists.

- Work at listening to criticism of your work, in writing groups or classes, without getting defensive. It can be helpful—and put you at a temporary emotional remove from your story, if participants describe the main characters as "protagonists."

- Read *Pushcart's Complete Rotten Reviews and Rejections: A History of Insult, A Solace to Writers* (Pushcart Press: 1998), edited by André Bernard and Bill Henderson. This collection of mean-spirited letters and reviews is heartening because many of the authors receiving them became greatest successes, including Jane Austen, Herman Melville, and John Le Carré.

Other Types of Addictions

Dirty Secret: A Daughter Comes Clean About Her Mother's Compulsive Hoarding, by Jessie Sholl (Gallery: 2010). The author offers a psychological explanation of her mother's troubling compulsion.

Loose Girl: A Memoir of Promiscuity, by Kerry Cohen (Hyperion: 2008). Despite facing many dangers, the author, a teen hurt by her parents' divorce, uses sex to bolster her self-esteem. *Publishers Weekly* described this book as "deeply poignant."

Love Sick: One Woman's Journey Through Sexual Addiction, by Sue William Silverman (W. W. Norton: 2001). The author takes readers through the twenty-eight days she spent in a clinic for women with sex addictions. A victim of incest, she recognizes the connection between her abusive father and the men she chose in adulthood.

In each subgenre there is at least one book that we can look to as a learning experience. Following is a $$$Analysis of *What's Left of Us,* by Richard Farrell.

$Writing Chops

In an effort to understand what life is like for clients recovering from addictions, Brenda Richardson read several addiction memoirs and was most impressed with *What's Left of Us*. Although therapeutic language is seldom used, readers come away with a psychological understanding of an addict's inner life. Not everyone would agree. One reviewer reported that reading this book made him so angry he threw it across the room (before picking it up and finishing it). Brenda reacted differently, tucking the book into her purse and carrying it like a talisman. *What's Left of Us* chronicles Farrell's seven intensely painful days in detox for a heroin addiction. Now a filmmaker, journalist, and adjunct professor of English at the University of Massachusetts, Farrell explains that he started the book in response to learning that James Frey lied about his experiences in *A Million Little Pieces*. What bothered Farrell most seemed to be Frey's suggestion that recovery is easy to accomplish independently. Frey's problems may have given Farrell the incentive he needed to start the book, but reading it makes it clear why he finished it. As much as Farrell hates what drugs can do to people, he loves the addicts and wants to see them recover. A *Kirkus* reviewer wrote, "Though the book is powerfully, even entertainingly, written, reading it is about as pleasurable as a week in rehab must be—which may be Farrell's point." He closes with the recommendation that the story is, "probably best savored by addiction counselors and people in recovery."

The memoir earns 10 points for superb writing.

$Narrative Hook

Raised in a working-class Irish neighborhood in Massachusetts, despite a birth defect that weakens the right side of his body, Farrell is groomed mercilessly by his father to become a star athlete. The cruelty and pain he suffered in childhood and later financial setbacks in adulthood led Farrell to turn to heroin for relief. When he entered detox, recovery made his excruciating athletic training seem like a cakewalk.

This plot is clear but hardly memorable, in part because it lacks the high tension created when protagonists "lose everything." With working-class roots, a broken spirit, and a lifestyle supported by debt, Farrell was unlike most of the well-to-do protagonists of popular books in this subgenre. Readers expect the protagonist to experience a stunning fall from grace. Farrell didn't have a long distance to fall.

The narrative hook that might have been strengthened but went largely ignored can be found in Farrell's "Note to Readers." Farrell's explanation as to why he wrote his book and the connection to Frey's work was intriguing, as was Farrell's message that ending an addiction is too daunting to be carried out alone.

That message offered an opportunity for a strong hook that was not realized. It's true that three years had passed since the blowup over *A Million Little Pieces*, but Frey, the Don Imus of memorists, has not been forgotten. The power of the 12-Step movement, which is championed by Farrell, is to be found in the audacity of addicts joining together to help themselves. In the goal of recovery there is hope for redemption, of becoming one's highest self. The anonymous nature of these groups is a reminder that participants are not known as individuals but as part of a larger whole.

The memorability factor or hook of this work rates a 4-point score out of 10.

$Platform Strength

As an adjunct professor, Farrell is accustomed to standing before others and speaking, and he was listed as a blogger on the popular *Huffington Post* site. Still, it was not immediately apparent that he was heavily promoting his book. While *What's Left of Us* was not a bestseller in the years immediately after publication, Farrell's fans have reason to be hopeful. The author's award-winning documentary, *High on Crack Street*, caught the eye of actor and producer Mark Wahlberg, and Farrell later played a small role in Wahlberg's Academy Award–nominated film, *The Fighter*. Those Hollywood connections may help improve sales of *What's Left of Us*. It has been optioned as a film, and Channing Tatum of *Stop-Loss* fame has signed on to play Farrell's role. Farrell is scheduled to adapt his memoir for the big screen. Release of the film could elevate Farrell's platform and send readers in search of his book. *What's Left of Us* scores a 6 for platform. The book garners a total of 20 out of 30 points.

Concluding Advice for Writers of Addiction Genres

Knowing what's out there will help you decide what kind of emphasis to give your story. While it's true that Farrell's book did not become an immediate bestseller, the quality of his writing did open the door to getting his book published.

Other authors of this subgenre have been successful by making their substance abuse issues part of a larger story rather than the central narrative.

One writer praised for her lyrical writing is Kelle Groom, the author of *I Wore the Ocean in the Shape of a Girl* (Free Press: 2011). Her memoir details her alcoholism and recovery, but the heart of her story is the painful aftermath of her addiction. She is raped and gives birth to a son who is given to relatives before he dies of leukemia at fourteen months.

Nick Flynn's *Another Bullshit Night in Suck City* (W. W. Norton: 2004) follows an unconventional form. Flynn plays with different types of narratives, including one-act plays, interviews, and stream-of-consciousness. The author is the son of a homeless alcoholic on the streets of Boston. After he, too, turns to alcohol for comfort, Flynn fights against becoming his father. This book won the PEN/Martha award, given to American authors of a distinguished first nonfiction book. The story was made into a film entitled *Being Flynn*.

Finally, some addiction stories get ahead on sheer gumption and inspiration. One example is *A Piece of Cake*, by Cupcake Brown (Crown: 2006), one of the few addiction books featuring an African American protagonist that is published by a major house. Brown was no well-to-do professional who experienced a steep fall. As a child, following the death of her mother and the abandonment of her father, the author lived with a foster mother who encouraged her son to rape Brown repeatedly. A second foster parent traded the adolescent Brown drugs for oral sex. Brown became a multiuse addict, until awaking one day in a Dumpster and, amazingly, turning her life around by becoming a lawyer. Her book became a bestseller, and Brown is a sought-after speaker.

Five

Transformation Memoirs

IN TURNING TO THIS CHAPTER, MAYBE YOU'RE WONDERING, "What the heck is a transformation memoir?" If so, that's just the response we were hoping for, because it gives us a chance to explain. Some people call these books "survivor memoirs," but too often that is said with a note of disdain. Survivor memoirs are the Rodney Dangerfields of an already maligned genre. In addition to snarky irreverence, there is a vagueness associated with the term. Survivor memoir means something different to different people.

Some reviewers would be likely to slap the survivor label on many of the books presented in the preceding chapters that discuss coming-of-age and addiction narratives. It's true that many of those authors exemplify the notion of the ultimate survivors. Many would-be memoirists have told me that they are trying to write inspirational memoirs. I point out that this is not a subgenre category, but that many "survivor" memoirs are inspirational.

In chapter three we looked at the work of Mira Bartók. Raised by a tormented, schizophrenic mother, she has grown into a gifted writer and illustrator. There was also Wes Moore, the going-downhill-fast inner-city youth who rose to become a White House Fellow and army combat veteran. Chapter four included the story of Cupcake Brown, the abused foster child and drugged-up prostitute who awoke in a Dumpster, vowed to turn her life around, and earned a law degree. There was also Richard Farrell, a one-time homeless, thieving addict bent on suicide, now an adjunct professor and award-winning documentary producer-turned screenwriter, who is adapting his recovery memoir for the big screen. They and so many of their fellow memoirists do honor to the term "survivor." They seem highly deserving of respect. What is more often the case, though, is that when authors admit to having experienced hardship, the survival memoir label is bequeathed and the book is viewed as rife for derision.

The apotheosis of this scorn was reached back in 2008, when an English comic, calling himself Sunny McCreary, wrote a survivor memoir parody, *My Godawful Life: Abandoned. Betrayed. Stuck to the Window* (Macmillan UK: 2008). The title itself drew snickers, let alone McCreary's suffering protagonist, who is bullied by pigeons, starved, pounded with nails, prostituted, and ravaged by drugs. Pigeons? Of course that's silly. But note that the story serves as a reminder that even the most biting criticism offers learning opportunities. Talented memoirists do not indulge in maudlin displays of misery.

The larger problem is that McCreary and his readers aren't the only ones laughing. A lot of people refer to true-life narratives in the survivor category as "misery memoirs," "medical miseries," or "feel bad" stories. That last designation is puzzling, since these stories often accomplish just the opposite, making readers feel "good," by helping us to find meaning in loss.

Could classism lie at the heart of this brand of criticism? Do some reviewers disparage "survival" stories in the belief that only "common people" need these narratives to feel inspired? Talk about getting a good laugh. You can almost imagine a few literary critics looking over the tops of their *pince-nez* glasses and suggesting that if "those people" had stronger character they wouldn't have allowed themselves to get in those dreadful situations in the first place.

Sounding far less pugnacious, but echoing a similar sentiment in an NPR book review, Maureen Corrigan challenged this type of literary snobbishness. Reviewing Laura Hillenbrand's biography, *Unbroken: A World War II Story of Survival, Resilience, and Redemption* (Random House: 2010), Corrigan urged readers to resist being intimidated by some criticisms, and praised the "hard-won triumphs of so-called ordinary" people.

We quite agree, and for that reason suggest that the time has come for a reappraisal. On these pages we refuse to use the beleaguered survivor memoir label, and have replaced it with the more appropriate designation: "transformation memoir."

Why We Prefer "Transformation"

As you may know, a survivor is an individual who remains alive after others have died. That definition fits the stories in this chapter's subgenre, but only to an extent. These stories hinge on the idea that the main character has experienced an event or condition that can cause spiritual or physical death, and has not only survived, but is in the midst of a profound transformation. The success of these books depends upon the character recalibrating his relationship to most aspects of his life.

In contrast, the word "survivor" implies a holding pattern, stasis, and a period of inactivity. It's true that the protagonists were once victims and they survived, but these stories cannot succeed if the protagonist appears to be stuck in survivor mode. In a life shaped by tragedy, there is a bridge between victimization and transformation. Emotional stasis can feel like hell. The authors of transformation memoirs have paid the toll and crossed to the other side.

It may be important for you, too, as a memoirist, to resist the survival mantel. Psychologist Dr. Brenda Wade, creator of the Love, Money & Seva seminars, says, "The brain works like Google. Give it instructions and it will search for answers through whatever information is available. Describing yourself as a survivor is not self-empowering. That belief is limiting. Researchers studying the effects of conscious language have found that words create neurological patterns. The ways in which we characterize ourselves forge neurological patterns and influence our beliefs and habits of behavior."

Memories can feel dangerous because they have the power to draw the body and mind back into the rage and pain, as if the hurtful experiences had just occurred. As you recall insults and other difficult experiences, the memories may become so vivid, the rage and pain so fresh, that you feel you're spinning out of control. So take a moment to feel the difference between thinking of yourself as someone who has survived versus someone who has transformed.

Memoirs That Fit the Transformation Subgenre

While some writers may take umbrage at having their work measured by what they view as rigid categorization, that is what happens in the publishing world. Editors and agents discuss and purchase books according to specific subgenres. In the spirit of self-empowerment, let's end the vagueness among memoirs, and give due respect to each subgenre. Coming-of-age stories follow a particular developmental path, the journey from childhood to young adulthood. Addiction memoirs are self-explanatory; they're what the category name implies.

The designation of "transformation memoirs" should be reserved for stories in which a spontaneous development or series of events threaten to destroy the protagonist, but in the end make her stronger. Specifically, the existence of the protagonist is imperiled by events or impairments that would include (1) a catastrophe or attack, (2) illness, disability, or social impairment, (3) life-threatening adventures, (4) geopolitical turmoil, or (5) military action.

The difference between a transformation memoir and a coming-of-age story is evident when comparing two books in which the World Trade Center attacks play a significant role. Highly lauded, *The Tender Bar* (Hyperion: 2005), by J. R. Moehringer, details the author's life from childhood through his early twenties, a popular timespan for coming-of-age memoirs, and this book fills that criterion. Raised by a single mother and abandoned by his father, Moehringer seeks out the male companionship of an uncle working at a bar in their beloved hometown of Manhasset, on the North Shore of Long Island. The author offers such a strong feel for Manhasset's denizens that in the story's climax, when fifty townspeople are killed in the 9/11 attacks, readers feel the loss.

In contrast, in Lauren Manning's *Unmeasured Strength* (Henry Holt: 2011) we know from the start that a catastrophe is about to occur. There is little time for us to develop a relationship with this wife, mother, and financial executive before she enters the lobby of her firm, Cantor Fitzgerald, on September 11, 2001. She is immediately engulfed in flames that burn over 80 percent of her body. Readers come to know this heroic woman in the aftermath, in flashbacks that help explain the woman she became, and with the help of family and friends, she rebuilds her life and recovers from severe injuries.

A miracle of modern medicine, Manning displays formidable inner strength. In the cover photo, she wears high heels and a red dress, hands propped jauntily on her hips, a signal that she is returning to her old self, and yet, she has been transformed. This change is underscored in a *New York Times* E-Book Nonfiction listing of bestsellers that offers a capsulized description of Manning's story: "A 9/11 survivor recounts her recreation as a wife, mother and woman." "Recreation" works for this story. Manning is the embodiment of transformation protagonists. After surviving tragedy, she has re-created herself.

The experience of the protagonist can be shared. Although few readers will be tested to the same degree, when they do run into difficulty, they might feel inspired when recalling a character's stoicism. Someone might think, "I can get through this; look at what Lauren Manning went through—and *she* managed to turn things around."

The different kinds of books in the transformation subgenre—catastrophe or attack; illness, disability, or social impairment; life-threatening adventures; geopolitical turmoil; or military action—share seven crucial interrelated elements.

(1) INEVITABILITY

Readers know as they begin the story that something terrible will happen to the protagonist. In fact, the upcoming problem is a major plotline, which will be delineated in a subtitle or jacket blurb. One of the first details readers learn when looking at the information beneath author Scott Bolzan's blurred cover photo on *My Life Deleted* (Harper-Collins: 2011), is that after a blow to the head, the protagonist suffers from a severe form of amnesia.

A sense of inevitability is present in books in this subgenre, including adventure stories. With memoirs such as *The Ledge: An Adventure Story of Friendship and Survival on Mount Rainer* (Ballantine: 2011), readers don't have to wonder whether these two men will be imperiled, the "spoiler" is right in the title. For the most part, readers of this subgenre determine whether they want to buy a title on the basis of the tragedy that is highlighted. Readers of *The Ledge* learn that Jim Davidson and his best friend climb more than fourteen thousand feet up Mount Rainier, and that while descending, Davidson plunges into an eighty-foot-deep crevasse. We know that Davidson survives and that his best friend dies. The suspense is in the details of how the protagonist survives, and most significantly, how his life is changed by the experience. It's also important to remind you that in addition to the inevitable grueling experience, the character's life is expected to be reoriented. One powerful example is the protagonist in Cheryl Strayed's *Wild: From Lost to Found on the Pacific Coast Trail* (Knopf: 2012). This celebrated story tells of an inexperienced hiker's life-changing trek through California and Oregon.

(2) BONDING

An attachment between the reader and author must be forged almost immediately. Readers need to bond with the protagonist so they will stick with him during his upcoming tribulations. In Manning's story, quick brushstrokes suggest that she has much to lose: an infant, a husband, and a comfortable lifestyle. We're given glimpses of her humanity: she's impatient and is grumpy toward her husband. Making quick judgments, a reader might think, here's a woman who supposedly has everything, but she still argues with her husband. She really could be me.

That bond is unlikely to hold if a reader becomes convinced that a protagonist has invited trouble. (Adventure stories are an exception. "Armchair" readers expect to be taken for a ride by risk-taking, adrenaline-fueled protagonists.) For most books within the transformation category, there is little tolerance for what might be described as loss resulting from acts that defy common sense. If the plot chronicles the life of a teen who survives paralysis, for instance, readers might bond with him initially and might well feel sympathetic. However, they might also give up on his story if it becomes clear that his injuries are a result of him riding on the outside of subway cars. Enduring relationships in transformation memoirs require trust and respect.

(3) SUSPENSE

Suspense depends on the reader's curiosity about what's going to happen next, so authors of transformation memoirs face a particular challenge.

The reader believes he knows what's going to occur, so this is where the rubber hits the road and where the strength of the reader/protagonist bond is tested. Although readers may be fully apprised of details of the central event (9/11 attacks, getting lost on a freezing mountain, being trapped by alligators) your protagonist will surely find herself in other frightening situations. For instance, if she's a federal agent and the central event is that religious extremists kidnap her and hold her hostage, she might escape while being transported just before the ransom is paid. Readers who have bonded with this character may experience terrible dread. Their stomachs might clench, for instance, as she races through a dark tunnel, unable to see whether her captors are waiting around the next bend.

HONING YOUR CRAFT

Here are some approaches to heightening suspense.

- **MAKE THE MOST OF IMPENDING DOOM. In** Manning's case, it's significant that she ignores warning signs. Aware of 9/11 events, readers experience dread, the gut response elicited in horror and/or action films. We want her to return home, make peace with her husband, and linger over her infant. We want the taxi she's riding in to drive past Tower 1. When she enters the lobby, we want her to know that the "incredibly loud, piercing whistle," is not from a construction project. Yet she keeps going, and we steel ourselves for the inevitability.

- **SET UP A CONTRAST BETWEEN THE CHARACTER'S PERSONALITY AND THE EVENT THAT WILL TEST HIS STRENGTHS.** If a timid librarian travels to the Canadian wilds with members of his photo club to take pictures of rock formations, but gets trapped in a cabin surrounded by cougars, he would seem to be an unlikely survivor. Readers will want to know about his near misses and the details, such as how he found enough food to last through the winter, and what he did to get rid of the cougars.

- **TICKING CLOCKS ARE HELPFUL:** In building suspense, deadlines should be written in a way that is integral to the story. If the librarian must escape from the Canadian wilderness before the spring floods, that seems intrinsic to the plot.

- **USE FEAR OF THE UNKNOWN:** A stranger in the wilderness, the librarian has no real idea of what to expect from one minute to the next. Readers who bond with the character will be looking over his shoulder, more terrified even than he.

- **PACING IS ALWAYS IMPORTANT:** A manuscript feels dynamic when the author speeds up and slows certain scenes, a technique known as narrative pacing, which is essential for suspense. For instance, the pace might be moderate when the librarian first arrives in the wilderness. Out of the library and away from his beloved books, he takes great pleasure in the untamed outdoors. The author might describe the abundant vegetation that the protagonist is investigating by smelling, touching, even tasting unknown plants; something he'd never do back in Boston. Realizing he's lost, the librarian might remain calm, until he falls in the rocky terrain; when his heartbeat accelerates, as does the narrative. The pace can be further picked up with descriptions of physical sensations. He is sweating, breathing rapidly; he becomes hyperalert. Did he detect movement in the brush?

When the wildlife in question proves to be a posse of squirrels, the pacing slows again with humor. Relieved, the librarian asks the squirrels whether they've seen his traveling companions. He realizes the squirrels aren't scampering playfully, but escaping the bear now confronting him. Pacing speeds up, as do the librarian's thoughts, but not necessarily his physical being. He does instinctively what he's best at, using encyclopedic knowledge to classify this bear's species, and as if speed-reading, searching for what to do when approached by a bear.

This slowing and speeding suspense-building process is akin to the action you'd see in a movie house popcorn machine, when everything seems hushed before a few grains of corn fire off, building to a fusillade, and then . . . not yet. A few kernels float, hanging temptingly in the balance. Appetite whetted, you move closer, as if to catch that one escaped kernel—and then wham! There's your ten-year-old grabbing your thigh, demanding that you buy a bigger tub of popcorn and with extra butter.

......

(4) CHARACTER DEVELOPMENT

Characters are the beings (humans or dogs, for instance) that represent certain distinctions and passions. Characters possess traits that in conjunction with others make them unique. For example, a lot of people may be imperious, but a smaller percentage are imperious and lazy. Even fewer might be imperious, lazy, and prudish. The plot must reveal then how that imperious, lazy, and prudish character responds to conflicts.

Characters (like all people) are deemed to have or not have character—some might call it grit—marked by traits that would include courage, ingenuity, and persistance. This notion of character refers to an innate way of thinking; it shapes an individual's perspective, emotions, and behavior. It's what lies at the heart of a person. There's an old saying: character is what we do when no one is watching. Protagonists with strong character are key to transformation memoirs. These protagonists should be admirable, even if he or she doesn't appear to have those strengths in the beginning of the story. These traits should never be paraded.

The character of an individual is revealed in behaviors; strength of character is judged according to the ability of the protagonist to never surrender and to do what is morally right. An example can be found in *Lone Survivor: The Eyewitness Account of Operation Redwing and the Lost Heroes of SEAL Team 10*, by Marcus Luttrell, with Patrick Robinson (Little, Brown: 2007). In Northern Afghanistan in 2005, members of a Pashtun tribe risked everything to protect the badly injured sole survivor of a four-man team of Navy SEALs from the Taliban. Those Pashtun tribesmen had a lot of heart; it's what others describe as character. Of course, character isn't confined to military memoirs. Charlotte Gill's *Eating Dirt: Deep Forest, Big Timber, and Life with the Tree-Planting Tribe* (Greystone: 2012), celebrates the heroism of those who work as planters for logging companies and who plant seedlings to repopulate forests.

Readers want to know protagonists such as these as well as or better than they know their closest friends. That happens through character development—how that character grows and changes over time. Change and growth are of unparalleled importance.

In a coming-of-age story, character development occurs at a relatively relaxed pace. When readers learn that the acclaimed *One Day I Will Write About This Place* (Graywolf: 2011) is set in Kenya, they might assume the story is all about geopolitical turmoil. Instead, we are introduced to the author, Binyavanga Wainaina, at an early age, when one of his biggest problems is feeling off-kilter in middle-class Kenyan life. Growing up, he is advised to pursue medicine, law, science, or engineering, but he spends most of his time reading literature and studying others for his own "sensual comfort." He seems destined to become a writer, and with the suspense set on simmer, the question becomes: how will this come about?

In transformation memoirs, character development is decidedly different. Readers are initially given broad outlines of major characters; their development is influenced and fine-tuned after the story's major events. These kinds of stories have a forward thrust. The author is expected to provide glimpses of the past that offer enough information to understand the protagonist.

(5) TEMPORAL VICTIMIZATION

Victimization is essential to a transformation story, but it does not play a central role. Manning's victimization is used to contextualize her transformation. Because she was a 9/11 victim, she will never be the same person that she was, nor does she want to be. She has somehow managed to emerge better for her loss. Earlier in the story, moving forward must seem impossible. The details of how that transformation occurs should be conveyed.

(6) EMPATHY

In Mary Matsuda Gruenewald's *Looking Like the Enemy* (New Sage: 2005), the story of one of 110,000 Japanese Americans imprisoned in U.S. internment camps during World War II, the teenage protagonist is torn from her community. As is the case of protagonists in transformation stories, Gruenewald is stripped bare by tragedy. Readers are generally predisposed to feeling compassionate, and those who bond with the main character are more likely to feel what the protagonist is experiencing. This is known as an empathic response. Readers may see themselves in the character on the basis of what they have learned about this character's past, observed through her interactions, and gleaned from her insights. In the most successful transformation memoirs, tragedies test the humanity and the dignity of the protagonist.

The Diary of Anne Frank—originally published as The Diary of a Young Girl (Contact: 1947)—offers a powerful example of tragedy testing a character's humanity and dignity. The story takes place in the Netherlands, during the Nazi occupation, as young Anne and her immediate family go into hiding with four others. As she exposes her desires and criticizes her mother and others with whom she lives, the story provides an extraordinary opportunity for intimacy and empathy. We readers begin to feel that we are her "truest friends." At this point, the story achieves what even photographs, historic accounts, and war-tribunal transcripts cannot: We begin to grasp on the most personal level, the scale of loss and the horrific atrocities committed by the Nazis. It is for good reason that Anne Frank's story, which has been adapted for stage and screen, is considered one of the most significant books of the twentieth century.

(7) INSIGHT

This essential element is last on the list of requirements for transformation stories, but it is far from being the least. The life or death of memoirs depends upon a reframing of difficult events and giving readers something to take away that they can apply to their own lives. One bestselling memoir that uses insight as its theme is Jill Bolte Taylor's My Stroke of Insight: A Brain Scientist's Personal Journey (Viking: 2008).

After recovering from a debilitating stroke that incapacitated much of the left hemisphere of her brain, Bolte, a Harvard trained neuroanatomist, was able to offer a unique perspective of what happened in her brain. More surprisingly, she provided readers with enlightenment as to how her life had improved. She explained that her left brain (associated with logical, analytical thinking) had dominated the right side of her brain (associated with creativity and expressiveness). Liberated from her dominating left brain she experienced joy and a deep sense of peace, something that she has learned to cherish in her continuing life as a scientist.

TAKE THIS PERSONALLY

Memoirs are often critiqued for their level of insightfulness, and your manuscript will be insightful only if you are. Insightfulness is a quality that has to do to with your way of relating to the world and to yourself. Transformation assumes the capacity for change in your view of the world and yourself. Notice that the word contained within "insight," is "sight," which in this case is not physical, but emotional, having to do with awareness and seeing inwardly. Insight can help you develop a new perspective, which is also significant in transformation memoirs. Perspective and insight are linked to the fundamental notion of seeing as a way of knowing. These strengths can help you make sense of the inner-visual information that may seem to be flooding your brain. The two words also differ. Insight tends to be episodic; an awareness that comes upon you, as if in a flash of understanding. Perspective has a connotation of more duration, as in someone looking back over a period of time and having gained a sense of pattern and meaning in the whole of an experience.

As you write your story, record in a journal any realizations that come to light about how you survived and prevailed over difficulties. As you begin to feel less wary, you may become more . . .

playful—which can make you more spontaneous and open to new ideas

curious—which drives you to look beyond simplistic answers and explanations

open—which can send you down unexplored territory

self-accepting—not allowing yourself to be defined by your ordeal.

Get Inspired: Want to gain insight about the motivations of others? Go to YouTube or check Public Broadcasting Systems (PBS) to watch Anna Deavere Smith, award-winning dramatist and the recipient of the prestigious MacArthur Fellowship, the so-called genius grant. Solo plays are nothing new, but it was Deavere Smith's idea to interview people from various walks of life, study their words and body language, and then re-create these characters on stage. In her production, *Let Me Down Easy*, she morphs into twenty different characters, including Lance Armstrong, Lauren Hutton, and an unknown rodeo cowboy. While few of us have the talent to replicate Deavere Smith's work, we can become so inspired by her performance that we develop the courage to climb into the skins of our characters—people we thought we would never be able to understand, for the sake of re-creating them for readers.

Some writers are turning their memoirs into stage performances. Tania Katan wrote *My One-Night Stand With Cancer* (Alyson: 2005) after sacrificing both breasts to cancer. She turned her story into a one-woman play, *Saving Tania's Privates*, described by one critic as wildly funny and moving. Amy Ferris's memoir, *Marrying George Clooney: Confessions of a Midlife Crisis* (Sea Press: 2009), a humorous take on middle age, was also adapted as a play. Finally, Jeanne Darst, the author of *Fiction Ruined My Family* (Riverhead: 2011) writes one-woman shows based on her book, which she performs in bars and living rooms.

Role-play: While performing live, Deavere Smith is likely to have heard a congratulatory phrase used in some black communities. In the midst of applause, an audience member might call out "Anna Deavere Smith is *in* the house." It's a phrase that suggests a person has used ingenuity and talent to seize control of a situation, as represented by property of one's own. In Deavere Smith's case, the phrase might refer also to her controlling her body and the powers harnessed therein. Here's how you can take possession of your "house" to work through a scene or reveal a character's inner essence.

- Think of words that remind you of specific people and incidents.

- Write the words and a name on a paper slip—one incident per slip and place this within reach.

- Stand and feel yourself *in* your body. That may sound odd, but people who've experienced trauma often feel shame and emotionally disconnected from what they feel. Breathe deeply and relax, as if you are taking possession of your body.

- Reach out and retrieve randomly one of the slips of paper. As you read, say and do what comes to mind. Remember that your mind doesn't simply reside in your brain; it permeates your entire body. Let your mind/body re-create this person's words and the situation. What did he say? What did he want or feel?

- Recall how you responded: what you said, felt, how you behaved. The more comfortable you become in your body, the more you may recall. Some people seeking to become deeply attuned to their bodies and wanting to heal from trauma have turned to clinicians that utilize somatic therapy techniques. This mind/body approach focuses on the ways in which we "embody" our experiences; how we can tap into the feelings and emotions imbedded into our musculature and nervous system, and become more empathic with ourselves.

Patients are taught to learn from their body language, feelings, sensations, even breathing patterns.

- If re-creating events in any of these exercises makes you uncomfortable, you may want to forgo them or try them when you're with someone you trust. Should you try either or both of them, consider processing and recording what you're feeling in a journal. If you want to work with a somatic specialist, it is best to seek out a licensed social worker or psychologist trained in this specialty.

A Word to the Wise: What Makes Selling Some Transformation Memoirs Difficult

Ask publishers or editors about their most difficult reading matter, and there's a good chance they will mention what we call transformation stories. Why would these be more difficult to sell than other memoir subgenres? How might this tie in with the media's discomfort with these books? First let me mention that it may be difficult to read our thoughts about this, particularly if you're writing about trauma. Trust us, though—you'll need to hear this. Although it might not be easy to accept, it is always best to have as much information as possible so you can make choices accordingly.

While most publishing professionals won't admit it publicly, if you're going to write a commercially viable transformation memoir, you will need to know how to work around what we call the "cringe responses." Let me give you an example. In stories in which an individual is ill, it wouldn't be unusual for someone with a hacking cough to spit out a globule of red and green phlegm. Or picture what happened to Aron Ralston, the author of *Between a Rock and a Hard Place* (Atria: 2004).*

*This book was adapted into the film, *127 Hours*.

Stuck in a canyon, he cut off his arm to free himself. Disgusting, isn't it? And therein lies the problem.

According to Josie Glausiusz, writing for *Discover* magazine, the emotion of disgust appears to be universal, except for regional variations (for example, some people in India are revolted by seeing others kiss in public). Around the world, researchers found that spittle, feces, vomit, sweat, blood, pus, and sexual fluids repulse people. A growing body of research suggests that certain substances and certain animals make us mindful of diseases that can be contracted through viruses, bacteria, and pathogens. Rachael Herz, a Brown University researcher and the author of *That's Disgusting: Unraveling the Mysteries of Repulsion* (W. W. Norton: 2012), explains that of the six universal emotions (including happiness, sadness, anger, fear, and surprise) emotional disgust is the only one that is unique to humans, and the only one that is learned.

Publishing professionals aren't alone in being squeamish. The cringe response is connected to an instinct for survival that is born of biological programming (and let's not discount the power of Mom's early warnings). In transformation stories—where the readers' worst fears may be realized—the cringe response is extended to various types of losses, as readers are reminded of their own physical vulnerabilities.

So you might wonder how these books get published anyway. The answer is money. Publishing professionals know that there's a market for these books. In addition to those who are armchair adventurers, other readers are undergoing or have had similar experiences, or they know someone who has. These stories are especially popular among people who can relate to the illness, condition, or other harsh experiences that a protagonist might struggle through.

Of course, there are gradations of disgust. Some details are harder to read about than others. Since many transformation protagonists may suffer from wounds and diseases, burns, rape, and torture, are tormented by harrowing mental illnesses, or stranded in remote, hostile environments, publishing professionals aren't exactly eager to crack open these manuscripts. How can you move an agent or editor from "Eew" to "Yes"? Five suggestions follow.

1) DIFFUSE DISGUST WITH HUMOR

While humor isn't always appropriate, it worked for Josh Sundquist. At nine, he lost his leg to a rare form of bone cancer and then he became a paralympic skier. In Sundquist's memoir, *Just Don't Fall: How I Grew Up, Conquered Illness, and Made It Down the Mountain* (Viking: 2010), he employs absurdist humor. A popular and inspiring speaker, he made a hilarious video, "The Amputee Rap," which, he explained via e-mail, resulted in direct sales from viewers. Television stations played it on air. At the time of this writing, his video had been watched on YouTube 774,000 times. There is nothing disgusting about those numbers.

Cartoonists have also used humor successfully in transformation memoirs, notably in Marisa Acocella Marchetto's heartwarming and funny graphic novel, *Cancer Vixen* (Knopf: 2006). Although Marchetto's cartoons had appeared in *Glamour* and *The New Yorker* she had no health insurance when she was diagnosed with breast cancer. Friends and loved ones helped her out, as did her sense of humor.

2) SHORT-CIRCUIT DISGUST WITH UNIQUE REALISTIC DETAILS

There are a number of ways that you can ground your story in realistic and unique details. The most important strategy is to never exploit details for cheap shock value. Understatement should prevail. Maybe you have a teen protagonist who has lost both arms in an accident. While readers might think they would crumble under such duress, don't over-amplify the character's feelings. Instead, allow readers to "see" this young woman prepare for prom. What dress would she choose if she has been fitted with artificial limbs?

Also, consider events that might be considered ordinary and look at them from your character's perspective. How might she get her chores completed? Fill the story with details on how the protagonist manages his or her life. Describe special preparations. What precautions does she take before passing through airport security?

Most readers can accept even brutal scenes if the details serve a literary purpose. For example, in *A Long Way Gone*, by Ishmael Beah, readers are able to understand why the young and innocent protagonist turns into a soldier who is addicted to violence and drugs. He witnesses or becomes involved in one horrifying experience after another, including the one that follows:

> On one verandah we saw an old man sitting in the chair as if asleep. There was a bullet hole in his forehead, and underneath the stoop lay the bodies of two men whose genitals, limbs, and hands had been chopped off by a machete that was on the ground next to their piled body parts.

These kinds of details give the protagonist a sense of nobility, and resiliency, leaving readers wondering how he could have possibly survived war and transformed into a college student, author, and noted speaker. The strength of the human spirit is what makes these books inspiring.

A MARKETPLACE SURVIVAL TIP

"But it really happened." If you ever catch yourself saying this when someone has pointed out that a particular passage or the behavior of your character doesn't seem credible, keep in mind that credibility issues have little to do with what actually happened. They arise from insufficient development of a character or plot.

Here's an example. A persistently unemployed bachelor awakens to a raging inferno that cannonballs through his housing tenement. Before he can save his beloved grandmother she perishes in the flames. Despite shock and grief, he runs to warn other tenants about the fire. When the young daughter of one family passes out, he administers mouth-to-mouth resuscitation, and as she comes to, he leaves her with her parents. Our unlikely hero continues risking his life, helping other tenants escape before the fire crews arrive. He suffers third-degree burns, but thanks to him, no other lives are lost. After he recuperates, he's being celebrated publicly when the neighbor shows up at the press conference to announce that his hospitalized daughter has died. He says that he's suing the hero for using first aid on the girl, when he should have waited for emergency help. He accuses this young man of murdering his daughter.

After reading this manuscript, suppose an agent said he doesn't believe a grieving father would interrupt a press conference, threatening to sue. The author might have responded, "I'll show you a video from the TV news reports."

That response would mean the author didn't get it. What he would need to do is rewrite, perhaps develop the father's character, utilizing information that hadn't been included previously. Now imagine that it turns out that in the middle of this raging fire, the father had paid more attention to saving his valuables than his family. In this light, his press conference behavior would seem credible.

If you disagree with criticism about some detail not being credible, ask for opinions from a number of people who read your work, but resist the tendency to be dogmatic about how your story *must* be told. Authors of memoirs are often particularly reluctant to rewrite, because they often (and for good reason) take their stories so personally. What's not so good is hearing memoirists explain that no one can tell them how their book should be written. That may be true with stories written for family or friends or simply for the sake of healing, but if you want to sell your story, you may have to capitulate.

There's a scene in *Gone With the Wind,* which Brenda utilizes to teach memoirists to think of rewriting as an opportunity. In this famous Civil War novel, there's a point when Scarlett O'Hara wants a new dress so she can look her best when she asks Rhett Butler for money that she needs. Since Scarlett can't afford a new dress, her gaze lands on a set of beautiful window curtains and she pulls them down, assured that she has the material from which a new outfit can be fashioned. That dress comes to symbolize Scarlett's will to survive. When you have written a manuscript, see it the way Scarlett viewed those curtains. You already have something special, but first you must re-create.

3) SQUELCH SQUEAMISHNESS WITH A BIG FAN BASE

The idea of war and wounding might be the last thing some publishing professionals want to think about, but writer and photographer Fred Minnick, the author of *Camera Boy: An Army Journalist's War in Iraq* (Hellgate: 2010), was so tenacious about overcoming objections he became a literary version of the Energizer Bunny. Determined to build a sizeable fan base during the three years he tried to sell his war story, which recounts his battle with Post Traumatic Stress Disorder (PTSD), he remained certain there was an audience for his book, and he was right. Minnick explained in an e-mail that after becoming an expert on his subject matter, he began contacting the media, and was soon giving interviews about his war experiences and the symptoms of PTSD. He also spoke on panels, maintained a blog, and discussed his experiences with anyone who would listen. With each speech, each appearance, he gave out his contact information and added new names to his own mailing list.

Minnick explained that after he sold his book, he continued building his platform. "I started a Facebook fan page, set up a 12-city book tour, and sent press releases out to all military and health media." In addition to TV and press interviews, he wrote personal letters to the members of Veterans of Foreign Wars (VFW) inviting them to his book signings. At an average signing, he sold twenty-five books, and at one point, seventy-seven copies. Meanwhile, he continued blogging and writing essays for publications with targeted audiences, including *National Guard* and his alumni magazine. He concluded, "My Facebook postings, according to my calculations, resulted in an Amazon sale every other post. Of all my tactics, I found Facebook to be the most effective."

GOING VIRTUAL

While you will not want to disclose too many details before your manuscript is published, if you want to spread word of your ability as an expert who can weigh in on stories in the news, or if you are looking for an opportunity to pitch your book, pay attention to Internet radio, one of the most effective platform-building approaches available. Where else can authors find numerous opportunities for hour-long interviews that will be archived online and available for indefinite periods? In days leading up to your interview, hosts will spread word of your work at various internet sites, and may also post the show as a podcast on iTunes. When you become familiar with the terrain, you might want to sign up to host your own show.

- To get started, get familiar with popular sites such as www.BlogTalkRadio.com, www.voiceamerica.com, and www.wsradio.com.

- To interest others in your skills, e-mail hosts or station managers, describing your credentials and experience, and offer topic ideas for shows.

- Before interviews, rehearse until you sound knowledgeable and relaxed. Also prepare a list of questions, which your host may or may not opt to use.

- During interviews, mention your Web site address and book title (if you have one), so listeners sitting at computers can order your book while it's still on their minds.

- After interviews, write your host to express appreciation for being included.

Also, search the Web for online opportunities to participate in webinars and podcasts.

TRADITIONAL RADIO

Look into opportunities in traditional radio talk-show formats. In addition to local commercial stations check out public radio stations including NPR, where you are likely to find a concentration of book-buying listeners. For a list of public radio affiliates, go to: www.npr.org/stations and type in your zip code.

One memoir launched through an NPR connection is Darin Strauss's *Half a Life* (McSweeney's: 2010). At the age of eighteen, Strauss was driving a car with friends when, in the blink of an eye, his life changed, and someone else's ended. A classmate, riding past on a bicycle, swerved in front of his car. She died, and although this was deemed a no-fault fatality, Strauss knew that he had killed her. His is a story of half a life. In addition to suffering decades of self-blame and regret, he was plagued by severe stomach maladies. He managed to become a respected novelist, and tried to avoid the subject of the long-ago accident, until he wrote his memoir hoping for closure and healing. He explains that a friend talked him into submitting an excerpt to *This American Life*, a weekly public radio show that is broadcast on more than five hundred public radio stations to about 1.7 million listeners. His story drew widespread critical praise and the attention of publishers. For information on submitting a story to *This American Life*, go to www.thisamericanlife.org.

Finally, another venue in which you can get accustomed to telling your story is StoryCorps, an oral history project that places value on the stories of "everyday" people. For details on where you can record and read your story, make an online reservation at storycorps .org. When the stories become available, their links can be sent to publishing professionals.

4) WRITE SO COMPELLINGLY READERS BYPASS DISGUST AND GO DIRECTLY TO INVOLVED

Who would have thought that a story about a young woman's incestuous relationship with her father that begins when she is twenty could become a bestseller? Novelist Kathryn Harrison accomplished that feat with *The Kiss* (Random House: 1997). A critic for *The Atlanta Journal-Constitution* compared Harrison's work to literary giants William Faulkner and Emily Dickinson. Absent of graphic sexual detail, Harrison's story dwells on her deep despair and yet she fashioned a page-turner.

Don't chalk up Harrison's achievement to her experience as a novelist or her memoir's controversial subject matter, because then you would be hard put to explain the praise heaped upon first-time author Lucy Grealy for her memoir *Autobiography of a Face* (Houghton Mifflin: 1994). Margo Jefferson of *The New York Times* wrote that, "A really good [memoir] . . . like 'Autobiography of a Face,' makes you feel there is more to ask and learn. You are not just seeing the writer; you are not trying to see yourself. You are seeing the world in a different way."

Nor was Grealy's subject matter easy for her to discuss. When she was nine, cancer severely disfigured her face. With more than a third of her jaw removed, and only flesh remaining on the lower right side of her face, she became the object of cruel taunts. Determined to succeed and resisting self-pity, she began writing poetry, burnishing her literary skills. Grealy also universalized her theme, turning it into a meditation of society's preoccupation with beauty. She died in 2002 at the age of thirty-nine.

HONING YOUR CRAFT

One of the best gifts you can give yourself is a memoir-writing class. In addition to learning opportunities and critical feedback, you may bond with others of similar skills and become part of a supportive writing community. We generally advise people to first look for classes or workshops offered through colleges and universities, situations in which the teachers have been tested by students and professionals. Alice Sebold was a graduate student in a writing program at the University of California, Irvine, while working on her highly praised memoir, *Lucky* (Charles Scribner's Sons: 1999), which depicts a brutal rape. Sebold mastered the craft of making a difficult-to-discuss subject palatable by recounting the attack and subsequent trial with precise, almost journalistic language. She universalized her theme by delving into the subjects of Post-Traumatic Stress Disorder and the racial tensions surrounding her trial.

Writing programs can teach skills that can help authors expand stories to interest wider audiences. Lindsay Harrison, whose memoir, *Missing* (Scribner: 2011), recounts the forty days in which she learns that her mother is missing, and the eventual discovery that her mother's corpse was dumped into the ocean. At twenty-five, Harrison, a recent graduate of Columbia University's MFA program, began writing her story as a way to cope with this brutal and untimely death.

In or out of the classroom, keep in mind that there is great value to be found in communities of writers. Frank McCourt, the author of *Angela's Ashes*, got his start because of a fellow writer. After finishing his manuscript, he turned it over to a friend, novelist Mary Breasted. She stayed awake all night reading and then phoned her agent, who told her that Irish books by new writers weren't selling. Unwilling to give up, Breasted contacted the mother of her babysitter, a well-known agent, who was also reluctant to read McCourt's manuscript, though she finally agreed. The manuscript was purchased eventually, although the publisher didn't expect it to be a bestseller. The rest is publishing history. *Angela's Ashes* is credited with starting a memoir boom.

If your schedule makes it difficult to enroll in brick and mortar classrooms, and you are searching for a distance course, consider the Web site of the National Association of Memoir Writers (www.namw .org), sponsors of online writing seminars and teleconferences, and workshops. You can also find online instruction from the Gotham Writers Workshop, which can be found at www.WritingClasses.com. *The New York Times* also teams up with various universities to offer online writing classes. More information can be found at www.nytimes .com/knowledge.

Whether you meld with a community in the classroom, in online workshops, on in weekend writing seminars, don't ignore the writer communities forming on the Web. You can have your work critiqued and join with others in the writing life at www.reviewfuse.com.

A Listing of Transformation Memoirs

Catastrophes or Attack

Crash Into Me: A Survivor's Search for Justice, by Liz Seccuro (Bloomsbury USA: 2011). Twenty-one years after being drugged and raped at a college frat party, the author receives a letter of apology from one of her attackers. She presses charges against him.

Missing Sarah: A Memoir of Loss, by Maggie de Vries (Penguin Canada: 2003). One of sixty-nine women who went missing in Vancouver in the 1990s, Sara is mourned by her sister, the author.

Fifty Years of Silence: The Extraordinary Memoir of a War Rape Survivor, by Jan Ruff-O'Herne (Random House Australia: 2008). When the Japanese invaded Java in 1942 the author was abducted and forced into sexual slavery in a military brothel.

If I Am Missing or Dead: A Sister's Story of Love, Murder, and Liberation, by Janine Latus. (Simon & Schuster: 2007). After her sister is strangled by a boyfriend, wrapped in plastic, and buried, the author explores her own relationships with abusive men.

Psychological Disorders and Mental Illness

History of a Suicide: My Sister's Unfinished Life, by Jill Bialosky (Atria: 2011). A novelist, poet, and editor, the author experiences many losses, including her twenty-one-year-old sister. Bialosky's grief is compounded by the death of two newborns.

Learning to Breathe: My Yearlong Quest to Bring Calm to My Life, by Priscilla Warner (Free Press: 2011). This story of the author suffering from panic attacks is filled with information and humor. After testing several different tools and methods she brings an end to her debilitating episodes.

Finding Rosa: A Mother with Alzheimer's, a Daughter in Search of the Past, by Caterina Edwards (Greystone: 2009). When her mother shows signs of dementia, the author embarks on a search for the meaning of their past and present-day lives.

Hurry Down Sunshine: A Father's Story of Love and Madness, by Michael Greenberg (Vintage: 2009). At fifteen, the author's daughter began suffering from manic episodes. Greenburg writes compellingly about her condition.

The Day I Stopped Being Pretty, by Rodney Lofton (Strebor: 2007). An African American gay male suffering from depression, the author awakens in an emergency room after a suicide attempt. He reflects on his brutal past, and an HIV-positive diagnosis.

Life Inside, by Mindy Lewis (Atria: 2002). At fifteen, the author was deemed rebellious, and was institutionalized and diagnosed as schizophrenic. Released at eighteen, she attended college, tried various therapies, and joined the Mental Patients Liberation Project.

Losing My Mind: An Intimate Look at Life with Alzheimer's, by Thomas DeBaggio (Free Press: 2002). This book allowed the author to preserve his past before he forgot it, and serves as a first-person account of the daily struggles for those with Alzheimer's.

Prozac Nation: Young and Depressed in America, by Elizabeth Wurtzel (Houghton Mifflin: 1994). The author describes her struggle with major depression. The title refers to the antidepressant medication, Prozac, which was prescribed for her symptoms.

Girl, Interrupted, by Susanna Kaysen (Random House: 1993). In the 1960s the author, who was considered suicidal, was diagnosed with borderline personality disorder. This book chronicles her confinement in a psychiatric hospital. The story was adapted into a film.

Nobody's Child, by Marie Balter and Richard Katz (Perseus: 1991). Adopted by strict parents, the author was indigent at seventeen and confined to a mental hospital for two decades. She later attended Harvard, and married. Her story was the subject of a TV movie.

Dying to Be Me: My Journey from Cancer to Near Death, to True Healing, by Anita Moorjani (Hay House: 2012). After four years of fighting cancer, as malignant cells spread through her body, the author's organs began to fail and she hovered near death. It was during this time, she explains, that she discovered her inner strengths, awoke, and began to recover without a trace of cancer—defying medical diagnoses.

Physical Illness and Physical Impairments

Immortal Bird: A Family Memoir, by Doron Weber (Simon & Schuster: 2012). This book is atribute to the author's son, Damon, who died from a rare heart disease. It was selected by Amazon as one of the best books of February 2012.

The Boy in the Moon: A Father's Search for His Disabled Son, by Ian Brown (St. Martin's: 2011). The author's son, Walker, is born with a genetic disorder. At the age of twelve, still wearing diapers and unable to speak, he reminds his father of the man in the moon, because he fears that there is actually no one there. Despite his imperfections, his parents love him.

Black Smoke: A Woman's Journey of Healing, Wild Love, and Transformation in the Amazon, by Margaret De Wys (Sterling: 2009). When this composer and Bard College professor is diagnosed with breast cancer, she heads to the Amazon, where she works with a charismatic master of medicine.

How We Survived Prostate Cancer: What We Did and What We Should Have Done, by Victoria Hallerman (William Morrow: 2009). Hallerman has written the ultimate how-to-survive guide. Packed with beautifully phrased personal observations, this book also empowers readers at a crucial time in their lives.

Conquering Stroke: How I Fought My Way Back and How You Can Too, by Valerie Greene (Wiley: 2008). At thirty-one, this businesswoman suffered a stroke that paralyzed the left side of her body and robbed her of speech and hearing. Ignoring dire medical predictions, she battled her way back, achieving a 90 percent recovery.

Poster Child, by Emily Rapp (Bloomsbury USA: 2006). Born with a shortened leg, after surgeries and prosthetic fittings the author becomes a March of Dimes poster child. As an adult she seeks to come to terms with her differences.

Swimming with Maya: A Mother's Story, by Eleanor Vincent (Capital: 2004). The author, a single mother, rejoices when her nineteen-year-old wins a UCLA scholarship. Maya later rides a horse bareback, and when thrown, suffers brain damage and loses the ability to breathe. The author recounts her transformation born of loss and grief.

The Red Devil: To Hell with Cancer—and Back, by Kathleen Russell Rich (Crown: 1999). In this darkly comical story, the author, who begins struggling with breast cancer in her youth, defies predictions of her demise. She writes of her odyssey through what she called "Cancerland." With intermittent treatment, she lived nearly twenty-five more years before succumbing to the disease at fifty-six.

The Diving Bell and the Butterfly: A Memoir of Life in Death, by Jean-Dominique Bauby. (Knopf: 1997). This former editor-in-chief of *Elle* suffers a stroke to his brain stem. With only his left eye available, he blinks out the narrative, one letter at a time. The story of his remarkable accomplishments was made into a film.

Geography of the Heart, by Fenton Johnson (Scribner: 1996). When this novelist loses his partner to AIDS, he recounts his own beginnings, as well as his partner's, and pays tribute to him as a masterful high school teacher.

Social Impairments

All I Can Handle: I'm No Mother Teresa: A Life Raising Three Daughters with Autism, by Kim Stagliano (Skyhorse: 2010). As the title makes clear the author puts a humorous spin on her complicated life, which is made more difficult by financial insecurity.

Born on a Blue Day: Inside the Extraordinary Mind of an Autistic Savant, by Daniel Tammet (Free Press: 2007). There seems to be some confusion by reviewers as to whether this fine book is a memoir or autobiography. It's true that the story details some events in the author's infancy and adolescence, and takes us through to his adulthood. But these details are important backstory to help put Tammet's life into context. The author has an extraordinary ability to perform calculations in his head, and he is among the most successful of polyglots. These are but a few of talents of this high-functioning Brit.

Thinking in Pictures: And Other Reports from My Life with Autism, by Temple Grandin (Doubleday: 1995). As a highly functioning autistic, the author offers a view from the inside out. With a Ph.D. in animal science, and teaching animal sciences at Colorado State University, she uses her heightened ability to make sense of the world by constructing concrete visual metaphors.

Let Me Hear Your Voice: A Triumph Over Autism, by Catherine Maurice (Knopf: 1993). The pseudonymous author tells of using behavior modification to raise two autistic children to live normal lives. According to the author, these techniques can benefit measurably about 50 percent of autistic kids.

Geopolitical Events

The Pianist: The Extraordinary True Story of One Man's Survival in Warsaw, by Wladsylaw Szpilman (Picador: 1999). Originally published in Polish in 1945, this Holocaust memoir was suppressed for years by Communist authorities. Szpilman, a classical pianist, survived the deportation of Jews to extermination camps. In matter-of-fact mesmerizing tones he describes the grim life of a Jewish ghetto under Nazi occupation. In one scene, a young Jewish smuggler is squeezing through an opening in a wall when his body becomes stuck. On one side, where his legs dangle, a German policeman administers harsh blows; on the other side, the author grabs the boy's arms and tries to pull him through. The child makes it to the other side, but by then his spine is shattered. Still, acts of humanity grace this story. A German officer saves Szpilman's life after he hears him play a Chopin nocturne on a piano found among the rubble. The story was adapted into an award-winning film.

Brother, I'm Dying, by Edwidge Danticat (Knopf: 2007). The celebrated Haitian author writes of the uncle who raised her and later fled the island, following a battle between United Nations peacekeepers and gang members that destroyed his church. In Miami, during a plea for temporary asylum, he collapsed and began vomiting. The medics refusal to treat him cost him his life.

Adventure

Swimming with Crocodiles: The True Story of a Young Man in Search of Meaning and Adventure Who Finds Himself in an Epic Struggle for Survival, by Will Chaffey (Arcade: 2011). In Australia, the author treks through harsh countryside, exhausted, running out of food, and then struggles with a hungry crocodile.

Crazy for the Storm: A Memoir of Survival, by Norman Ollestad (Ecco: 2009). An eleven-year-old survives a plane crash in the San Gabriel Mountains in a blizzard, using the survival techniques taught to him by his deceased father.

Touching the Void: The True Story of One Man's Miraculous Survival, by Joe Simpson (Perennial; revised: 2004). This is the gripping account of the author's near-death experience in the Peruvian Andes, as he travels with a friend/climbing partner. The story was adapted into a film.

Into Thin Air, by Jon Krakauer (Villard: 1997). On assignment for *Outside* magazine, the author accompanies a climbing group up Mount Everest. Eight are killed and several others stranded by a rogue storm. This bestselling story was made into a film.

War/Acts of Terrorism:

American Sniper: The Autobiography of the Most Lethal Sniper in U.S. Military History, by Chris Kyle, with Scott McEwan and Jim DeFelice (William Morrow: 2012). A highly decorated fighter keeps the emphasis on his battlefield experiences during the Iraq war, with some time-outs for "getting hitched and a honeymoon," and reflections from his bride, Taya, who closes her final note with words of admiration.

I Lost My Love in Baghdad: A Modern War Story, by Michael Hastings (Scribner: 2008). The author's girlfriend, Andi, joined him in Iraq, where he worked for *Newsweek*. Andi was killed in a kidnapping.

With the Old Breed: At Peleliu and Okinawa, by E. B. Sledge (Presidio: 1981). This bestselling account of combat in the Pacific during World War II is based on notes the author kept with him inside a pocket-sized Bible that he carried into combat.

A Helmet for My Pillow, by Robert Leckie (Bantam: 1957). Written by a marine veteran, author, and military historian, this story follows the author through boot camp, shortly after the bombing of Pearl Harbor, to Pacific deployments. This story, and *With the Old Breed* (see above title), became the basis for the HBO miniseries *The Pacific*.

We close with an $$$Analysis of Howard E. Wasdin and Stephen Templin's *SEAL Team Six: Memoirs of an Elite Navy SEAL Sniper* (St. Martin's: 2011).

$Writing Chops

In this story, by a SEAL Team Six member, Wasdin or "Waz-man" as he is known, goes long on military images and short on philosophizing. He and his coauthor, Stephen Templin, do such a good job of writing for their audience that at least one of the training routines might make readers gasp.

In one scene, an instructor teases the recruits that they will love the next routine. "Drown-proofing is one of my favorites. Sink or swim, sweet peas." Wasdin then ties his feet together; a partner ties his hands behind his back, and the instructor intones:

> When I give the command, the bound men will hop into the deep end of the pool . . . You must bob up and down 20 times, float for five minutes, swim to the shallow end of the pool, turn around without touching the bottom, swim back to the deep end, do a forward and backward somersault underwater, and retrieve a face mask from the bottom of the pool with your feet.

Interestingly, another memoir on the Navy SEALs was released at about the same time. Eric Greitens is the author of *The Heart and the Fist: The Education of a Humanitarian, the Making of a Navy SEAL* (Houghton Mifflin Harcourt: 2011). Although he is assigned to a different team of commandos, his book also includes details of the brutal training regimen. Unlike Wasdin, Greitens, a Rhodes scholar, takes a more cerebral approach in this bestselling memoir. Before signing up with the navy Greitens earned a Ph.D., researching humanitarian movements and relief efforts. He has worked in refugee camps, visited projects in Rwanda, and met Mother Teresa in India. The two books seem to be aimed at different audiences. *SEAL Team Six* may have been written for those who love military thrillers. A *New York Times* reviewer described *SEAL Team Six* as "visceral and as active as a Tom Clancy novel." This memoir earns 10 points for well-executed writing.

$Narrative Hook

St. Martin's senior editor Marc Resnick, who specializes in military nonfiction, says that when he began reading the manuscript more than two years before publication, it had a different title, which included no mention of SEAL Team Six, the most elite members of the navy's special operations forces. So it came as a wonderful surprise to him when he realized early on that the story offered an insider's view of this highly secretive team.

Resnick points out that with today's books competing for attention with video games, cell phones, and the Internet, the uniqueness of a hook is tremendously important for commercial viability. "An editor's job is to acquire books that will sell. A strong hook grabs a reader's attention, and strong writing holds it."

After acquiring the manuscript, along with its newly bequeathed title—*SEAL Team Six: Memoirs of an Elite Navy SEAL Sniper*—Resnick joked with his colleagues at St. Martin's that he loved the book, and that if the SEAL Team Six members ever captured Osama Bin Laden, the company would have a bestseller on their hands.

A confluence of events worked to the publisher and author's advantage. Who could have guessed that the SEAL Team Six—Wasdin's former team—would kill Osama bin Laden on May 1, 2011? As a blogger for *The New Yorker* wrote: "Everyone wants to know more about SEAL

Team Six." The book had been scheduled for release later in May, but St. Martin's moved the release date up by a few weeks and tripled the print run. At a time when everyone wanted to know more about the highly secretive team that had taken out America's number one enemy, Wasdin put a face and a heart to the story. This book rates a 10 out of 10 on the strength of the narrative hook.

$Platform Strength

Although Wasdin didn't have a highly developed platform, Resnick was impressed with his insider knowledge of SEAL Team Six operations. As it turned out, Wasdin's confidence about his subject matter proved to be crucial in marketing this book. In the first three days after the book's release, Wasdin gave an estimated one hundred interviews. Strong writing and a hook strengthened by uncanny timing meant that the author's interviews were all over the Web, and highlights of the book ballyhooed around the world, online, on TV, radio, and in print publications. This book scores 10 points for platform.

Thanks to strong writing, a unique hook, and an author prepared for a media onslaught, the book sold more than 250,000 copies in hardcover and 125,000 e-books, and this was all prior to the release of the paperback and a Young Adult edition. With all three rating categories combined, *SEAL Team Six* earns 30 out of 30 points.

Six

Travel and Food Memoirs

TRAVEL AND FOOD HAVE BEEN LINKED SINCE EXPLORERS took to the high seas. In the late 1400s, Europeans began sailing home with the holds of their ships loaded with potatoes, chili peppers, corn, beans, chocolate, vanilla, and allspice; they even brought tomatoes. But what if they'd never made it back home? Can you imagine Italy without tomato sauce? Let's not even go there. And yet, go the explorers did, outward and to worlds beyond.

Today, in both travel and food memoirs, a journey or meal is viewed by the author as an occasion for interior and exterior contemplation. Still, there are differences between the two subgenres. Many travel memoirists are propelled by craving and seem to be satisfied only temporarily; after catching their breath they hunger for more. Food memoirists are often filled with an intense desire to move backward in time, to replicate flavors and tastes that evoke memories of the past. That is not always the case, of course. Some authors offer a mélange: combining their taste for travel and food. These books retain their roots, nevertheless. They can either be travel books with recipes or detailed meal discussions; or food memoirs, with some authors traveling to foreign climes. Rather than confuse you in your writing efforts, we won't attempt to blend the two subgenres. We will begin by focusing on travel memoirs.

Most people remember Charles Dickens for his vividly rendered Victorian-era fiction, which demonstrated his knack for creating unforgettable characters. Few realize that the author of *A Tale of Two Cities* applied his prodigious talents to travel writing, and established a tone for memoirs to follow. In *American Notes* (Chapman & Hall: 1842), Dickens populated the chronicle of his first visit to America with fully realized portraits based on the people he encountered. Touring a factory in Lowell, Massachusetts, he trained his observant eyes on the workers. He wrote of a group of female mill workers:

> These girls, as I have said, were all well dressed: and that phrase necessarily includes extreme cleanliness. They had serviceable bonnets, good warm cloaks, and shawls; and were not above clogs and pattens.* Moreover, there were places in the mill in which they could deposit these things without injury; and there were conveniences for washing. They were healthy in appearance, many of them remarkably so, and had the manners and deportment of young women: not of degraded brutes of burden.

By giving power to the people, Dickens conveyed to readers the character of the United States.

A few years later, in 1844, British historian Alexander William Kinglake couldn't find a publisher for *Eothen, or, Traces of Travel Brought*

---

*"Pattens" is defined by the Merriam-Webster online dictionary as "A shoe or clog with a raised sole or set on an iron ring, worn to raise one's feet above wet or muddy ground when walking outdoors."

Home from the East, so he published it himself. In 1849, after this chronicle of his journey through Syria, Palestine, and Egypt had proved to be popular, GP Putnam publishers purchased the book.

In the introduction to a later edition of Kinglake's book, Barbara Kreiger explains that the author broke many of the rules that at the time were expected in travel narratives, and created a model for many of those to come. *Eothen* was conversational, humorous, and written to entertain.

These days, whether traveling by bicycle, ship, motorcycle, car, train, plane, or on foot, travel memoirists still leave behind their familiar worlds and allow readers to settle in and experience new adventures.

A MARKETPLACE SURVIVAL TIP

Here's what publishing professionals look for in travel memoirs:

1. **A protagonist driven by a desire or circumstance to know a particular place, region, or mode of transportation.**

2. **That the protagonist has a strong point of view, and the courage to voice an opinion, even at the risk of offending (but not alienating) readers.**

3. **A protagonist with whom readers can bond (this does not mean this person should be flawless) so we can see a place through her eyes.**

4. **Writing that opens the way to sensory experiences, allowing readers to not only see, but hear, taste, feel, and smell new pleasures as well as discomforts.**

5. **Writing that includes the thrill of new discoveries—even in well-traveled cities—of notable features, such as terrain, architecture, etc.**

6. **The historical, geographical, political, and cultural context of a place.**

7. Encounters with people who are revealed in well-drawn portraits and who reflect a particular place.

8. A dynamic, insightful protagonist with interior and exterior story lines, making the trip both a contemplative and physical journey.

9. A journey that serves as a catalyst for change and growth, altering the way the protagonist sees himself and this particular place or places.

10. A protagonist as an integral part of a story that ties together all of the above.

The Biggest Challenge to Writing a Travel Memoir

You may recall that this book opened with a message that memoirs are more than just an interesting story. Well, here's what many writers forget about travel memoirs: They must tell about more than just an interesting journey or destination. Something has to happen to the protagonist. In *Tout Sweet: Hanging Up My High Heels for a New Life in France* (Sourcebooks: 2011), Karen Wheeler doesn't just move to the beautiful French countryside. When her heart is broken, this British fashion and beauty writer starts a whole new life in France. Her story is not simply about changing locations; she changes, too. She leaves behind the artifice of the fashion world and creates a life that is more genuine. That's called a plot, and no travel memoirist, or author of any story, should leave home without one.

Too often, Brenda and I have read (or at least started to read) a travel memoir manuscript, and found ourselves thinking that the story lacked a discernible plot. Authors seem to get so excited about the lush descriptions of their journeys that they forget they aren't putting together travel brochures. Memoirs don't include bullet points. It's important to remind you that *all* memoirs require the same literary elements that have been noted throughout this book, including themes and character development—and plot construction.

When it comes to plot construction, travel memoirists can claim at least one distinction, which is that the author must make an outer and inner journey. In Susan Brind Morrow's *The Names of Things* (Riverhead: 1997), the author's early life is spent in rural New York. Eventually, she moves to the deserts of Egypt and the Sudan, before traveling extensively in the Middle East and Africa. At the same time, she undertakes an inner journey—moving from a distressed emotional state, as a result of losing her siblings—and searches for inner peace. As such, she embarks on both geographical and spiritual journeys.

HONING YOUR CRAFT

Travel memoirs are usually capped by the beginning and ending of a journey, but no matter your subgenre, there is always a beginning, middle, and end, sometimes called the three acts of a story. As you plot your three acts, keep these points in mind:

- Characters and setting can be established in the story's opening.

- A conflict should soon arise that will take the protagonist out of her comfort zone.

- Nothing should happen randomly. The conflict should arise from the reaction of the character who is under pressure.

- The character has an urgent, personal goal. That means the author must reveal something of the protagonist to help readers understand her motivation.

- Consider which characters will have conflicting

agendas. Let's say, for instance, that the story opens in the comfort of a character's home (as opposed to her already being in the "place" she will travel to—which would also work). This woman, whom we will call Sara, wants to travel to Patagonia to oversee construction of a dam project. Her husband wants her to remain at home because she is three months pregnant and he worries about her safety and that of their unborn child. The government minister offering her the job is using her. He believes that Sara will be a sympathetic figure and that might mean the protestors in Chile are less likely to use violence once this controversial project gets underway.

- You can tease the readers forward by offering a brief foreshadowing. For instance, let's say that as Sara packs a wedding photo, she wonders whether she's making the worst mistake of her life. Later, she loses the photo at the airport.

- A Point of No Return makes the story feel compelling: Since Sara couldn't get her husband to agree to her taking the trip, she heads off to Patagonia, leaving a letter behind, explaining that she can't say no to this job offer. Now the character's world has changed forever. She will have to react to the new situation, which propels her toward the climax.

- Your story should reflect on the relationship of your protagonist to new environs. Consider, for instance, the ways that your protagonist might become isolated from society. Sara has just arrived in Patagonia and finds that few people in this Chilean city understand her rudimentary Spanish. The domestics serving Sara cannot understand why a pregnant, "wealthy" gringa would leave her husband for work, and they keep Sara at a distance. Sara despises the ex-pats she meets because of their racist attitudes. She's now isolated.

- Readers should finish with a better understanding of the country and its people—as well as the protagonist.

....

If you want to write about your travel experiences, get started by reading online sites for travel memoirists. For an overview of the lives of several popular travel writers, try Michael Shapiro's *A Sense of Place: Great Travel Writers Talk About Their Craft, Lives, and Inspiration* (Travelers' Tales: 2004).

Many of the memoirists mentioned below have since written other travel memoirs. The thirteen classics that follow were selected to relate to suggestions that can help you frame memoirs and move you in the right direction.

1. SHARE YOUR HARDSHIPS BUT KEEP THE FOCUS ON YOUR TRAVELS

After losing his job and his wife, William Least Heat-Moon packs up a van and takes a thirteen-thousand-mile trip down America's back roads, visiting tiny and "forgotten" towns in *Blue Highways* (Random House: 1982). Rich with well-drawn portraits of characters that Heat-Moon meets along the way, the book is also chock-full of historical details.

2. VISIT THE COUNTRY OF YOUR ANCESTORS

Barbara Grizzuti Harrison's *Italian Days* (Grove: 1989) details her journey to Italy, as she searches for her ancestral past. She depicts the personalities of various Italian cities through sly observations about local culture. Readers know without her having to say so that this Queens, New York, native is not feeling quite at home when she writes of Milan:

> One may not get to one's destination by walking either to one's left or to one's right. No set of directions is ever issued the same way twice. No one, except those who live in a vaguely bohemian quarter . . . ever says I live in such and such a neighborhood. People live in the vicinity of museums or in the vicinity of publishing houses or near the fashionable shopping streets but one hears little of neighborhoods . . .

3. PLAY WITH THE "FISH OUT OF WATER" IMAGE

A Year in Provence, by Peter Mayle (Knopf: 1990), tells of a British couple purchasing and renovating a house in Provence, France. The author arrives with certain expectations, particularly when it comes to getting his house remodeled, and that soon leads to dashed hopes. Mayle's new neighbors operate on a different scale of time: seasons, as opposed to hours, days, or weeks. Not surprisingly, that turns out to be problematic for this cynical Brit and makes for difficult communication between him and his laid-back contractors. This, and so much more, is a recipe for great hilarity. The book was adapted into a BBC miniseries.

4. IF YOUR PROTAGONIST LOVES THE CUISINE OF THE NEW LAND, CONSIDER INCLUDING RECIPES

Under the Tuscan Sun: At Home in Italy, by Frances Mayes (Chronicle: 1996), also uses a house remodeling project—this one an abandoned villa in rural Tuscany—to structure the story, but there is so much more. Mayes writes poetically of her observations, and includes recipes, some with delicious sounding titles: "Bruschetta with Pecorino and Nuts,"

"Wild Mushroom Lasagne," "Cherries Steeped in Red Wine," and "Sage Pesto."

Mayes's vivid writing, every bit as appetizing, is evident in this description of Santa Maria del Calcinaio:

> . . . this church is situated on a broad terrace below the town. From the Montanina road, I'm looking down at its fine-boned shape, rhythmic curves, and graceful dome, a deeply glazed aquamarine and bronze in the sun.

5. ELEVATE SCENERY FROM BACKDROP TO CENTER STAGE

Readers are not likely to describe Jonathan Raban as a people person. He sometimes seems harshly judgmental toward those he meets in his travels, but readers will surely remember this English-born, now Seattle-based, author for bringing to life places and scenery they might never have imagined to be of such great interest. *Passage to Juneau: A Sea and Its Meanings* (Pantheon: 1999) is the author's account of sailing the inside passage between Puget Sound and Juneau, Alaska. His descriptions are lush and nuanced, and often mirror his inner state. A *Salon* reviewer described this book as, ". . . lively, engaging, fiercely personal and vastly well-informed, filled with history both cultural and natural, tart social observation and entertaining riffs . . ."

6. PORTRAY YOUR PROTAGONIST AS DEVELOPING AN UNDERSTANDING OF A NEW LAND

Sometimes it takes a while to fall in love, and that's what happens to Australian Sarah Macdonald in *Holy Cow: An Indian Adventure* (Broadway: 2004). This author first traveled to India at the age of twenty-one, and upon leaving, was not keen on returning. Years later, when her boyfriend is sent to India for work, she joins him, reluctantly, and is no more impressed the second time around—not at first, anyway. Later, she develops friendships and falls in love with the country. For her own sake (and that of readers), she discovers the real India.

7. DEPICT THE TRANSFORMATIVE POWER OF TRAVEL

In her third decade, life had soured for Elizabeth Gilbert, and her publisher agreed to finance a yearlong trip for her. The resulting book, *Eat, Pray, Love: One Woman's Search for Everything Across Italy, India, and Indonesia* (Viking: 2006) became a major bestseller and a popular film. At trip's end, the author feels self-sufficient and spiritually grounded.

TAKE THIS PERSONALLY

Sure it sounds exotic to travel someplace new with writing in mind, and this can be a life-changing experience. To remain safe, you will need to take precautions. You may want to follow these tips, so you can return safe and sound and write about your experiences.

- Join AAA. This organization offers traveler's insurance (necessary, if you need to be flown to medical care), as well as a VISA money card and an international driver's license.

- Scan your itinerary, insurance papers, and passport, and leave copies with people you trust.

- With some of the same people, arrange a regular Twitter or Skype check-in.

- Set up a Twitter account and or a foursquare account to keep in touch with friends and family through accounts that whet their appetite for your upcoming manuscript.

- Ask your health provider for recommendations for inoculations.

- Use networking skills to get the names of contacts in the area, and look up and record contact information at consulates, should you need help in an emergency.

- Purchase a cell phone that works in the countries you plan to visit—or set up phone service upon your arrival and program those contact numbers so you can speed-dial if necessary.

- Keep emergency cash and documents in a money belt that's tucked out of sight.

- Go online in advance to check out ground transportation in your destination.

- If you depend on any prescriptions, get duplicates for the length of your stay and separate these among carry-ons and packed baggage.

- Don't leave valuables (passports, credit cards, etc.) in hotel rooms; check them into a safe or carry them with you.

- Purchase, read, and follow applicable suggestions in *Staying Safe Abroad: Traveling, Working and Living in a Post-9/11 World*, by Edward L. Lee II (Sleeping Bear: 2008).

Continuing with suggestions for framing your travel memoir:

8. MAKE 'EM LAUGH.

Bill Bryson, an Iowan returning to the States after two decades in England, decides to hike the twenty-one-hundred-mile Appalachian Trail in *A Walk in the Woods: Rediscovering America* (Broadway: 1998). The author is no outdoorsman at heart, but he does such a fine job of translating his bewilderment into comical scenes that readers plunge into the wilderness with Bryson and his cranky companion, Katz.

9. CAST YOUR JOURNEY AS A TRANSITION BETWEEN STAGES OF LIFE

Mary Morris travels down the Mississippi River in *The River Queen* (Henry Holt: 2007), a journey undertaken in midlife, after her daughter has left for college and when she is still feeling the loss of her deceased father. The author fills us in on her past life, shaped by a love of reading and high-level curiosity for places located far from tourist haunts.

10. SET UP YOUR TRIP AS A CHALLENGE

In Tim Cahill's *Road Fever: A High-Speed Travelogue* (Random House: 1991), the author and a professional long-distance driver try to break a Guinness Book record for a road trip from the tip of South America to Prudhoe Bay, Alaska. The two travel a total of fifteen thousand miles in a record-breaking twenty-three and half days.

11. DON'T FORGET THE IMPORTANCE OF EXCELLENT WRITING

Long before the prolific author Paul Theroux had made a mark on the literary scene he wrote what is still considered one of the finest travel memoirs, *The Great Railway Bazaar* (Houghton Mifflin: 1975), chronicling a twenty-eight-thousand-mile intercontinental railway journey from London to Tokyo and back. Even today, at a time when people are insistent on getting from one place to another as fast as possible, readers of the travel subgenre still cite this memoir as among the best.

12. "DISCOVER" A PLACE

In *Korea: A Walk Through the Land of Miracles* (Prentice Hall: 1988), bestselling author Simon Winchester is determined to know more about South Korea. He journeys by foot from the southern tip of the country to the North Korean border, armed with historical facts and geographical detail.

13. CHALLENGE WHO YOU'RE SUPPOSED TO BE

It is thrilling to learn in Kira Salek's *Four Corners: A Journey to the Heart of Papua New Guinea* (National Geographic: 2004) that this British explorer traveled to a remote Pacific island in the 1920s, and even more so, when we tag along with her adventures as she travels by canoe and on foot.

Here's a listing of other popular travel writers and books listed by travel region:

Borneo: *Shooting the Boh: A Woman's Voyage Down the Wildest River in Borneo*, by Tracy Johnson (Vintage: 1992)

Colorado: *Canyon Solitude: A Woman's Solo River Journey Through the Grand Canyon*, by Patricia McCairen (Seal Press: 1998)

Cuba: *Trading with the Enemy: A Yankee Travels Through Castro's Cuba*, by Tom Miller (Atheneum: 1992)

Europe: *Without Reservations: The Travels of an Independent Woman*, by Alice Steinbach (Random House: 2000)

The Far East and beyond (partially by ship): *Give Me the World*, by Leila Hadley (Thomas Dunne: 1999)

The Far East and Russia: *All the Right Places*, by Brad Newsham (Villard: 1989)

Fiji and beyond: *Kite Strings of the Southern Cross: A Woman's Travel Odyssey*, by Laurie Gough (Travelers' Tales: 2000)

France: *Two Towns in Provence*, by M. F. K. Fisher (Vintage: 1983)

Greece and France: *Traveling with Pomegranates: A Mother-Daughter Story*, by Sue Monk Kidd and Ann Kidd Taylor (Viking: 2009)

Greece: *Harlot's Sauce: A Memoir of Food, Family, Love, Loss, and Greece*, by Patricia Volonakis Davis (Harper Davis: 2008)

Ireland and beyond: *The Good Girl's Guide to Getting Lost*, by Rachel Friedman (Bantam: 2011)

Japan: *36 Views of Mount Fuji: On Finding Myself in Japan*, by Cathy N. Davidson (Duke University Press: 1993)

Madagascar: *Muddling Through in Madagascar*, by Dervia Murphy (Overlook: 1989)

Newfoundland (and Canada by mishap) *Seaworthy: A Swordboat Captain Returns to the Sea*, by Linda Greenlaw (Viking: 2010)

The United States, Minnesota to California: *Zen and Now: On the Trail of Robert Pirsig and the Art of Motorcycle Maintenance*, by Mark Richardson (Knopf: 2008)

The United States, crossing the country: *The Road to Somewhere: An American Memoir*, by James A. Reeves (W. W. Norton: 2011)

The Continental Divide from Banff, Alberta, Canada to Antelope Wells, New Mexico: *Eat, Sleep, Ride: How I Braved Bears, Badlands,* *and Big Breakfasts in My Quest to Cycle the Tour Divide*, by Paul Howard (Greystone: 2011)

Crossing the Equator (including the territorial waters of fourteen countries): *The Voyage of the Rose City: An Adventure at Sea*, by John Moynihan (Spiegel & Grau: 2011)

World travel: *Miles from Nowhere: A Round-the-World Bicycle Adventure*, by Barbara Savage (Mountaineers: 1983)

Food Memoirs

In many food memoirs, the protagonist travels to a new country and embraces the nation's food. The question that arises is: how can we tell the difference between a travel and a food memoir?

TO BE OR NOT TO BE: TRAVEL OR FOOD?

Maybe you've wondered how you can make your intent clear in your own memoir. It's helpful to consider Frances Mayes's *Under the Tuscan Sun*, because this author writes about traveling to foreign shores and there are copious descriptions of food, as well as recipes. It is known as a travel memoir, but why?

As with most of these commercially viable books, the answer can usually be found in the theme, which drives a story. In *Under the Tuscan Sun*, Mayes restores an Italian villa, but the story is actually about self-restoration and self-discovery. Mayes is transformed by her life in a new land and the new friends that she makes in this lovely setting. Had this story been a food memoir, gastronomic experiences would have driven her theme. Just as importantly, the subtitle signaled her intent. The full title of Mayes's bestseller is *Under the Tuscan Sun: At Home in Italy*. Her home became symbolic. The story isn't solely about working on a house in Tuscany. Once there, she learns who she is and how and where she wants to live.

Notice the difference in emphasis that Fuchsia Dunlop employs in *Shark's Fin and Sichuan Pepper: A Sweet-Sour Memoir of Eating in China* (W. W. Norton: 2008). In this story about a woman traveling to China, the title spells out the book's intent, which is further clarified with a cover photo of the author drinking from a bowl and holding chopsticks. Even if the title and cover had been more opaque, a reader need only scan the headings in the table of contents to understand the story's thrust: "The Chinese Eat Everything," "Mouths That Love Eating," "First Kill Your Fish," "Only Barbarians Eat Salad."

While *Shark's Fin* does depict this British author's evolving attitude toward China, what seems paramount is her determination to eat everything she is offered during her travels, no matter how unusual it might seem, even if it offends her Western sensibilities. As she eats, she develops a better understanding of China. She even winds up enrolling at a Sichuan cooking school.

Another food memoir with a traveling protagonist who develops an affinity for the people and the food is Joan Fry's *How to Cook a Tapir: A Memoir of Belize* (University of Nebraska Press: 2009). Dayna Macy also travels in *Ravenous: A Food Lover's Journey from Obsession to Freedom* (Hay House: 2011), but her journey is propelled by food. Describing herself as a "lifelong overeater," Macy travels back to her Upstate New York childhood home and along the California coast to understand the origins of her cravings.

Similarly, Kate Moses takes readers along on a gustatory journey in *Cakewalk* (Dial Press: 2010), detailing comfort foods that she came to know and love while traveling the roads of childhood, from Pennsylvania to California. A reviewer for *The Chicago Tribune* praised *Cakewalk* for being "lyrical and delectable."

Despite offering dissimilar plots, the stories by Moses, Dunlop, and

Macy underscore the most important and often overlooked rule for writing a food memoir—the story must be about food, whether that includes theoretical or gastronomic musings, or events that involve lots of cooking and/or eating. Rather than think of this rule as limiting, consider it a hook upon which you can hang your story.

The plots of the most popular food memoirs make a statement about . . . you guessed it, food. It is true that Robert Farrar Capon, an Episcopal priest, may share theological insights in *Supper of the Land: A Culinary Reflection* (Doubleday: 1969), but readers also learn tips about serving leg of lamb and cutting onions, among other food topics.

Anyone who writes about food in a halfhearted attempt usually fails commercially. This is more true today than in years past. At a time when people care so much about food that the subject seems to dominate many conversations, memoirists seem to be proud of their passions, and eager to translate them into the written word.

In fact, if memoirs could talk, many of the most popular ones would explain how food plays a major role in their stories. Let's imagine what the following books might say:

- **"*This food story has been a lifetime in the making*." These words might have been spoken by *Tender at the Bone: Growing Up at the Table* (Random House: 1998), written by Ruth Reichl, the former editor of *Gourmet Magazine*. The popularity of this memoir is credited with launching a food memoir boom. If that is so, Reichl has taken wise advantage of an interest that she spurred. Reichl takes readers through her passage to adulthood with recipes and events involving food. Those meals are so closely tied to her developmental life that when Brenda, a fan, heard descriptions of Reichl's culinary adventures, she knew which recipes were connected to particular stories and what the author was experiencing at that point in her life.**

- *"I wanted to pursue my passion for cooking and became a chef."*
  It's easy to imagine these words coming from Jonathan Dixon's
  *Beaten, Seared, and Sauced: On Becoming a Chef at the Culinary
  Institute of America* (Clarkson Potter: 2011). Out of money and
  without direction, Dixon woke up one day and, realizing that he
  had to do something with his life, decided to follow his passion
  for cooking. Enrolling in what many consider the top culinary
  school in the United States, Dixon developed more than culinary
  knowledge. He learned to persevere, even when feeling beaten
  and seared.

  A similar desire to pursue her passion led Kathleen Flinn to
  attend the famed French cooking school Le Cordon Bleu, which
  resulted in *The Sharper Your Knife, The Less You Cry: Love,
  Laughter, and Tears at the World's Most Famous Cooking School*
  (Viking: 2007). The author left her corporate job and moved to
  France.

- *"I used food as a lure to my homeland."* Madhur Jaffrey re-creates
  the memories, feelings, and images of the India in which she was
  raised in *Climbing the Mango Trees: A Memoir of a Childhood in
  India* (Knopf: 2006). An actress and cookbook author, she was
  praised with a starred review by *Publishers Weekly* for depicting
  a "vivid landscape of an almost enchanted childhood . . . the
  bittersweet sorrows of puberty, the sensual sounds and smells
  of the monsoon rain . . ." (The recipe section included at the
  end of this and some other memoirs is referred to as "lagniappe,"
  pronounced *lan-yap*. With roots in Louisiana French and
  Americanized Spanish, the word is defined as a small gift given
  at the end of a purchase, something extra a merchant might
  offer.)

  A deep longing for home can be felt also in Donia Bijan's

Maman's Homesick Pie: A Persian Heart in an American Kitchen
(Algonquin: 2011). According to the *National Geographic Traveler*,
this coming-of-age food story offers a re-creation of the author's,
"memory-menu of her life, incorporating recipes for the dishes that
most poignantly capture the past for her."

◆ "*I wanted to learn how to prepare Italian Food.*" Bill Buford leaves
his deskbound job at *The New Yorker* to become a line cook in
Manhattan's three-star Babbo restaurant. The literary result was
*Heat: An Amateur's Adventures as Kitchen Slave, Line Cook,
Pasta-Maker, and Apprentice to a Dante-Quoting Butcher in Tuscany*
(Knopf: 2006). Reviewing the book, Anthony Bourdain wrote that
Heat offers readers a, "unique appreciation of not only what is truly
good about food—but as importantly, who cooks—and why."

◆ "*I expose the truth of what happens with food behind the kitchen
door.*" Anthony Bourdain's *Kitchen Confidential: Adventures in
the Culinary Underbelly* (Bloomsbury: 2000) doesn't seek to
impress. Bourdain shares may unpleasant truths about the
behind-the-kitchen-door restaurant scene, and is equally as
candid about his own life and how he fell prey to a drug habit.
Well known for the Travel Channel's culinary program, *Anthony
Bourdain: No Reservations*, he has been described as an
anticelebrity chef.

◆ "I was willing to risk my life to keep cooking." That story line is
expounded upon in *Life, on the Line: A Chef's Story of Chasing
Greatness, Facing Death, and Redefining the Way We Eat*, by Grant
Achatz and Nick Kokonas (Gotham: 2011). Recognized as one of
the country's top chefs, Achatz, chef and owner of Chicago's Alinea,
had fulfilled his lifelong dream: His establishment was named
among the top restaurants in the country. But at thirty-two, he was
diagnosed with stage-four mouth cancer. An oncologist advised
removing his tongue, which would have made his job as a chef

virtually impossible. Achatz opted instead for an experimental protocol of intensive chemotherapy and radiation. His coauthor/ business partner, Kokonas, helps narrate this dramatic story.

- *I understand the pleasure and comfort derived from eating good food.* Gabrielle Hamilton, the owner and chef of New York's Prune restaurant, may have been reluctant to become a chef, but she showed no hesitancy to become a writer. In fact, she earned a MFA in writing before moving on to the field that claimed her. She turns out to be not only a great chef, but a marvelous writer as well. Many critics view *Blood, Bones & Butter: The Inadvertent Education of a Reluctant Chef* (Random House: 2011) as one of the best memoirs to have been written by a chef.

- *"I'm obsessed with food."* We didn't have to manufacture that quote, it's practically right there in the title of Michael Lee West's *Consuming Passions: A Food-Obsessed Life* (HarperCollins: 1999). Louisiana born, this author was raised listening to her aunts "dreaming up recipes," she writes. "Some were designed to lure men, and in a few cases they were made to repel them." In adulthood, West was attending a funeral, when her Aunt Hettie commented, "What a shame." Of course West assumed that this referred to the deceased relative, but not in this food-obsessed family. Aunt Hettie moaned, "She's taken her gingerbread recipe to the grave . . . Men could not resist that dish."

- *I wanted to remember my childhood by the food I ate."* A British bestselling book, Nigel Slater's *Toast: The Story of a Boy's Hunger* (Gotham: 2004) recounts the details of what he ate in childhood, while equating his quest for gastronomical gratification with his need for emotional satiety. Early in his life, his mother died, and his father physically abused him. He eventually became a respected food writer in England, and also penned the popular *The Kitchen Diaries: A Year in the Kitchen with Nigel Slater* (Gotham: 2006).

This section could just as well be called "Food Writers Publishing Professionals Expect You to Know." If you discuss writing a food memoir with anyone knowledgeable expect the following names to be bandied about.

- M. F. K. Fisher: Few familiar with her work would hesitate to call Mary Frances Kennedy a brilliant writer. If you doubt this, read her meditation on the lowly mollusk, *Consider the Oyster* (Duell, Sloan & Pearce: 1941). Fisher was among the most celebrated of twentieth-century American food writers. She died in 1992, but not before turning out more than twenty-five books on food, travel, and literature. Her autobiographical works include: *Long Ago in France: The Years in Dijon* (Simon & Schuster: 1991), a memoir of Fisher's first years as a newlywed; *The Art of Eating* (Macmillan: 1979), a blend of culinary musings; and *The Gastronomical Me* (Duell, Sloan & Pearce: 1941), a series of essays chronicling her coming-of-age as a foodie.

- Julia Child: Sixteen years after Fisher landed in France, along came Child, who was also accompanied by her husband. At the time, Child knew almost nothing about cooking or about her newly adopted country, but none of that stopped her from taking cooking classes and, later, joining up with Simone Beck and Louisette Bertholle to write one of the most influential cookbooks of all time, the two-volume *Mastering the Art of French Cooking* (both published by Knopf: vol. 1, 1961, vol. 2, 1970). Many will remember Child as a tall, squeaky-voiced television chef; others will remember her life, which was adapted into the popular film, *Julie and Julia*. Child compiled her autobiography, *My Life in France* (Knopf: 2006) before her 2004 death. Alex Prud'Homme, her husband's grandnephew, completed the book.

- Earlier in this section, we mentioned Ruth Reichl and her coming-of-age story, *Tender at the Bone*. Her influence should not be underestimated. She is also the author of other books detailing her culinary adventures: *Comfort Me with Apples: More Adventures at the Table* (Random House: 2001) and *Garlic and Sapphires: The Secret Life of a Critic in Disguise* (Penguin: 2005). One of the finest food writers of our time, she is now a Random House editor.

- Although this next name is not familiar to most, Diane Jacob is an important one for those hoping to write food memoirs. Jacob is the author of *Will Write for Food: The Complete Guide to Writing Cookbooks, Blogs, Reviews, Memoir, and More, 2nd Edition* (Da Capo Lifelong: 2010). Updated from the original book for the sake of including the increasingly popular use of social networking, this is a title many publishing professionals recommend to aspiring food writers.

- Speaking of blogs, those dedicated to food have proven highly popular. Prior to approaching a publishing professional, consider launching a food blog to boost your platform. Should you do so, a book to peruse is *Food Styling: The Art of Preparing Food for the Camera* (Wiley: 2010), by Delores Custer, designed to help you present appealing images of your culinary creations.

Bloggers have published a number of cookbooks, the most famous of which is *Julie and Julia: 365 Days, 524 Recipes, 1 Tiny Apartment Kitchen* (Little, Brown: 2005), by Julie Powell. This author's success is tied to the popularity of food blogs. In 2002, Powell began her blog, the Julie/Julia project, dedicated to cooking every recipe in Child's *Mastering the Art of French Cooking*. Powell soon gained a following. This led to the publication of her book, and the film *Julie and Julia*.

Since that time, other food blogs have helped to launch memoir careers, including Molly Wizenberg's *A Homemade Life: Stories and Recipes from My Kitchen Table* (Simon & Schuster: 2009), and David Lebovitz's *The Sweet Life in Paris: Delicious Adventures in the World's Most Glorious—and Perplexing—City* (Broadway: 2009). Lebovitz also microblogs on Twitter.

With Lebovitz's blog getting an estimated four hundred thousand hits a month, it is no surprise that he is involved in the Food Blog Camp (http://foodblogcamp.com), an annual event that is described as an opportunity to, "practice, learn & have fun with other food bloggers."

◆ Finally, another way to convince an editor of your gastronomic gravitas is to write a story that's published in a food magazine. Of course you should try for the prestigious *Bon Appétit* or *Food & Wine*, but there are also a number of Web-based food magazines, and a community of print food magazines that publish locally with titles that begin with the word "Edible." These lushly illustrated magazines are published in more than sixty localities. To look for an *Edible* in your area, go to www.ediblecommunities.com/content/edible -publications.

◆ To learn how to write effective magazine stories, check out *The Complete Idiot's Guide to Publishing Magazine Articles*, by Sheree Bykofsky, Jennifer Basye Sander, and Lynne Rominger (Alpha: 2000).

If you're still at loss as to what aspect of your life is best suited to a food memoir, remember that you are only limited by your imagination. Writers have fashioned food memoirs in a variety of different guises, some of which are suggested below.

The Struggle of War

Day of Honey: A Memoir of Food, Love, and War, by Annia Ciezadlo (Free Press: 2011). The author lived in Baghdad and Beirut over a period of six years. In depicting food and eating rituals, Ciezadlo brings to life the Middle East that few outsiders glimpse.

Secrets of the Red Lantern: Stories and Vietnamese Recipes from the Heart, by Pauline Nguyen (Andrews McMeel: 2008). Part visual narrative and part memoir, this book offers a culinary account of the author's immigration from Vietnam.

Romance

I Loved, I Lost, I Made Spaghetti, by Giulia Melucci (Grand Central: 2009). Passionate about cooking, this Italian-American former publishing executive loves to feed men. Her story moves through a range of relationships, each one accompanied by recipes.

The Butcher and the Vegetarian: One Woman's Romp Through a World of Men, Meat, and Moral Crisis, by Tara Austen-Weaver (Rodale: 2010). This vegetarian author experienced a health crisis and followed a doctor's advice to eat meat. Her experiences led her to attractive butchers, and eco-friendly ranches populated by appealing cowboys.

Transformation Stories

Season to Taste: How I Lost My Sense of Smell and Found My Way, by Molly Birnbaum (Ecco: 2011). Shortly before matriculating at the Culinary Institute of America, the author was struck by a car, and among multiple injuries, lost her sense of smell. Birnbaum gave up on plans to attend cooking school and a restaurant job, set off to explore the science of smell, and started a new and delicious life.

A Tiger in the Kitchen: A Memoir of Food and Family, by Cheryl Lu-Lien Tan (Voice: 2011). Laid off from her job as a fashion reporter for *The Wall Street Journal*, the author returned to her native Singapore to learn to prepare the traditional dishes from her childhood. Along with learning to make pineapple tarts and other delicacies, she rediscovers a culture that speaks to many of her most cherished values.

Coming-of-Age

Charlotte au Chocolat: Memories of a Restaurant Girlhood, by Charlotte Silver (Riverhead: 2012). The author was raised in a restaurant—owned by her parents and a business partner—which happened to be housed in the same building as Harvard's renown Hasty Pudding Club.

My Nepenthe: Bohemian Tales of Food, Family, and Big Sur, by Romney Steele (Andrews McMeel: 2009). A granddaughter of the creators of the Nepenthe restaurant in Big Sur, California, Steele opened her own outdoor café on the grounds of the popular eatery. Her story celebrates her family's history through food.

Cooked: From the Streets to the Stove, from Cocaine to Foie Gras, by Jeff Henderson (William Morrow: 2007). A former cocaine dealer, after a prison incarceration where he was assigned to kitchen duty, the author becomes an award-winning chef.

Stealing Buddha's Dinner, by Bich Minh Nguyen (Viking: 2007). Born in Vietnam and raised in Grand Rapids, Michigan, the author hungers for an American identity, and by extension, American junk food, such as Pringles, Jell-O, Kool-Aid, and Kit Kat bars.

The Language of Baklava, by Diana Abu-Jaber (Pantheon: 2005). The author shares stories of growing up in Upstate New York, with trips to Jordan. She includes a sampling of recipes that formed her character, such as baklava, shish kebab, and bread salad.

Daughter of Heaven: A Memoir with Earthly Recipes, by Leslie Li (Arcade: 2005). According to *Publishers Weekly*, which gave this collection a starred review, "The essays lyrically show the tension in Li's family between her father and mother, between herself and her father, and most of all, between Li's American ways and her Chinese history. Li uses the food of her family to tell her stories."

We close with an $$$Analysis of *A Spoonful of Promises: Stories & Recipes from a Well-Tempered Table*, by T. Susan Chang (Lyons: 2011).

$Writing Chops

This coming-of-age story is told in a series of linked essays. According to the Purdue online writing lab, "Where the personal essay explores, free from any need to interpret, the memoir interprets, analyzes, and seeks the deeper meaning beneath the surface experience of particular events. The memoir continually asks the following questions: Why was this event of particular significance? What did it mean? Why is it important?" What then should be expected from a compilation of food essays?

Memoirists such as Chang continue to expand the boundaries of the personal essay. Her stories include details of childhood memories and scenes from her current-day life that are intended to cohere into a memoir-like ensemble. The author explains in the introduction that she began writing the essays while on a fellowship in 2006. One essay in particular, "The Once and Future Apple Cake," is exceptional.

The author recalls how her mother baked dark, moist apple cakes. Returning home as a girl, she would find one of the freshly baked cakes waiting, "on the linoleum counter, its warm invitation extending beyond our door." When eating it, Chang would "feel loved, and deserving of love." Sadly, during Chang's adolescence, her mother died. In adulthood, the author discovers that her mother's apple cake recipe is missing. Year after year, she tries to replicate the recipe, only to fail. At some point an acquaintance passes along a satisfying recipe, and when Chang bakes the cake and removes it from the oven, it smells so good that she has to resist tearing it apart with her fingers. Instead she waits, and shares it with her children. The author's experience and discipline are apparent in this story. Her sentiments and passion are clear, but she employs skill rather than sentimentality.

A writer of Chang's talent leaves readers longing to be treated as confidants. The essays might work well as stand-alone piece, but the difficulties that arise with this collection have to do with the decision to recycle and package essays that do not cohere into a thematic whole.

This beautifully presented volume, its front and back covers decorated with irresistible black-and-white photos of the author's daughter Zoe, contains several recipes. One author's review that runs on the book jacket observes that recipes of foods have been included that Chang loves, "some totally and happily beyond reason."

This quote raises legitimate questions. As the blurb suggests, recipes have been included that seem "beyond reason." In fact, very few of the recipes are presented in a manner that helps readers experience their significance in Chang's life. That is especially important in this work because similar recipes can be found on the Internet, while others might fit into cookbooks for beginners: pumpkin bread, sautéed spinach, roasted potatoes, and applesauce. Personal writing about food is at its best when it evokes a flow of layered images and sensations true to both the palate and the memory. In using essays the whole should be greater than the sum of its parts.

When followed, the recipes in *A Spoonful of Promises*, lead to dishes that are as good as promised, making it clear that they have been exhaustively tested. It is not unusual for ordinary food to be included in memoirs, as in Kate Moses's previously discussed *Cakewalk*. Moses and Chang are both highly skilled writers. Chang's essays in *A Spoonful of Promises* garners 6 points for the writing score.

$Narrative Hook

Raised in a Chinese American family, the author explains that her relatives didn't talk much about the past that had brought them to America. Chang adds that, "as the family propagated and throve in our new home, bits of cultural habits dropped away." One of the attractions of this book is that the life that unfolds is post-racial, presenting a range of readers with the opportunity to recognize their own stories framed by Chang's recollections. Yes, there are stories in *A Spoonful of Promises* that make us crave Wonton Soup and New Year's Dumplings, but these would not be unusual in many other American homes.

Chang's approach may send curious readers in search of food essays in which heritage *is* relevant to the cuisine. *We Are What We Ate: 24 Memories of Food*, a collection of essays edited by Mark Winegardner (Mariner: 1998) is written by authors who were asked to recall how food defined their families and made them who they are today. In "Picky Eater," novelist Julia Alvarez explains why she didn't grow up thinking that restaurant food was something she would enjoy. She writes:

> This was a carryover from my childhood in a big Dominican family in which the women prided themselves on the fact that nobody could put a meal on the table like they could put a meal on a table. You went out for the special purpose of seeing and

being seen by your friends and neighbors, but you never went out to have a good meal. For that you stayed home . . .

One post-racial point of view is that society should move beyond racial identification. As the Alvarez story makes clear, some particulars of a racial group can be viewed as part of the bouquet of life. That isn't said to imply, of course, that Chang's story should be presented as something that it's not. But it is important to remember that whenever there is an absence of something in a story, it's up to the author to fill the void, to come up with something unique.

A narrative hook that was only partially developed pertains to the interplay of Chang's maternal memories and the immediate sensations of feeding her own children. By viewing the author within the orbit of her mother's kitchen, where the foods prepared were so powerful they made a girl, "feel loved, and deserving of love," the recipes for what Chang now serves her family—Chicken Pot Pie, Make-Ahead Marinade, Cold Green Bean salads—bring her life into focus, and the circle binding past and present feels complete. *A Spoonful of Promises* scores 5 points for the strength of its narrative hook.

$Platform Strength

Chang's energetic work in her field has strengthened her platform. She reviews cookbooks for *The Boston Globe*, contributes regularly to NPR's "Kitchen Window" column, and also delivers biannual roundups of cookbooks for this national public station. Chang also reviews and blogs for the cookbook-indexing Web site Eat Your Books, and the AOL Kitchen Daily Web site. A freelance journalist, she writes for a variety of national and regional food publications. *A Spoonful of Promises* garners 10 points for the strength of the platform, bringing Chang's overall score to 21 out of 30 points.

Seven

Religion and Spirituality Memoirs

G IVEN THAT MATTERS OF RELIGIOUS BELIEF CAN CAUSE
great controversy, we confess to being tempted to skip this subject
all together, like a hotel elevator bypassing the thirteenth floor. Let's face
it, though—this category is too important for us to pretend it doesn't
exist, especially as it pertains to the memoir.

We've already discussed how the bond between reader and memoirist
is an outgrowth of the human desire for connection. The best memoirs
give readers the sense that they are not alone. Additional consideration
concerns the human capability that distinguishes us from other members
of the animal kingdom. We are prone to worrying about the future—one
that cannot be predicted in detail. Memoirs offer us something difficult
to live without: hope.

That brings us to the subject of this chapter, religious and spiritual memoirs. Perhaps especially during times of loss, fear, change, or doubt, or when faced with difficult decisions, religious and spiritual memoirs can remind us that we are connected to something larger and more comprehensive than ourselves. As with love, people are attracted to that which transcends mundane experience, while at the same time they are terrified of it. Since even the most complicated relationships require interaction, many readers turn to memoirs in search of a dynamic communion with the Unknown.

Challenging Aspects to Writing Spiritual/Religious Memoirs

Significant factors challenging those hoping to write, market, and sell this subgenre require learning to negotiate a landscape on which the personal can quickly become intensely political. Consider the culture wars incited by religion and spirituality and the angry debates over the role of religion in shaping public policy. Adding to the mix are disheartening headlines about clerical leaders with feet of clay.

It is no surprise that religion is losing its luster. A significant segment of the larger culture is exhibiting an almost allergic reaction to the public face of religion. Still, research suggests that many are unwilling to relinquish this significant dimension of life. More than 90 percent of people surveyed in the United States say they believe in God or a Higher Power, a figure that is down only slightly since the 1940s, according to the results of a June 3, 2011, Gallup Poll.

Yet while the United States may be a nation of believers, many draw a line between spirituality on the one hand, and religion on the other. Back in 1997 Meredith McGuire's essay, "Mapping Contemporary American Spirituality: A Sociological Perspective," cited a survey of changed religious views in the U.S. in which many respondents agreed with the statement, "I'm not a very religious person, but I consider myself a spiritual person."

Those who are "spiritual" are among the Americans who have become less tied to formal religion, with many viewing it as old-fashioned and out-of-date. Younger Americans, ages eighteen to twenty-nine, are considerably less religious than others. A February 17, 2010, Pew Research study found that one in four interviewees born after 1980 is unaffiliated with a particular religious tradition.

This shifting of sand may impact RU authors. For decades, religious titles written by RUs were seldom known outside the network of bookstores specializing in faith-themed titles. The Christian Booksellers Association and the Evangelical Christian Publishers Association have long represented a major segment of the religious market. Both organizations publish bestseller listings.

Manhattan's publishing industry long maintained a hands-off approach to religious fare. Occasionally, recognition was given to clerics with their own following, such as The Reverend Billy Graham or Rabbi Harold Kushner, the author of the bestselling *When Bad Things Happen to Good People* (Random House: 1981). For the most part, though, religious books were not tracked for patterns of sale or considered for inclusion on nationally known bestseller listings.

The rise of the Christian Right changed that scenario. Religious books were ushered into the mainstream with the success of the Christian novel series *Left Behind*, by Tim LaHaye and Jerry Jenkins, first published by Tyndale House in 1995 and later adapted for the big screen, as well as the Reverend Rick Warren's *The Purpose-Driven Life* (Zondervan: 2002), which has sold more than twenty-five million copies.

Bestselling memoirs followed, including: *The Boy Who Came Back from Heaven: A Remarkable Account of Miracles, Angels, and Life Beyond*, by Kevin Malarkey and Alex Malarkey (Tyndale House: 2010); *90 Minutes in Heaven: A True Story of Death and Life*, by Don Piper and Cecil Murphey (Revell: 2007); *Heaven Is for Real: Lessons on Earthly Joy—from the Mom Who Spent 90 Minutes in Heaven*, by Don Piper and Cecil Murphey (Berkeley: 2007); *Same Kind of Different As Me: A Modern-Day*

Slave, an International Art Dealer, and the Unlikely Woman Who Bound Them Together, by Ron Hall and Denver Moore, with Lynn Vincent (Thomas Nelson: 2006).

With a Gallup Survey of December 23, 2011, indicating that 78 percent of religious American adults identify with some form of Christianity, while less than 2 percent are Jewish, and 1 percent are Muslim, it is no surprise that Christian books are big business. Mark Kuyper, chief executive of the Evangelical Christian Publishers Association, forecast in 2011 that the Christian book market would generate annual sales revenue of $1.4 billion, up slightly from 2010. One sign of the publishing world's faith in the continued success of this subgenre is that several major publishing houses now have religious imprints. In 1998, HarperCollins purchased Zondervan, a major religious publisher based in Grand Rapids, Michigan. The company later acquired Thomas Nelson, the publisher of Billy Graham and the megabestseller *Heaven Is for Real.* Random House owns the religious imprint WaterBrook Multnomah. Simon & Schuster's Howard Books serves the religious market, and Hachette has FaithWords. For more information about writing for the Christian book market and to learn more about the many religious independent publishing houses and agents, read: *The Christian Writers Market Guide—2012* (Tyndale House: 2011).

One explanation for the stunning commercial success of some Christian books is that the authors understand their audience. A great many readers are Protestant evangelicals, loosely affiliated groups, which in the aggregate include tens of millions of adherents worldwide.

A MARKETPLACE SURVIVAL TIP

A factor that helps fuel sales of religious books is that the authors know where to find passionate audiences—in houses of worship. From the time Saint Augustine took to the pulpit, religious memoirists have been spreading the word. Today, a number of

bestselling religious authors owe their success to face time at houses of worship, where they preach to the choir—and anyone else beneath vaulted ceilings. According to a December 2009 Pew study of U.S. religion, 35 percent of respondents said they attend religious services regularly, 9 percent attend occasionally, 26 percent attend services at more than one location, and most of these (24 percent overall) sometimes attend religious services of a faith different from their own.

Don Piper, the author of *90 Minutes in Heaven,* has spoken to three thousand audiences around the world, according to his Web site. Traveling and speaking at different venues, often churches, has paid off for him. His Web site explains that over five million copies of *90 Minutes in Heaven* have been sold in forty languages, with the book remaining on *The New York Times* bestseller listings for nearly four years.

Piper's success is a reminder that in religious settings in particular, face-to-face contact can translate into sales. Unlike Moses, these authors aren't using stone tablets—they're also on the Web and Twitter, sending out inspirational blasts or blog entries to e-mail addresses collected from congregants and other audience members that have heard them speak.

Memoirists are often welcome in religious settings because they bring real world experience that can put a fine point on rich historical teachings. Increasingly, authors of religious titles are also speaking at parochial high schools and colleges. In the fall of 2011, Immaculée Ilibagiza, the author, with Steve Erwin, of *Left to Tell: Discovering God Amidst the Rwandan Holocaust* (Hay House: 2006), spoke at a Catholic high school in Oakland, California, where tickets for the event and books were sold. In the days leading up to her appearance, Ilibagiza's photo and a plot summary were featured on the school's Web site. The details of Ilibagiza's story are dramatic. In 1994, she hid in a bathroom with seven other women for ninety-one days, during the period of Rwandan genocide. She remained sane, she explains, through constant prayer and with the help of rosary beads. Her faith helped her to forgive her tormentors and those who murdered her family members. To fellow believers, Ilibagiza's story serves as an illustration of faith in action.

Another popular African memoirist, Leymah Gbowee, wrote, with Carol Mithers, *Mighty Be Our Powers: How Sisterhood, Prayer, and Sex Changed a Nation at War* (Beast: 2011). Gbowee organized Christian and Muslim women to pray for peace, a protest movement that eventually ended the dictatorship of President Charles Taylor and Liberia's brutal civil war. Inspired by her story, Leonard Riggio, the chairman of Barnes & Noble, financed Gbowee's book tour to churches and college campuses in eight cities. Gbowee's voice was heard beyond her tour. She was awarded a 2011 Nobel Peace Prize.

Your Audience: Religious or Spiritual?

People who are religious tend to observe a system of historical beliefs, formalities, ritual worship, and practices that are usually social and institutional. Their "interior lives" are largely intelligible within the practices of a community. In the United States, religion is often associated with monotheistic traditions, including Christianity, Judaism, and Islam. Other major religions include Buddhism, in which the major religious figure is Buddha, and Hinduism, a religious and cultural tradition that has origins in the Indian subcontinent.

When people describe themselves as "spiritual," this often means something different to different people. The word was used originally in a Christian context, referring to the work of the Holy Spirit. It was about becoming more Christlike, as in Jesus's way of relinquishing power, the giving up of the self to find God, and the fruitfulness of life that is associated with this approach. The notion of spirituality has since been adapted to a wide variety of traditions.

Philip Sheldrake, the author of *A Brief History of Spirituality* (Blackwell: 2007), believes that the word "spirituality" seems elusive because it is increasingly detached from religious traditions and its Christian roots. He writes that, "Spirituality refers to the deepest values and meanings by which people seek to live." He further explains that the word now implies, "some kind of vision of the human spirit and of what will assist it to achieve full potential."

Those who are "spiritual" often describe themselves seeking individual paths as they search for purpose and meaning, sometimes through contemplation, meditation, or prayer. The notion of spirituality has expanded to include the attributes of self-awareness, creativity, rationality, moral consciousness, and action.

TAKE THIS PERSONALLY

Religious and spiritual adherents have long emphasized gratitude as an important virtue. Gratitude might also help improve your writing. How is this possible? Research by Dr. Robert Emmons, of the University of California, Davis, has found in experiments conducted with Michael E. McCullough of the University of Miami that gratitude can lead people to feel less anxious, less depressed, and more satisfied with life. To some extent, these findings might help to explain the success of Gretchen Rubin's spiritual memoir, *The Happiness Project: Or, Why I Spent a Year Trying to Sing in the Morning, Clean My Closets, Fight Right, Read Aristotle, and Generally Have More Fun* (Harper: 2009), which became a bestseller almost immediately after publication.

The author began her quest as a somewhat discontented mother and wife, and through her individual efforts became more appreciative of what she already had. You, too, can reframe the way you view your life. As a writer, for example, it may help to think of the difficult times you have experienced as narrative conflicts, which can keep readers turning pages. Here are some specifics to help you make lemonade out of lemons:

- The next time you're stuck at a traffic light, use the time to think of some aspect of your life or work for which you are grateful, perhaps even having the luxury of time to write your memoir.

- Start a gratitude journal, digitally, or in a paper notebook, and contribute to it daily. As you think about what to record, consider even small kindnesses: the driver who stopped to allow you to pull out of your driveway, or the professor who gave you an additional day to finish your assignment. What about experiences that further your ability to tell your story?

- Try not to let "positive thinking" blind you to learning opportunities. For instance, if members of your writing collective negatively criticize a particular scene or approach in your manuscript, don't convince yourself that no matter what, your story will sell. Even if you don't use the advice that's offered, accept the criticism as a gift from someone who cares enough about your work to risk making a comment.

- Write an entry in your journal about someone who hurt you, incorporating details about aspects of the experience that turned out to be collateral benefits. For instance, a workshop participant said that for sixteen years her mean-spirited grandmother shamed her into sitting through two excruciatingly long Sunday church services. She had always thought of those services as a waste of time. Now she realizes that one collateral benefit of six hours of having endured fire and brimstone was that these were times when, forced to sit still, she exercised her imagination and started "thinking like a writer."

- Search back in your religious/spiritual traditions or experiences for role models whose lives were enriched by gratitude. If possible, download a photo or illustration of this person onto your phone, or print and paste it inside a gratitude journal, as a face that serves as a reminder that gratitude can work in your favor.

- Read *One Thousand Gifts: A Dare to Live Fully Right Where You Are*, by Ann Voskamp (Zondervan: 2011). The author, a mother of six married to a pig farmer, wondered what it would mean to be Christlike when your days are long and gritty. She began what became a transformative ritual of chronicling God's gifts and expressing gratitude for the life she already had.

Some authors might wonder whether—since "religious" people seem passionate about buying religious memoirs and are clearly an easier audience to target and given that they tend to show up for worship services, as compared to "spiritual" people who march to their own beat—a savvy author shouldn't try to appeal to the largest possible audience.

The most important answer is: to thine own beliefs be true. Tell your story with integrity and follow your own religious and/or spiritual path. Should you doubt the commercial wisdom of this advice, look to Bruce

Feiler's bestselling *Walking the Bible: A Journey by Land Through the Five Books of Moses* (William Morrow: 2001). A fifth-generation Jewish son raised in the South, he embraced his heritage, traveling ten thousand miles to biblical landmarks, reconnecting with the faith of his ancestors. Feiler, inspired by a truth in early verses of Genesis, writes:

> Abraham was not originally the man he became. He was not an Israelite, he was not a Jew. He was not even a believer in God—at least initially. He was a traveler, called by some voice not entirely clear that said: Go head to this land, walk along this route, and trust what you will find.

His book inspired the spinoffs *Walking the Bible (Children's Edition): An Illustrated Journey for Kids Through the Greatest Stories Ever Told*, with illustrations by Sasha Meret (HarperCollins: 2004), and *Walking the Bible: A Photographic Journey* (William Morrow: 2005), and became the subject of a PBS miniseries.

You'll create a stronger story by striving for religious and spiritual balance. The truth is, religion without spirituality can feel moribund, smug, reflecting un-graced judgment. Spirituality in and of itself, absent of historical and cultural roots, can feel superficial and bland. Many people describe themselves as purely spiritual without realizing that their self-understanding doesn't come out of a vacuum, but in many cases has been shaped by history and culture, a mix of elements from diverse religions.

Some authors ignore the need for religious/spiritual balance. Some write religious memoirs devoid of spirituality that are overly dogmatic and out of touch with universal emotions. The purely spiritual books smack of saccharine, feel-good piety. Employing spirituality without religion, or vice versa, is like holding a telescope and ignoring the stars. But using one to enhance the other can give you an expanded view of the universe.

Four Books Illustrating Religious/Spiritual Balance

Plenty of personal narratives tip toward the prosaic when they might have instead been more inspiring. Here are four memoirs that will provoke discussion.

1. *The Devil in Pew Number Seven*, by Rebecca Nichols Alonzo, with Bob DeMoss (Tyndale: 2010): Although the plot makes for difficult reading, *Devil* became an e-book bestseller. During the early '70s, a disgruntled parishioner tormented Alonzo's father, Robert Nichols, a handsome, good-natured pastor of a North Carolina church, his adoring wife, Ramona Nichols, and their children. The five-year reign of terror began with threatening phone calls, ratcheted up to bombings, and culminated with the shooting of the author's mother. She died from her wounds. To those who do not share the couple's religious beliefs, the Nichols's certainty that faith would shield them from harm may make them seem out of touch with reality. Those who do share their beliefs will view them as admiringly devout.

The author often quotes scripture to explain her parents' thoughts. In one scene, Ramona Nichols makes an effort to "take a stand against anxiety," and the concern of others who fret, "over what might happen to her and her family," by reading Psalm 91, which is presented in the story in uppercase:

I WILL SAY OF THE LORD, HE IS MY REFUGE AND MY
FORTRESS: MY GOD; IN HIM WILL I TRUST. SURELY
HE SHALL DELIVER THEE FROM THE SNARE OF THE
FOWLER...THOU SHALL NOT BE AFRAID FOR THE
TERROR BY NIGHT; NOR FOR THE ARROW THAT
FLIETH BY DAY...

The story makes clear the parents' courageousness—and the author's compassion. Later, she quickly accepts the killer's apology. *The Devil* is a religious story with touches of spirituality. Like a leavening agent, spirituality can be employed by memoirists to help readers understand why some people are capable of rising up beyond the circumstances of the world. The portrayal doesn't have to be romantic; it doesn't have to depict a robust interchange with a divinity. It does call for a connection to be made with a source beyond the everyday experience of the world.

As tragic as their decisions turned out to be, the Nicholses used robust prayer to pursue a life beyond space and time, as we know it. They inspired others, not by words, but by example. Faith for them was far more than religious observances. After enduring ten bomb attacks in two and a half years, it might have seemed to others that this killer had imprisoned this couple with fear. Yet faith allowed the Nicholses to move beyond the pedestrian needs of life, and experience what for them may have felt like perfect freedom.

2. *The Seven Storey Mountain*, by Thomas Merton (Harcourt Brace: 1948). One of the bestselling religious autobiographies in history, Merton's story invites readers into his spiritual wrestling match. Merton was European born, and as a young man fathered a child out of wedlock (both mother and child were said to have been killed during World War II). Expelled from Cambridge, Merton enrolled at Columbia University and pursued his interests in jazz, Harlem, film, and writing.

Continuing restlessness led Merton to turn to spiritual matters, and he later chose to be baptized as a Catholic. This was a big leap for someone who grew up hearing disdainful remarks from his grandfather about Catholicism and Judaism. After conversion, although Merton wasn't willing to give up worldly enjoyments for his faith without a fight, love of God continued to pull him in a different direction. Visiting a church in Cuba, he heard children chanting, "*Creo en Dios...*" (I believe in God) and the words struck him, "like a thunderclap." He became aware of a light, "so profound and so intimate ... It was as if I had been suddenly illuminated by being blinded by the manifestation of God's presence." Merton eventually entered a Trappist monastery.

The Seven Storey Mountain quickly became a bestseller, but according to publishing editor Robert Giroux, *The New York Times* refused to include the title in the weekly listing, "on the grounds that it was a religious book."

The book's continuing popularity surely has something to do with its transcendent arc, and this, too, can be a reminder of the importance of spirituality. Transcendence is about connecting with a source of reality beyond the everyday experiences. It lies at the heart of conversion stories, those that force protagonists to change direction in character, behavior, or conviction, occurring in response to a spiritual interaction.

3. *The Autobiography of Malcolm X: As Told to Alex Haley* (Grove Press: 1965), by Malcolm X and Alex Haley. Although it is not often recognized as a religious story, this book is told in the tradition of the conversion narrative. A page-turner, it, too, has sold millions of copies, and millions more after the book was adapted into a film.

While in prison, Malcolm X was introduced to the teachings of the Nation of Islam, with its message that whites were evil by nature. Upon his release, he converted to the Nation of Islam, and his oratorical gifts and message of black supremacy helped him become one of black America's most revered leaders.

This story might have been interesting if it had simply ended at that point, but something profound occurred that caused Malcolm X to undergo a second conversion. Disenchanted with the leadership of the Nation of Islam, he traveled to Africa and to the Middle East, where he made a pilgrimage to Mecca. During this period, when he witnessed Muslims of all races worshipping together, Malcolm X embraced Orthodox Islam. This understanding led to a spiritual rebirth. Returning to the United States, he espoused changed beliefs, and among several issues raised, he disavowed racism and indicated his support of white participation in the struggle for black emancipation. Soon afterward, he was shot and killed by members of the Nation of Islam.

Malcolm X's story and his renunciation of hate didn't die with him. The experience of the kindness and fidelity that he found to be universal in the Islamic people put Malcolm X in touch with something that spoke to a larger core of reality than what he had tapped into before. This transcendent moment allowed him to reinterpret all manner of experiences. That this experience was centered in his faith reoriented his life.

4. *Devotion*, by Dani Shapiro (Harper: 2010). The title of this spiritual book contradicts the opening scenes of Shapiro's story. The word "devotion" suggests, of course, that she is enthusiastically religious and highly observant of the tenets of her faith. Readers are disabused from this notion from the first pages, when Shapiro is visiting a psychic who claims to channel the spirit of the author's father. Cynical as the author is, she cries at the thought of her father hovering nearby. As it turns out, it was he who was devoted—to Orthodox Judaism and to his family. Shapiro says of her religious memories, "As a child, I was told what to believe." Her father died when Shapiro was a young woman, before she'd had a chance to change her life for the better. In *Devotion*, Shapiro, a wife and mother, struggles to experience something outside the confines of her own comfortable life, something to which she can become devoted. A confident and artful writer, she charts deftly the rough waters between religion and spirituality.

It's understandable why aspiring memoirists struggle with dialogue. Charged with telling the truth, they can't simply pretend that their characters said something. At the same time, they are often expected to reconstruct conversations from decades past. Getting at the truth can actually be fun, if you learn to "channel" your characters' dialogue. That's not a euphemism for "making stuff up." It's a writing technique employed by some of the best memoirists. Here's how it works:

First of all, it might help you relax to know that you will recognize when you've created authentic characters. They'll wake you, insisting that you get up and write down what they want to say. That is not fanciful thinking. Ever hear of someone traveling to a new country and getting so immersed in the food, attitudes, history, and language that he or she starts dreaming in that foreign tongue? That happens to some travelers. Similarly, authors experience this kind of effect when immersed in a character's life.

Elmore Leonard, whose bestselling books have been adapted into memorable films, like *Get Shorty*, told an interviewer that he'd started smoking Virginia Slims because one of his characters started smoking them, and every once in a while he would say, "I think I'll have a Slim." Leonard's character had gotten under his skin. Of course Leonard is speaking from the point of view of a novelist, which makes him a literary cousin of sorts. A memoirist has to have the instincts of a novelist, and think like an autobiographer.

With your senses attuned as you communicate with others online, and read news articles, journals, and books, you will begin to hear phrasing that could have come straight out of your characters' mouths. You will "hear" your characters as you listen to others speaking in public, on television and radio, at parties and other events. This will strengthen your memory.

By the way, just because Leonard writes fiction, doesn't mean that you can't learn from this grand master. You may want to Google his essay for *The New York Times* in 2001, "Easy on the Adverbs, Exclamation Points and Especially Hooptedoodle." This list of eleven rules of writing is often discussed in creative writing classes—and some of it is pertinent in nonfiction writing.

Here are three pointers for helping you develop dynamite dialogue:

1. Dialogue doesn't sound like a verbatim conversation with long complex sentences and proper grammar. Helen Fremont's *After Long Silence* (Delacorte: 1999) is the story of a girl raised Roman Catholic by parents who hide their Polish-Jewish roots in response to horrendous Holocaust experiences. As a girl, Fremont is confused as to why her mother attends church service and then mocks what she believes is the priest's poor grammar. In one scene, she recalls her mother:

   > "Jesus died for you and I!" she would exclaim. "For you and *I!*" She would shake her head in a rage. "An idiot he is!"

2. Dialogue works best when the words fit the character's personality, but surprise us nevertheless and endear us to that character. In *Traveling Mercies: Some Thoughts on Faith*, by Anne Lamott (Pantheon: 1999), the author's dialogue is in keeping with her experiences and her irreverent tone. In one scene, Lamott is concerned about the daughter of a friend, Olivia, a two-year-old diagnosed with cystic fibrosis. Rather than phoning Olivia's home, Lamott prays. She says to God,

> "Look I'm sure you know what you're doing, but my patience
> is beginning to wear a *little* thin . . ."

3. Internal dialogue is every bit as important as what a character
   might actually say aloud. In *The New York Regional Mormon
   Singles Halloween Dance*, by Elna Baker (Dutton: 2009), the
   protagonist doesn't have quite the tone one would expect
   when picturing a young, observant Mormon. Elna's
   mischievous personality is apparent after her mother worries
   aloud about her attending college in New York City. "Elna,"
   she says nervously. "The first thing that will happen when
   you move to New York is, you might start to swear."
   Elna thinks: "Oh, *shit*, really?"

Following is a list of religious and spiritual books not mentioned
earlier in this chapter, listed alphabetically:

*An American Requiem: God, My Father, and the War That Came Between
Us*, by James Carroll (Houghton Mifflin: 1996). This story won the author a National Book Award. Now a novelist, columnist, and poet, this
former priest came of age just in time to thrust his interest in religious
activism into the 1960s antiwar movement, and to lock horns with his
father, one of the most powerful men at the Pentagon.

*An Invisible Thread: The True Story of a 11-Year-Old Pandhandler, a Busy
Sales Executive, and an Unlikely Meeting with Destiny*, by Laura Schroff
and Alex Tresniowski (Howard Books: 2011). Like many New Yorkers,
ad executive Schroff was accustomed to passing people begging for help,
but when she stops to help the young and hungry Maurice Mazyck both
of their lives change. Theirs is a story of faith in action.

A Stitch and a Prayer: A Memoir of Faith Amidst War, by Phyllis Tickle
(Paraclete: 2003). The founding editor of the religion department of

Publishers Weekly, the author writes of her father's pre–World War II experiences, and by extension, her own life. Tickle's father crochets a coverlet and continues to stitch until war's end.

Adam's Gift: A Memoir of a Pastor's Calling to Defy the Church's Persecution of Lesbians and Gays, by Jimmy Creech (Duke University: 2011). After a long and heartfelt conversation with an openly gay parishioner, this United Methodist pastor in North Carolina defied his church's teachings that homosexuality was a sin. His ordination credentials were revoked.

Blue Like Jazz: Nonreligious Thoughts on Christian Spirituality, by Donald Miller (Thomas Nelson: 2003). The author, a speaker, campus ministry leader, and former evangelical who developed progressive political views, writes of Jesus's relevance in his everyday life. This memoir was recently made into a film.

The Bread of Angels: A Journey to Love and Faith, by Stephanie Saldana (Doubleday: 2010). An American scholar arriving in Syria in 2004 struggles to feel connected to and trusting in God. A *Publishers Weekly* starred review praised the author's knowledge of Christianity, Islam, and Judaism, and described the book as an *Eat, Pray, Love* for the intellectual set.

Children of Dust: A Memoir of Pakistan, by Ali Eteraz (HarperOne: 2009). This coming-of-age story opens with the author's father promising Allah that if God gives him a son, the youth will become a leader and servant of Islam. The Pakistani-born Eteraz struggles to come to terms with his relationship to Islam in adventures that *O* magazine described as a, "heavenly read."

Choosing My Religion (originally *Turbulent Souls: A Catholic Son's Return to His Jewish Family*), by Stephen J. Dubner (William Morrow: 1998). Like his seven siblings in this Catholic family, the author was named after saints, and a brother served as an altar boy. Dubner's *New York Times* essay about discovering that his parents were born Jewish and converted to Christianity attracted a slew of letters. He later converted to Judaism.

Chosen By God: A Brother's Journey, by Joshua Hammer (Hyperion: 1999). This *Newsweek* correspondent's brother followed his troubled teenage years with an arranged marriage and life in an ultraorthodox Jewish sect in Upstate New York. After years of estrangement, the author wanted to understand his brother's choices.

Dakota: A Spiritual Geography, by Kathleen Norris (Tickle & Fields: 1993). An award-winning poet with a many admirers, Norris writes of moving from New York to a house in Dakota built by her grandparents. She then undertakes a reevaluation of her heritage and her religion,

Do Not Go Gentle: My Search for Miracles in a Cynical Time, by Ann Hood (Picador: 2000). When her father is diagnosed with inoperable lung cancer, Hood, who was raised Catholic, searches for a cure. In Chimayo, New Mexico, where each year thousands of pilgrims travel to a tiny chapel known as a site of miraculous cures, the author is desperate for answers. She finds solace in reclaiming her spiritual heritage.

Escape, by Carolyn Jessup, with Laura Palmer (Broadway: 2007). The author was raised in a polygamist sect and married at eighteen to a fifty-year-old with three wives. More than a decade later, she fled the church and her marriage, and successfully sued for custody of their children.

Growing Up Amish, by Ira Wagler (Tyndale: 2011). The author experiences life both inside and outside Amish worlds. He writes of the discontent many young people feel in the confines of an Amish settlement. Wagler chose ultimately to leave the community, and in this story recounts his early life.

Hannah's Child: A Theologian's Memoir, by Stanley Hauerwas (Wm. B. Eerdmans: 2010). Like Hannah in the Book of Samuel, the author's mother prayed for a child whom she would raise to be of service to God. Now a respected theologian, the author has written a work praised as highly inspiring.

Higher Ground: A Memoir of Salvation, Found and Lost, by Carolyn S. Briggs (Bloomsbury USA: 2002). Becoming a born-again Christian as an adult, the author joins a community of self-described "Jesus Freaks," a group that incorporates religious fundamentalism with a countercultural lifestyle. Eventually seized with doubt, the author leaves her marriage and the community. This story was made into a film.

House of Prayer No. 2: A Writer's Journey Home, by Mark Richard (Nan A. Talese: 2011). Born with crippling physical disabilities and viewed by many in the 1960s South as mentally disabled, the author heads, in adulthood, to New York City. Despite misbehavior, he learns to write and discovers the power of faith.

Jesus, My Father, The CIA, and Me: A Memoir . . . of Sorts, by Morgan Cron (Thomas Nelson: 2011). The confused, emotionally abandoned boy at the heart of this story grows up to become an Episcopal priest and father. He shows his own children the love that he learns through faith.

Jesus Land, by Julia Scheeres (Counterpoint: 2005). A white child in racist rural Indiana, the author is raised with two black adopted brothers. Their father is violent and their mother seems more passionate about church missionaries than her parental responsibilities. The author and one of her brothers are sent to a religious reform school in the Dominican Republic. The book won an American Library Association Award.

The Last Days: A Son's Story of Sin and Segregation at the Dawn of a New South, by Charles Marsh (Basic Books: 2001). Raised in a conservative Mississippi family, where one town resident is the Imperial Wizard of the White Knights of the Mississippi Ku Klux Klan, Marsh recalls his minister father's moral complicity during a period of racial violence. A professor of religion, the author writes with remorse of this period of injustice.

Leaving Church: A Memoir of Faith, by Barbara Brown Taylor (Harper-Collins: 2006). One of the first women ordained in the Episcopal Church, Taylor served as a rector for two decades, until the job began wearing her down. She became a college professor, who continues to write for the spiritual but not necessarily religious crowd.

Man Seeks God: My Flirtations with the Divine, by Eric Weiner (Twelve: 2011). The author means it when he says he is "flirting with the Divine." After a health scare, this award-winning journalist travels the world to explore religions, in hope of finding one that will give him a better understanding of God.

Mennonite in a Little Black Dress: A Memoir of Going Home, by Rhoda Janzen (Henry Holt: 2009). The author, a college professor, at odds with her conservative Mennonite community, gives readers plenty of reasons to laugh, and may leave some longing to have been involved in this tradition.

Plain Secrets: An Outsider Among the Amish, by Jack Mackall (Beacon: 2007). A writer and English professor, the author approaches the Amish with an outsider's eye, but develops a deep respect as he got to know neighboring Amish families. The book won high praise from critics.

Unorthodox: The Scandalous Rejection of My Hasidic Roots, by Deborah Feldman (Simon & Schuster: 2012). The author—a child of a mentally disturbed father and a mother who fled from their religious community—is raised by conservative grandparents. Contraband classic literature and a college classes whet her appetite for a life that is not filled with harsh restrictions, and she breaks free. Many members of the

Hasidic community have challenged the veracity of this story, heightening the controversy and calling attention to the book.

The Vow: The Kim and Krickitt Carpenter Story, by Kim Carpenter (Broadman & Holman: 2000). Two years into their marriage and following a catastrophic car accident, massive head injuries left Krickitt Carpenter with no memory of her husband. The two are devout Christians, and Kim Carpenter remains determined to honor their wedding vows—he does so even as the going gets rougher. The book was made into a film, which led to the 2010 bestselling repackage: *The Vow: The True Events That Inspired the Movie.*

GOING VIRTUAL

Worried about how to develop a religious or spiritual audience in cyberspace? Let faith be your guide. Lee Rainie, director of the Pew Research Center, told *The New York Times,* "Spiritual groups are one of the oldest forms of social networks. They understood a fundamental truth about networks eons before the Internet existed: The most effective way to get things done and to survive is to form a community." Your message may be based on teachings thousands of years old, but that doesn't mean you can't attract an audience in the new millennium. According to Beliefnet, in August 2011, the number one most active page on Facebook was "Jesus Daily." These posts of inspirational words from Jesus has over 8.3 million fans and four million weekly interactions.

If you feel inspired by this finding, perhaps you will be moved to start your religious or spiritual memoir as a blog, building your story event by event. Once you've hit upon a theme, plan posts in advance so you can stay on message. Begin with an author's bio and an introduction of your theme, and then add posts regularly, the more often the better. It's best to begin after you have cultivated a list of e-mail contacts, and as you continue writing you can ask followers to recommend you to others. Work at keeping your quality high, remembering the importance of the three essentials: quality writing, strong hook, and strong platform.

With excellent writing and a strong narrative hook, Anna Broadway's Sexless in the City blog helped her build a digital platform. Her title is, of course, a nod at the racy cable TV series *Sex and the City*, which she enjoyed watching. A young evangelical Christian, Broadway's blog was propelled by her determination to remain chaste.

Describing her conflict as "God versus sex," she understood her audience members. Like her, they were young, college-educated women searching for love but determined to remain consistent with the values of their faith. Discovering that the romantic novels she'd read had not prepared her for the real world of dating, Broadway wrote of struggling through difficult relationships. The blog attracted a significant following, and the religious division of Random House acquired Broadway's memoir, *Sexless in the City: A Memoir of Reluctant Chastity* (WaterBrook: 2008). *Publishers Weekly* described the book as a "spicy and funny Gen-X memoir." Broadway has since signed off on the blog, but aware of the importance of a Web presence, she maintains a Sexless in the City Web site: www.sexlessinthecity.net.

Salvation on Sand Mountain: Snake Handling and Redemption in Southern Appalachia, by Dennis Covington (Perseus: 1995). A liberal *New York Times* journalist travels to the South where a minister is on trial for attempting to murder his wife with rattlesnakes. During the trial Covington befriends snake-handling locals.

Thin Places, by Mary E. DeMuth (Zondervan: 2010). Perhaps one miracle of this coming-of-age story is that DeMuth recognizes God's goodness despite the loss of her biological father, years of neglect, and sexual brutality. She takes refuge in her faith.

Things Seen and Unseen: A Year Lived in Faith, by Nora Gallagher (Knopf: 1998) The author arrives as a tourist in search of peace at Trinity Episcopal Church, Santa Barbara. During the ensuing spiritual struggle she uses the Christian calendar as a compass.

The Year Mom Got Religion: One Woman's Midlife Journey into Judaism, by Lee Meyerhoff Hendler (Jewish Lights: 1998). Raised culturally Jewish, in midlife Hendler is drawn to exploring her religion. The author embarks on a study of the Hebrew language, the Talmud, and Torah, and develops a spiritual connection with God.

Of Water and the Spirit: Ritual, Magic, and Initiation in the Life of an African Shaman, by Malidoma Patrice Somé (Penguin: 1995). In this exceptional story, Dr. Somé, born in Burkina Faso, but taken from his tribe at the age of four by Jesuit missionaries, reconnects with his religious and cultural heritage.

We end this chapter with an $$$Analysis of *Take This Bread: A Radical Conversion*, by Sara Miles (Ballantine: 2007).

$Writing Chops

A journalist who has traveled to war-torn Central-American countries, Miles writes deftly about her missionary grandparents (on both sides of the family tree) and her parents, who were antireligious products of their missionary upbringing. Keenly aware that the best narratives do not meander but offer stories that build upon one another, Miles keeps her eyes on the theme of hunger.

Born in comfortable circumstances, she edges toward the subject of hunger in her early work as a restaurant cook, and learns from memorably colorful coworkers the soul craft of preparing food efficiently and well. Later, traveling to war-torn countries, she experiences what she might not have described at the time as the spiritual power of breaking bread with strangers. Miles was moved when she shared meals with people who were so impoverished that invitations to their tables were acts of grace. After returning to the States, she does what longtime leftist friends deem outrageous: She walks into an Episcopal church in San Francisco, St. Gregory's of Nyssa, where priests are audaciously generous during communion, welcoming all, barring none. At her first taste of sacramental bread, as an *O* magazine reviewer wrote, Miles, "got religion . . . or rather, discovered her own consuming need for it."

Miles converted and became a leader at St. Gregory's. Her spiritual call to action has since inspired many in the San Francisco Bay Area. She addressed the problem of physical hunger by requesting food donations, and St. Gregory's parishioners brought tons of groceries that were piled on the altar and given away without qualification. Over the years, she and her supporters have started nearly a dozen food pantries in the most impoverished areas of the city. Miles said in a telephone interview, "I see the food pantries as a way to build community around food, and that essentially is what we do in a church." This relevant and inspiring story helps readers recognize hunger, both specific and spiritual. *Take This Bread* scores a full 10 points in the writing category.

$Narrative Hook

This story promotes a vision of Christianity that resists exclusion, a graciousness of faith. Perhaps because of the abstractness of this idea, Miles's personal background was employed as a narrative hook. She is a self-proclaimed blue-state, secular-intellectual lesbian, with left-wing politics. It is all wonderfully true about her, but Miles is so much more than labels. Besides, this doesn't seem to be a relevant message in a denomination and a city in which being leftist, intellectual, and a lesbian is hardly a standout issue. The book does have a strong narrative hook, but it was not marketed sufficiently. The radical message of *Take This Bread* is an understated irony: In a nation with an abundance of religion and food (for some), too many are starving spiritually and physically. This memoir earns 7 points for the strength of the narrative hook that was emphasized.

$Platform Strength

As a book that was rejected by some publishers on the grounds that it was too liberal for Christian bookstores and too Christian for secular trade, it's clear that the Random House editor who purchased Miles's book understood that the author's powerful writing, oratorical gifts, and her message of radical hospitality could carry the day. Fortunately for Miles and her readers, the book remained in hardcover for a year before being issued in paperback, and sold thirty thousand copies. Miles, who can preach as well as she writes, is often invited to speak about her work and vision. Her Web site http://saramiles.net promotes her message by inviting donations to the nonprofit Food Pantry program that she founded in 2000, to provide free groceries to more than twelve hundred families around the altar at St. Gregory's. With 10 points for platform strength, *Take This Bread* garners a total of 27 points.

Eight

Outlier Subgenres

IF EVER THERE WAS A SIGNAL THAT MEMOIRISTS REFUSE TO BE boxed in, this chapter should do the trick. These pages are devoted to exploring outlier narratives, those that extend beyond the boundaries of the most popular subgenres that were explored in chapters three through seven. You will find that some of the various titles listed in the outlier categories could also be grouped in the already discussed major categories, but they don't necessarily make for an easy fit. Depending on trends, some of these categories can be more difficult to market and sell, perhaps for a reason as basic as booksellers not knowing where to shelve them.

There's good news concerning outlier stories. Despite some initial difficulties, many RU outsider authors are finding audiences and publishers for their works. As trends come and go, outlier memoir categories are sure to change. At the time of this writing, we identified eleven outlier categories:

1. biblio
2. canine
3. comedic
4. family saga
5. gardening
6. grief
7. incarceration
8. information-based
9. parenting
10. romance
11. venture

Let's examine these subgenres one at a time through representative titles.

1. Biblio Memoirs

What could be a better bet than writing a story about the importance of books and literary subcultures?

The Possessed: Adventures with Russian Books and the People Who Read Them, by Elif Batuman (Granta: 2011). Growing up in New Jersey, Batuman developed a passion for Russian literature. In a collection of essays, the author travels to Russia, and through readings and research confronts some mysteries of life. A *Booklist* reviewer praised Batuman for her ability to celebrate, "the invaluable and pleasurable ways literature can increase the sum total of human understanding."

So Many Books, So Little Time, by Sara Nelson (Putnam: 2003). Nelson, a readaholic, sets a goal for herself to read a book a week for a year, while questioning how the narrative intersects with her life experiences. While she doesn't necessarily follow her self-assigned list, she does discover some treasures, including, the memoir *Turning Japanese: Memoirs of a Sansei*, by David Mura (Anchor: 1992), which helps her to better understand her husband. This work inspires readers to—you guessed it—read more.

Reading Lolita in Tehran, by Azar Nafisi (Random House: 2003). Would you risk your life to read? That is the question seven young women must consider when they begin to meet secretly in Iran. Nafisi, their former professor who left the country in 1997, leads their book group. Understandably, given the risk they're taking by defying religious prohibitions, the women are initially shy and uncomfortable before they begin speaking up, voicing their opinions, hopes, and disappointments. Parallels are drawn between book group members and the characters in their literature: *Daisy Miller*, *The Great Gatsby*, *Lolita*, *Pride and Prejudice*, and *Washington Square*.

2. Canine Memoirs

If the stars of these books didn't have four legs they would qualify for the romance category. The themes that run through "dogoirs" usually touch upon how these furry companions change the lives of the people who care for them. One indication of the popularity of this category is a *New Yorker* parody, with stories entitled, "Tess the Orphan Earthworm" and "My Plant Skippy." In the latter story, with tongue planted firmly in cheek, *New Yorker* contributor Bruce McCall writes:

> This book is my way of making amends . . . to all the valiant
> spider plants on windowsills and end tables all over the world,
> cheerful companions who never harmed anyone or anything,
> who were born only to sit there radiating uncritical,
> unconditional joy.

The authors of the I-love-my dog stories that began hitting the best-seller lists in 2010 have a memorable precedent: John Grogan's *Marley & Me: Life and Love with the World's Worst Dog* (William Morrow: 2005), which recounted the thirteen years that the author and his family spent with their "untrainable" Labrador retriever. The story sold six million copies, in more than forty languages, and in addition to being made into a film, produced several spinoffs, including a children's board book.

Years later, the success of Alexandra Horowitz's bestselling *Inside of a Dog: What Dogs See, Smell, and Know* (Scribner: 2009), a mix of dog cognition research and the author's personal observations about her own dog, was an early entry in a tide of canine-centered nonfiction titles. Many in the marketplace wondered how long the trend would last.

A MARKETPLACE SURVIVAL TIP

Book sales are subject to trends, and that includes outlier titles. No matter your category, it can be beneficial to observe marketplace trends. Here, we examine the canine craze.

It's hard to pinpoint what reignited interests in dog books in the late 2000s, but it did coincide with a period of reduced economic activity in the United States. What comes to mind from a literary standpoint is John Steinbeck's *Of Mice and Men* (Covici Friede: 1937), set in California during the Great Depression. One of the book's central characters is Lenny, who takes comfort in stroking soft textures, like rabbit fur. Fast-forward several decades, when research has found that pets can be highly beneficial therapeutically. It's interesting to make the connection between consumers feeling anxious during a period some refer to as the Great Recession, and the trend of people taking comfort in stories about the unconditional love of dogs—and other furry and feathered friends.

It takes more than idle speculation to explain what sparks a trend, but RU authors in particular should work at staying informed about the marketplace, so they have an inkling of whether they're barking up the wrong tree. Ultimately, the author has to make the call as to what changes in consumer interest might signal when it comes to pursuing a particular story line. The five strategies that follow can help you figure out whether a trend has run its course or will hold steady for the next several years:

1. Consider whether the subject has attracted heavyweight authors. For example, two entrants in the dogoir sweepstakes are bestselling author Dean Koontz's *A Big Little Life: A Memoir of a Joyful Dog* (Hyperion: 2009), and *New York Times* executive editor Jill Abramson's *The Puppy Diaries: Raising a Dog Named Scout* (Times Books: 2011).

2. Consider whether the trend has produced literary offshoots. Just when you might have thought there was no room in the market for one more dog title, along came Susan Orlean's bestselling and critically acclaimed historical biography of the film star *Rin Tin Tin: The Life and the Legend* (Simon & Schuster: 2011). Dogs, though, aren't the only pets to have taken center stage. A couple of feline memoirs clawed their way to the top first. There was the bestselling *Dewey: The Small-Town Library Cat Who Touched the World*, by Vicky Myron and Bret Witter (Grand Central: 2008) and *Homer's Odyssey: A Fearless Feline Tale, or How I Learned About Love and Life with a Blind Wonder Cat*, by Gwen Cooper (Delacorte: 2009). There are also bird memoirs: *Wesley the Owl: The Remarkable Story of an Owl and His Girl*, by Stacey O'Brien (Free Press: 2008) and *An Eagle Named Freedom: My True Story of a Remarkable Friendship*, by Jeff Guidry (William Morrow: 2010).

Of course some animal lovers prefer an entire menagerie—which brings us to the popular *We Bought a Zoo: The Amazing True Story of a Young Family, a Broken Down Zoo, and the 200 Wild Animals That Change Their Lives Forever,* by Benjamin Mee (Weinstein: 2008). This story of a husband and gravely ill wife trying to meet the needs of their children, along with those of a jaguar, pumas, tigers, lions, wolves, bears, boa constrictions, and a tarantula was made into a film.

3. Keep your ear to the marketplace about acquisitions. Stay informed through an agent or editor, and/or by reading major industry Web sites by Publishers Marketplace and *Publishers Weekly.* Some authors like mingling with crowds at BookExpo (not a conference, but an exposition) where publishers display new titles to librarians and booksellers. Sponsored by the American Booksellers Association, it is held each year in a different city. For information, go to: www.bookexpoamerica.com.

Late in 2011 the marketplace was rife with stories about dogged acquisition deals, including the titles:

- *What the Dog Knows: The Fascinating World of Working Canines,* part memoir, by Cat Warren, purchased by Touchstone for an amount described as "an aggressive six figures."

- *Weekends with Daisy,* a prison dog story, by Sharron Kahn Luttrell, acquired by Simon & Schuster, with film rights sold to CBS Films.

- *New York Times* reporter Sarah Kershaw's *Watch My Six,* the story of a troubled Iraq War veteran and the dog that helps him overcome PTSD, acquired by W. W. Norton, for what was described as "a significant deal."

4. **Track unit sales of RU titles.** Use resources mentioned in the previous suggestion to learn about what's selling in your subject matter. In 2011, successful titles included:

- Luis Carlos Montalvan's *Until Tuesday: A Wounded Warrior and the Golden Retriever Who Saved Him* (Hyperion: 2011) sold 44,000 hardcover copies in seven months.

- Lisa Rogak's *The Dogs of War: The Courage, Love, and Loyalty of Military Working Dogs* (St. Martin's Griffin: 2011) sold 73,857 copies in paperback in ten months.

5. **Be sure to pay attention to the narrative hooks of popular titles.** Larry Levin's bestselling *Oogy: The Dog Only a Family Could Love* (Grand Central: 2010) chronicles the story of a dog thrown in a shelter cage and left to die, until a family brings him back to life. As *Time* magazine's Kate Pickert pointed out, *Oogy* is more than just a story about a dog, it's about second chances—for the dog and for his owners. Oogy had been left for dead before being rescued, and the author and his wife experienced four miscarriages before they adopted twin baby boys.

....

MORE DOGOIRS WITH UNIQUE APPEAL:

Part Wild: One Woman's Journey with a Creature Caught Between the Worlds of Wolves and Dogs, by Ceridwen Terrill (Scribner: 2011). This associate professor of science writing and environmental journalism blends her personal story with information. She pulls readers forward by creating an atmosphere of suspense.

Thunder Dog: The True Story of a Blind Man, His Guide Dog, and the Triumph of Trust at Ground Zero, by Michael Hingson, with Susy Flory (Thomas Nelson: 2011). This bestseller recounts 9/11 events from the standpoint of a man who has been blind since infancy. His guide dog, Roselle, led him and others to safety from the seventy-eighth floor of the World Trade Center's Tower 1 shortly before it crumbled.

You Had Me at Woof: How Dogs Taught Me the Secrets of Happiness, by Julie Klam (Riverhead: 2010). In this hilarious story the author learns important lessons through her interactions with Boston Terriers.

Huck: The Remarkable True Story of How One Lost Puppy Taught a Family—and a Whole Town—About Hope and Happy Endings, by Janet Elder (Broadway: 2010). After years of resisting their son's plea for a dog, this busy couple relented, a life enhancing decision for the family.

From Baghdad with Love: A Marine, the War, and a Dog Named Lava, by Jay Kopelman, with Melinda Roth (Lyons: 2008). Amid destruction and loss, Kopelman, a marine stationed in Iraq, finds love in the guise of a stray dog discovered in the wreckage of Fallujah.

3. Comedic Memoirs

Powerful emotions may lie beneath the surface of these stories, but the authors prefer to keep readers laughing. While the characters might seem over the top, these stories—as with all commercial memoirs—should employ universal themes and plausible narratives.

How to Be Black (HarperCollins: 2012), by Baratunde Thurston. In satirizing the complexities of racial politics, Thurston, a comedian, uses his own thought-provoking personal experiences to remind readers of the importance of being true to themselves.

You Don't Sweat Much for a Fat Girl: Observations on Life from the Shallow End of the Pool, by Celia Rivenbark (St. Martin's Griffin: 2011).

According to an Amazon fan, this book of essays—which pokes fun at everything from Southern culture to family—made her laugh out loud ("fairly loudly, much to the alarm of my husband, who rushed in to see what was wrong when he heard my shrieks") in multiple places. Others seem to agree. Another of Rivenbark's books, *We're Just Like You, Only Prettier* (St. Martin's: 2004), won a Southern Independent Booksellers Alliance (SIBA) Book Award and was a finalist for the James Thurber Prize for American Humor.

When it comes to comedic memoirs, Rivenbark is far from being an anomaly. Laurie Notaro, another comedic memoirist also attracts a loyal following, with a series of titles that include *It Looked Different on the Model: Epic Tales of Impending Shame and Infamy* (Villard: 2011).

My Mom Is a Fob: Earnest Advice in Broken English from Your Asian-American Mom, by Teresa Wu and Serena Wu (Pedigree: 2011). This book, which began life as the highly popular blog mymomisafob.com, chronicles life with a parent who continues to speak and behave as if she is, according to the authors, "Fresh Off the Boat" (a Fob). The story includes snippets of parental advice in mangled English. The authors may be Asian, but they somehow manage to remind all readers of the mothers they had—or wish they'd had.

I Am Not Myself These Days, by Josh Kilmer-Purcell (Harper Perennial: 2006). An advertising executive by day and an alcoholic drag queen by night, the author struggles to make life work with a crack-addicted male escort. The premise is funny, the descriptions hilarious. This book became a bestseller.

4. Family Sagas

There's a world of difference between family sagas and family histories. The latter might be of interest to members of a particular family, in chronicling the lives and relationships of progenitors. On the other hand, family sagas, which chronicle the lives and experiences of a family over a specific period of time, deal with universal themes and are written with all the narrative elements we've discussed, with an eye on appealing to a broad audience. Two sample titles include:

The Hare with Amber Eyes: A Family's Century of Art and Loss, by Edmund de Waal (Farrar, Straus and Giroux: 2010). The objects of the title comprise a collection of ornamental Japanese carvings, an inherited collection acquired by an art connoisseur, who was an ancestor of the author. A world-renowned potter and curator, de Waal has written a dazzling and exquisite bestseller.

On Gold Mountain: The 100-Year Odyssey of a Chinese-American Family, by Lisa See (St. Martin's: 1995). This page-turner offers a sweeping family portrait filled with memorable characters, including the author's paternal great-grandparents, a Chinese merchant and his white wife who were wed when interracial unions were especially unwelcome. *The New York Times* named this bestseller a Notable Book.

5. Gardening Memoirs

This subject is particularly well suited for memoir writing. Gardeners are often observant, contemplative, and introspective, desired traits in a memoirist.

The Way of a Gardener: A Life's Journey, by Des Kennedy (Greystone: 2010). A former monk, the author leaves monastery life behind and takes up a vocation that has been referred to as Church of the Earth. Living in the rural Northwest, after constructing a home from recycled and handmade materials, he creates a garden where he raises food for the body and the spirit.

Gardening at the Dragon's Gate: At Work in the Wild and Cultivated World, by Wendy Johnson (Bantam: 2008). A Zen Buddhist, the author has served as head gardener for San Francisco's Green Gulch Farm Center, where she employed her meditational practices to help grow a productive garden. Part memoir, part how-to, this book is organized around seven principles that demonstrate respect for the land through organic gardening and ecologically supportive practices.

The Quarter-Acre Farm: How I Kept the Patio, Lost the Lawn, and Fed My Family for a Year, by Spring Warren (Seal Press: 2011). Disgusted by a widespread salmonella outbreak in 2008 and wanting to be more ecologically responsible, the author challenges herself to grow 75 percent of her family's food. After mistakes and setbacks, the author's edible experiment proves successful. Complete with recipes and illustrations, this book is humorous and delicious.

LITERARY OFFSHOOTS: STORIES OF GROWING SPECIFIC FRUITS OR VEGETABLES

Heirloom: Notes from an Accidental Tomato Farmer, by Tim Stark (Broadway: 2008). A former management consultant, Stark began growing heirlooms as a hobby, and he continued growing them. His tomato crop is now showing up on highly regarded tables.

The $64 Tomato: How One Man Nearly Lost His Sanity, Spent a Fortune, and Endured an Existential Crisis in the Quest for the Perfect Garden, by William Alexander (Algonquin: 2007). Rather than sharing a story of serene memories from the garden, Alexander found himself facing off with everything from herds of deer, beetles, worms, maggots, and occasional menacing landscaping contractors. Fortunately for readers, he maintains his sense of humor.

LITERARY OFFSHOOT: HOMESTEADING

Some observers might have wondered why bestselling author Barbara Kingsolver would switch from fiction to write a memoir about moving with her husband and teenage daughter to a farm in Virginia, with a vow to start eating locally. That is, they might have wondered *until* the publication of *Animal, Vegetable, Miracle: A Year of Food Life* (HarperCollins: 2007), by the author, her husband, Steven L. Hopp, and her daughter, Camille Kingsolver. A critical and commercial success, the book was named by *Time* magazine as one of the Top Non-fiction Books of 2007.

Sheepish: Two Women, Fifty Sheep, and Enough Wool to Save the Planet, by Catherine Friend (Da Capo: 2011). This is the author's second memoir about the life she shares with her partner on a Minnesota farm. As with the first, *Hit By a Farm: How I Learned to Stop Worrying and Love the Barn* (Da Capo: 2006), *Sheepish* is a hilarious reminder of how people are shaped by what they do.

The Dirty Life: On Farming, Food, and Love, by Kristin Kimball (Scribner: 2010). A Harvard graduate and freelance journalist, the author met her future husband, a farmer in Upstate New York, when she interviewed him for a story. Her transition from unattached city dweller to farm wife proves as daunting as the task of smoothing out the wrinkles in a new love relationship.

The Blueberry Years: A Memoir of Farm and Family, by Jim Minick (Thomas Dunne: 2010). The author chronicles the story of founding an organic pick-your-own blueberry farm. He and his wife prevail over the challenges that arise in farming without the use of pesticides and fertilizers.

The Bucolic Plague: How Two Manhattanites Became Gentleman Farmers: An Unconventional Memoir, by Josh Kilmer-Purcell (HarperCollins: 2010). When the author makes plans to start a new life in the country with his partner, Dr. Brent Ridge, they renovate their country mansion into a working farm, and hilarity and tenderness ensue. In 2010, the Discovery Network debuted *The Fabulous Beekman Boys*, a series based on Kilmer-Purcell and Dr. Ridge's life together.

6. Grief Memoirs

Renowned author Joan Didion is most often associated with first-person elegies. In the bestselling *The Year of Magical Thinking* (Knopf: 2005), she chronicles the sudden death of her husband, acclaimed author John Gregory Dunne, after he suffers a massive heart attack in 2003. The couple's privileged lifestyle and celebrity status is a reminder that no one is immune to loss. Didion's grief was magnified by the hospitalization of her daughter, Quintana Roo, thirty-nine, who lay unconscious from pneumonia and septic shock. Roo died subsequently, deepening the author's sense of loss and leading her to write *Blue Nights* (Knopf: 2011). With grief weighing upon her, Didion deftly created narratives that contemplate relationships loved and lost. *A Year of Magical Thinking* was adapted into a Broadway play.

Let's Take the Long Way Home: A Memoir of Friendship, by Gail Caldwell (Random House: 2010). This bestseller chronicles the author's best friendship with fellow writer Caroline Knapp, who died of lung cancer at forty-two, in 2002. *Publishers Weekly* gave this book a starred review and described it as, "a quiet, fierce work" in which the author writes of a, "desolating time with tremendously moving grace."

Lives Other Than My Own, by Emmanuel Carrère, translated from French by Linda Coverdale (Metropolitan: 2011). The author is reminded of the fragility of life when he befriends a couple whose daughter has died in a tsunami and after learning that his girlfriend's sister is dying from cancer. A *New Yorker* critic wrote that the author had created, "powerful portraits that celebrate ordinary lives."

Tolstoy and the Purple Chair: My Year of Magical Reading, by Nina Sankovitch (HarperCollins: 2011). Raised in a family of book lovers, this mother of two, grieving over the death of her eldest sister, cleared her appointment calendar and committed to reading a book a day for a full year. In the story, whose title refers to the armchair in which she often sought refuge, the author writes of the redemptive power of books.

Love Is a Mix Tape: Life and Loss, One Song at a Time, by Rob Sheffield (Crown: 2007). The author, a music journalist who eventually becomes a *Rolling Stone* contributing editor, recounts his romance with his future wife. He was a Catholic-born music geek from Boston; she, a "loud" and "impulsive" Southerner. The two bond over a mutual love of music. Collapsing after a pulmonary embolism, she died in 1997.

7. Incarceration Memoirs

Like most literary agents, I receive many unsolicited incarceration manuscripts. It may be difficult for the authors to learn that this is the most difficult of all outlier categories to sell. It is often a challenge for readers to muster sympathy for protagonists who might be convicted criminals. And with imprisonment high on the list of the greatest fears, few readers want to imagine that they are walking in these protagonists' shoes. Celebrity helps to sell these books, as was the case with convicted murderer Jack Henry Abbott, whose *In the Belly of the Beast: Letters from Prison* (Random House: 1981) is based on letters that he wrote to Norman Mailer after the two struck up a correspondence. Acclaimed by critics and adapted for the stage, this bestselling account of twenty-five years behind bars helped Abbott secure early parole. Not long afterward, Abbott committed another murder and was re-incarcerated. In 2002, he committed suicide by hanging himself in his cell.

Another well-known and controversial prisoner is former journalist and Black Panther Mumia Abu-Jamal. Many of his supporters from around the world believe Abu-Jamal was unjustly convicted of murdering a policeman in 1981. His book of essays, *Live from Death Row* (Perseus: 1995), sold more than eighty thousand copies. That was followed by a faith-based collection of spiritual reflections, *Death Blossoms: Reflections from a Prisoner of Conscience* (Plough: 1997).

Difficult as it is to sell a manuscript of this subgenre, especially those written by RUs, it does happen, if only occasionally, and only when offering unique hooks. It is important for anyone writing these manuscripts to get familiar with Son of Sam laws, which prohibit those who have been convicted from profiting from their crimes, including through book sales.

A Woman Doing Life: Notes from a Prison for Women, by Erin George (Oxford University Press, USA: 2010). The author, an inmate at Virginia's Fluvanna Correctional Center for Women, writes about the daily challenges that she faces as a woman incarcerated for life. George also includes stories of other inmates.

A Question of Freedom: A Memoir of Learning, Survival, and Coming of Age in Prison, by R. Dwayne Betts (Avery: 2010). From the age of sixteen, Betts was incarcerated for nine years in an adult prison in Virginia. His story reflects on his crime (carjacking) and confinement, as well as his salvation through books. Betts, who has earned an MFA in writing, runs a creative writing program, and is a national spokesman for the Campaign for Juvenile Justice.

Chasing Justice: My Story of Freeing Myself After Two Decades on Death Row for a Crime I Didn't Commit, by Kerry Max Cook (William Morrow: 2007). Wrongfully accused of a brutal murder in Tyler, Texas, the author's trial was derailed by corrupt members of the criminal justice system. Cook wound up on death row, but a *pro bono* attorney fought for and won his freedom after twenty years of imprisonment.

You Got Nothing Coming: Notes from a Prison Fish, by Jimmy A. Lerner (Broadway Books: 2002). A wise-cracking Jewish boy from Flatbush, Brooklyn, with a wife, two kids, and an MBA degree isn't a typical ex-con, yet the author spent three years behind bars in Nevada for manslaughter. His story of surviving incarceration when his fellow inmates, who deemed his reading and writing skills as valuable, has been described as akin to "Dilbert goes to prison." The manuscript was sold for a reported $100,000 advance.

Newjack: Guarding Sing Sing, by Ten Conover (Random House: 2000). A journalist who was determined to discover what it was like to work as a prison guard, the author enrolled in a guard-training program and was assigned to work at one of the most notorious prisons. In addition to writing about strip searches, lock downs, and intense hostility, Conover writes convincingly of how prison life can be improved and made more beneficial for the good of all.

The Prisoner's Wife, by Asha Bandele (Scribner: 1999). The child of college administrators, this author was raised in a sheltered middle-class home. As an adult she writes poetry and, when reading her work aloud in a correctional facility, strikes up a friendship and a letter-writing correspondence with a prisoner, whom she eventually marries. It is testimony to Bandele's lyrical power that this book attracted a wide and sympathetic audience.

8. Information-Based Memoirs

The personal stories woven throughout these books enliven the information they were meant to impart. In the Information Age, this is a subgenre that seems destined to grow in popularity.

Moonwalking with Einstein: The Art and Science of Remembering Everything, by Joshua Foer (Penguin: 2011). Who doesn't want to remember "everything," you might wonder, and publishers seem to have asked the same question. The author—a freelance science journalist who won a U.S.A. Memory Championship in 2006, and set records by memorizing a deck of cards in 1 minute and 40 seconds—received a reported $1.2 million advance, and film rights were sold to Columbia Pictures.

The Pain Chronicles: Cures, Myths, Mysteries, Prayers, Diaries, Brain Scans, Healing, and the Science of Suffering, by Melanie Thernstrom (Farrar, Straus and Giroux: 2010). The author makes the point that chronic pain is not a condition, but an actual disease that plagues more than seventy million Americans daily. Interweaving stories of her own struggle, the author looks at the subject through the ages and reports on the most advanced research.

Poser: My Life in Twenty-three Yoga Poses, by Claire Dederer (Farrar, Straus and Giroux: 2010). The author, a wife and mother, sought to do something for herself, and yoga beckoned. Dederer's ability to laugh at herself and serve up information for beginners makes this an entertaining and easy read.

9. Parenting

If you're raising children, the one thing you know for sure is that you'll never know enough about how to do it right. There's no such thing as a perfect parent, but it can't hurt to try and become one.

Bringing up Bébé: One American Mother Discovers the Wisdom of French Parenting, by Pamela Druckerman (Penguin HC: 2012). In this bestseller, the author writes of raising her children in France and employing the often frowned upon (by many Americans) strict French parent-centered methods of child rearing. Not surprisingly, the book caused a literary ruckus and ratcheted up sales.

French Kids Eat Everything: How Our Family Moved to France, Cured Picky Eating, Banned Smoking, and Discovered 10 Simple Rules for Raising Happy, Healthy Eaters, by Karen Le Billon (William Morrow: 2012). Another in a line of French-praising books—(kicked off by megabestseller, *French Women Don't Get Fat,* by Mirelle Gulino (Knopf: 2004)—this is a story of a family's culinary transformation. For readers dissatisfied with the "American" diet of processed, high-calorie foods and beverages, this book will provide a welcome alternative.

Battle Hymn of the Tiger Mother, by Amy Chua (Penguin: 2011). This book answers a question that has crossed so many minds: Why do so many Asian kids excel in school? Amy Chua's answers won't please all parents, but she sure gives them something to talk about. Her story, which chronicles exploits that have since become internationally known, describes tough love methods that few would be willing to own up to.

Losing My Cool: Love, Literature, and a Black Man's Escape from the Crowd, by Thomas Chatterton Williams (Penguin: 2010). This book is as much about the parenting this author received as it is about the importance of relentless parenting. Raised in a New Jersey home crammed with books, the author's childhood is akin to being enrolled in a yearlong unofficial prep course, run by his sociologist father, who passes on an appreciation for education. As an adolescent, the author has other areas of interest, such as "hoes" and clothes, values exemplified in the hip-hop culture. In the end, both father and son win. Williams studied philosophy at Georgetown and received a master's degree from NYU.

Crazy U: One Dad's Crash Course in Getting His Kid into College, by Andrew Ferguson (Simon & Schuster: 2011). Ferguson uses his son's search for a college as an opportunity to explore the admissions process. The story is informative, heartwarming, and memorable.

10. Romance

Ghosts by Daylight: Love, War, and Redemption, by Janine di Giovanni, (Knopf: 2011). The author, an American correspondent operating in major war zones in the Middle East and Africa, falls in love with Bruno, a French reporter. Their decadelong love affair is punctuated by armed conflicts, and ghosts of war haunt the couple as they try to forge a peaceful life.

The Triumph of Love Over Experience: A Memoir of Remarriage, by Wendy Swallow (Hyperion: 2004). The author, a divorcée, finds herself falling in love again and considering another marriage. Swallow's new love seems almost too good to be true. Intimidated by fears of a second divorce, the author interviews friends and experts and shares their advice with readers.

11. Venture Memoirs

The protagonists of these narratives generally elect to undertake a risky or daring experience, and the outcomes are uncertain. Unlike the children or adolescents in coming-of-age stories, the protagonists of venture memoirs are able to exert a measure of control over their lives. A venture protagonist might be a Columbia University graduate who gives up his Wall Street job to move to Vegas and become a professional card counter—a plot that describes Josh Axelrad's *Repeat Until Rich: A Professional Card Counter's Chronicle of the Blackjack Wars* (Penguin: 2010). Venture memoirs should not be confused with adventure or travel memoirs. While some venture protagonists may travel to distant lands, the focus of the story is not about a physical journey, or physical survival. Venture stories depict emotional odysseys. Venturing into the unknown, many of these characters are courageous, while others are naive.

Some Girls: My Life in a Harem, by Jillian Lauren (Plume: 2010). An aspiring actress, Lauren was nineteen and an NYU theater school dropout when she heard about a gig working with a rich businessman in Singapore that paid $20,000 for two weeks. The author spends the next eighteen months in a prince's harem in Borneo.

In the Land of Invisible Women: A Female Doctor's Journey in the Saudi Kingdom, by Qanta Ahmed, MD (Sourcebooks: 2008). When denied a visa renewal that will allow her to continue practicing medicine in the United States, this British-born Muslim woman of Pakistani heritage is offered a job in Saudi Arabia, and she accepts on a whim. Readers share Ahmed's astonishment over the country's rigid traditions, and at the same time, her admiration for many of the people she encounters.

Batboy: Coming of Age with the New York Yankees, by Matthew McGough (Anchor: 2007). This book recounts the two years the author spent fulfilling his dream as a high school student, beginning in 1992, working at Yankee Stadium, and getting to know the members of this legendary team. This might never have occurred had it not been for the author's persistence. After writing the Yankees and asking to be hired as a batboy, he kept calling the office over a period of weeks, until he was finally interviewed and hired.

My Own Country: A Doctor's Story, by Abraham Verghese (Simon & Schuster: 1994). A native of Ethiopia, this author and physician moves with his wife and newborn son to Johnson City, Tennessee. Although he has no patients initially, as the AIDS epidemic takes a toll on the residents of this small city, his practice is in great demand by people that some would consider least likely to contract the disease. This book was made into a film, and was a finalist in 1994 for the National Book Critics Award.

The Devil's Teeth: A True Story of Obsession and Survival Among America's Great White Sharks, by Susan Casey (Henry Holt: 2005). Most folks get out of the way when they hear of sharks, but not this author. Casey, a journalist who heard about two biologists conducting pioneering research on sharks in the Farallon Islands, nicknamed the Devil's Teeth, traveled to the islands to observe the scientists up close. Amazon .com reviewer Kim Hughes wrote of the book, "Despite the plethora of factoids on offer, Casey's style is consistently digestible and very amusing."

Black Ice, by Lorene Cary (Knopf: 1991). Although published in the early 1990s, this story continues to resonate with new readers. At fifteen, Cary left behind her family in an African American suburb of Philadelphia, and a part-time job in a fast food restaurant, to become a scholarship student—only the second African American woman—at the elite St. Paul's boarding school in New Hampshire. Despite periods of isolation and some difficulties, Cary excelled as a student, and later, as an adult.

HERE'S WHAT ELSE
YOU NEED TO KNOW

RUs Working
with Collaborators

COLLABORATING WITH ANOTHER WRITER CAN BE ONE OF the best experiences of your literary life. You've heard the expression that two minds can be better than one, and that can be true in collaboration efforts. It can also be comforting to have an interested party share the workload. And if you're really fortunate, you'll have a coauthor who knows how to cheer you up during discouraging times.

But—and I'm sure you knew there was a "but" coming—coauthoring can also be hell, especially for RUs unfamiliar with the territory. I have seen literary collaborations destroy friendships and family relationships. I've watched promising deals go up in smoke when two (or more) collaborators grew so resentful that they could no longer talk to one another, let alone agree on anything. Brenda and I know two collaborators who had to go into therapy together before they could go on the road to market their book.

Passion is good, but let's work on channeling it so you aren't distracted. Begin by picturing yourself as one of two collaborators (or more) on a warm evening, walking along a peaceful country road, sharing ideas, and feeling so simpatico toward one another that you're practically finishing one another's sentences. The image may be alluring, but the truth is, if you want to reach the end of the road with your relationship intact, you need a couple of high-wattage flashlights that can help you pick out the impediments in the road. Good communication can be illuminating. To that end, you will find a number of questions and responses that are designed to get you talking, so you'll be just as excited about your collaboration when you finish as when you begin.

Whose story is it? And who gets to tell that story?

As you know, memoirs can be told in more than one voice. So who gets to *tell* the story is a particularly relevant issue when it comes to working with a collaborator. A lot of the answers depend on whether your story focuses on the experiences of one individual or more.

Let's look at another collaborative writing relationship involving two parties, which is most often the case. The Reverend Don Piper tells of his near-death experiences in the hugely bestselling *90 Minutes in Heaven: A True Story of Death and Life* (Revell: 2007). It is clearly Reverend Piper's story, and yet he explains in the acknowledgments that after writing three unsuccessful drafts of the story, he turned to Cecil Murphey to partner with him. He points out that Murphey's, "passion for the project is felt on every page." That kind of language is authorspeak, and folks in the business will generally understand who *really* wrote the bulk of a book. There's no need to spell it out. Respect is what's important here.

In a telephone interview, Murphey—who has coauthored and ghostwritten more than one hundred books in various genres and teaches at approximately twenty writing conferences a year—explained that the key to a smooth collaboration is being clear about whose story is being told. That's seldom a problem in Murphey's writing, since people generally hire him to write their stories.

The situation is different, of course, when more than one protagonist tells a story. Note that the memoir *The Kids Are All Right* (Crown: 2009) was described as "multivocal." Alternating sections of this memoir are told in the voices of Diana, Liz, Amanda, and Dan Welch, who happen to be siblings. On a Web site devoted to their work (http://thekidsareallrightbook.com) the Welches explain that sisters Liz and Diana started the original collaboration, and then invited Amanda and Dan to share their versions of events. According to an O magazine reviewer, the Welches, "deftly pass the narrative baton from one to another, and the resulting book is both well crafted and beautifully written, not to mention tremendously engrossing and moving."

Please note that only one story should be told in a memoir. In *The Kids Are All Right*, the plot involves events that led to the siblings being orphaned and separated, but a singular story can be told in one or more voices. After collaborators determine who the narrator or narrators will be, it helps to spell that out in a collaboration agreement.

Who will be recognized as the author?

Once you establish who's telling the story, the conversation will quite naturally lead you to a subject that so many collaborators shirk from discussing, because the conversation can be emotionally fraught. Before tabling the conversation test the waters, because the way you handle this may offer insight into whether this collaboration will work.

If one of you is a writer for hire, the person who is signing the checks often gets to make the decision. She may want to establish up front that the only name that will appear on the book is hers. She may also offer explanations for her preference. All of her explanations might sound logical, but there is usually another truth that folks don't like to admit, and it has to do with ego. Some people like to pretend that they can write books completely on their own, convinced that this will make them look more impressive. What they fail to take into account is that dogmatic dictates about credits often breed so much resentment that a book's quality can be compromised. I, and just about any agent, have overheard unacknowledged coauthors grumble about how they didn't give manuscripts their best shot, because they felt offended about being left out on the cover.

Give yourself time to think before you agree. RUs, eager to seal a deal, often quickly agree to writing without being acknowledged. Months, sometimes years later, after laboring on a book, they may have changed their minds. Somewhat like women who lend their wombs (for hire or out of friendship) to carry a baby to term, they are often surprised at how emotions interfere with their best-laid plans.

There is also the workload to consider. If you are collaborating to help tell that person's story and handling most of the writing, your job will be particularly difficult. Although a memoir focuses on one story, it draws upon a cache of memories. You can better understand that point through Brenda's experiences in collaborating with a physician on a religious memoir. Based upon the experiences of Dr. Raymond Mis, the story tells (in his voice) of him losing his vision, and how relatives, members of their Catholic Church, and patients in his small town rescued his life and his medical practice. Tentatively entitled *Now I See: An Easter Story of Conversion Through Faith, Family, and Friends* the story can only be told successfully if it relays something larger than the events of the year in which Dr. Mis experienced tragedy and a religious conversion.

Like a quilt maker piecing together patches cut from garments worn over a family's lifetime, Brenda is seeking to understand the larger symbolic picture of the story. A credible literary voice is one that is informed. To that end, she has interviewed Dr. Mis extensively, studied how he thinks and behaves, read the medical diagnoses of his vision loss; interviewed family members; researched the historical period during which he came of age; studied his old Brooklyn neighborhood and the one in which he now resides; read books and papers about his ethnic group and Roman Catholic practices; visited his medical office and the hospital where he works; studied his medical procedures, and even spent time in the office of another physician with a similar practice.

In helping to write a memoir, which covers a slice of Dr. Mis's life, Brenda will include a small percentage of the information she has gleaned. She has coauthored nine other books, but says that the bar for what she needs to know to write someone else's memoir is higher than most. That is because when someone writes her own memoir, she carries a frame of reference in her head. However, that protagonist may not have the instincts of a writer. He or she may not be calling their collaborator and saying, "You might need to look into so and so . . ." If the collaborator is the member of the team doing the writing, he or she may be starting from scratch.

This is not said to discourage collaborations. Brenda is enjoying the assignment with Dr. Mis. Immersed in his story, she's a walking encyclopedia of his life, sometimes astonishing him with how much she knows, including ancestral details. We are sharing this information to make a particular point about the conversation in which you engage concerning authorial credit on a memoir, and so you will give a lot of thought before you sign a contract as to how you want to be recognized.

There is also the question of whether you will use "and" or "with." Depending on the degree of your involvement in a story, or your relationship to the protagonist, you may be comfortable seeing your name prefaced by the "with" designation. To some authors, this feels like a putdown, but in truth it is standard in the marketplace. "With" is usually reserved for a writer for hire and the person on the team who is not the expert on the book's subject. In memoir, the "expert" is the person whose story is being told.

The authors of *90 Minutes in Heaven* use "with" to credit coauthor Murphey, who was hired to help Reverend Piper write the book. Murphey said this sits well with him, and pointed out that when he first started collaborating with authors several years ago, he didn't care how he was listed. However, after writing a celebrity book for which he was not acknowledged, Murphey said, "I had to struggle over that a few days." The book he'd ghostwritten subsequently won awards, and that particular celebrity was given "all the credit."

As a result, Murphey's days of ghostwriting have ended, as soon will Brenda's. She turned down a lucrative book offer that she was asked to ghost. She laughed when she said, "When a book you helped write is published without your name, it's a bit like seeing a child you gave up for adoption look right through you, not knowing who you are."

The highest credit designation that collaborators may settle upon includes "and," to signal to readers and those in the marketplace that you are equal partners. Sometimes the story centers on the story of only one of the authors, but the "and" is given as a sign of gratitude. The "and" may be acceptable if both of you are responsible for getting the story to the marketplace, and depending on who carried the weight of the workload. In the end, the decision about crediting is almost always decided by the authors. So weigh in early with what you want and need, but remain flexible. As always, good communication is the key to making a collaborative relationship work.

Who will write the book?

There are two practical ways to approach this question. If the parties involved are both writers, and familiar with (and approving of) one another's work, they can divvy up the work. When that happens, it's always best to work from an outline, with the understanding that concepts change during the writing period. After all, collaborators might begin with one theme in mind and then begin moving in a different direction. That's something to discuss after you've made progress on the manuscript.

If you are just beginning, you can divvy up assignments. Be sure to divide the assignments into parts, even if only for the sake of making progress. Make the early chapters, for example, part one; another group of chapters might be designated part two, and so on. This way, you can write chapters within close proximity. If one writer is working on chapter one, for instance, the other one might work on chapter two. Continue in this manner, working in unison to complete each part. This will help you create a manuscript that feels as if it's lifted from one whole cloth. Since you may continue to struggle over concerns about meshing styles and tones, try turning to a writing coach or group for feedback.

Another approach to writing your memoir is that one of you does all the writing, while the other handles the research. You're already creative. That's why you're working on a book. It's up to the partners to divvy out tasks so you both feel supported and get the job done, but don't stop discussing details until you both imagine how you will be spending your days.

How do you handle deadlines?

If you're serious about finishing a manuscript, you will want to agree upon deadlines. Be aware that you will need to be flexible about time. Books almost always take longer than you might imagine at the onset. It does help if you are collaborating to discuss how you will handle personal emergencies. One of you might call the other crying, explaining about a calamity that occurred. When it was just a matter of friendship, you might have felt more understanding, but once a written collaboration has been agreed upon, the project is shaped by professional obligations. And you may be on the other end of the line, rolling your eyes, hissing to someone else, "Here comes another excuse."

This level of cynicism occurs in the healthiest collaborations, like a fallen log that stretches across your path. Set up a system for handling excuses and setbacks. For instance, agree that if you aren't going to get a chapter written by a certain deadline that you will inform one another via e-mail, followed up by a phone call, at least two days in advance. This is a subject that trips up a lot of collaborators. So if you are still walking dreamily down the country road, consider stopping and promising to one another that you will honor your deadlines, or contact one another when you cannot, and settle on a date when you can meet it.

Talk also about how you will proceed if the deadlines aren't met. This leaves a lot of people stymied. If you have a set date in mind, you should have a plan in place, such as: "If the setback slows X down for more than a month, our collaboration agreement is considered null and void and X is free to move ahead with the completed research and finish the project on her own." That might sound tough, but it's the kind of language that helps to get projects finished.

Brenda and I know two collaborators who secured a publishing contract, and one of the women had to stop contributing because her adolescent daughter was diagnosed with cancer. Despite tender feelings, the two agreed that development of the book should continue with only one writer. The woman with the sick daughter turned her share of the advance over to the writing author, and the book was published under both their names (using "and"). Their friendship remained intact, and best of all, the daughter recovered fully.

What happens if you're unhappy with what the other person is writing?

You should offer one another constructive criticism. No one likes to be criticized. I don't know about you, but if I were walking down that road, moving toward my endpoint, I would love it (no matter how much I might protest) if people stood on the side of the road and told me that I was doing a great job. Those kinds of experiences, though, don't allow writers to improve their craft. It might work better if someone on the sidelines shouted, "I love the main character, but I didn't agree with his rationale for why he quit."

First of all, that person acknowledged what she liked, and you get the sense she had read the sample in its entirety. Notice how the criticism is directed at the writing, and is not personal. The person along the side of the road also offered a suggestion about how this writing could be improved. Now that's constructive.

There are so many other issues that may trip up your collaboration. What about costs for proceeding with the book? Will there be travel expenses? What about securing admission to a university library or purchasing books? Who will handle the costs? The sooner you discuss this, the stronger your collaboration.

If you finish the manuscript, how will you communicate with an agent, so he is not hearing two different points of view?

This is one of those prized situations. You have an agent! Someone in the business is interested in your work! So take in the good news and work together to sort out different interests. Maybe one of you doesn't want to sell if the publisher is only offering a small advance. The other might feel that a "real" publisher is better than nothing. Work it out and then only one of you should respond. It can confuse an agent if he is corresponding with more than one author per project.

What if one of you, through your own efforts or luck, becomes more closely associated with the resulting book?

Even if each collaborator is doing what he can to sell and market the book, there's always a chance that one of you will appear more dominant.

Discuss this possibility. You may be entering a collaboration in which your partner expects little of you once the book is written. That may sound wonderful to some writers; to others, that may be a cause for complaint.

Cecil Murphey is more than satisfied with the way things turned out with his collaboration on *90 Minutes in Heaven*. His coauthor, Don Piper, makes more than two hundred appearances a year. "That makes sense for him," said Murphey. "They're on the road all the time . . . out making testimony."

Your coauthor, of course, may have other means of solidifying an audience of readers. She may start a blog, or write magazine articles using reflections based on your book. It's important to discuss beforehand how you will handle resulting book sales. Will you split all profits fifty-fifty, no matter what? If so, who and how will you measure profits? And what if your book is eventually published and years later the manuscript reverts back to you? Who *is* you in this case? Who will own the rights?

These are questions that may best be referred to an agent, or you may decide to write your own contract. What's important is that you do have a written agreement and formalize it based upon the many conversations that may have been instigated by this "walk down a country road." If you are looking for legal standardized forms, try *Business and Legal Forms for Authors and Self-Publishers* (Allworth: 2005), by Tad Crawford.

Here's hoping that you reach the end of your road in friendship, as Brenda and I have.

Ten

Contacting an Agent

T O PARAPHRASE THE FAMOUS PROVERB, ALL ROADS LEAD TO this chapter. Whatever your chosen subgenre, if your goal has been getting an agent to represent your work, this is where the rubber meets the road. The first time an agent begins reading your manuscript may be your one and only chance to grab that person's attention.

The significance of this moment was made clear by one of my colleagues, literary agent Katherine Sands, who edited a collection of essays written by forty agents and other publishing professionals, *Making the Perfect Pitch: How to Catch a Literary Agent's Eye* (Watson-Guptill: 2004). Katherine wrote in her introduction, "You can hire a caterer, a hit man, or a dominatrix. But you can't hire an agent. Literary agents must be enchanted, seduced, and won over to take you on as a client."

Yes, and it's important to add that somewhere out there during that moment in time, an overworked literary agent will read your correspondence with the unformed question that lies at the heart of this book: "*Are you* going to be a writer I should know?" It's our hope that your submission will speak in a loud, unqualified "Yes."

It's important to take the time to get this right, so let's walk through this step by step. The suggestions that follow are based upon the assumption that you have revised your manuscript a number of times, had it critiqued, and then revised it again.

You should also have completed a proposal and a minimum of three chapters of your manuscript, so you can e-mail it later, if the agent asks to read it. They know that editors will want to know that the story has a full arc and that the writing can stand on its own. They also want to be sure that even though there's a strong hook that there's enough of a story to hold the attention of the reader. Many great ideas turn out to be only sufficient for an article or blog.

The Proposal

You've spent months, perhaps even years, crafting your memoir so the next order of business (yes, business) is to write a proposal. A proposal can be viewed as the business plan for your memoir. It will outline why you wrote the book, who you are, who you believe your audience to be, and how you plan to get the attention of that audience. The proposal will help the editor and agent understand how to position your book in the marketplace. A proposal is a type of business plan that helps to sell a well-developed concept. Understand that these components are staples throughout most proposals, but are uniquely customized for every proposal. No two proposals are the same, and while the proposal is meant to "sell" to the publisher, it also gives a glimpse into the personality of the book, and what makes your project come to life.

Lastly, and perhaps, most importantly, no aspect of your proposal should be written in a question and answer format. Your proposal should be written as a narrative and capture the individuality and necessity of your memoir in the marketplace. It should be engaging and informative. In fact, after reading your proposal, the publisher should: have a very clear idea of what your book is about; be able to visualize what it'll look like; and have faith that you can effectively position the book in the marketplace.

Nonfiction Proposal Guidelines

Some of the main components that need to be clearly detailed within your proposal include, but are *not limited* to:

- **MARKET AND PUBLISHING RATIONALE:** Why do you think this book is needed in the marketplace? Who will it benefit and why? Why have you chosen to write it? This should describe the market opportunity (market, size, growth, etc.).

- **AUDIENCE:** Who are you publishing to? Why would they be interested in purchasing your book? A thorough description of your primary and secondary markets.

- **BRIEF DESCRIPTION:** A one-to-three sentence summary of the book. Think of this as potential back cover copy, which would describe the book in a nutshell.

- **BOOK DESCRIPTION/CHAPTER OUTLINE:** Should be a solid description of what the book is and what it's trying to achieve. This should include the table of contents with chapter heads and a brief description of each chapter.

- **KEY FEATURES AND SELLING POINTS:** Bulleted list of key reasons why this will be the best book on the market. Include "Special Editorial Features" and "Key Sales/Marketing Features."

- **AUTHOR PLATFORM AND BIO:** A profile of the author, which should include additional information that will help the publisher understand why you are the ideal person to write this book. Include information that shows you have the ideal platform to write this book. What is your current social media platform? How many Twitter/Facebook followers? You should include here a list of all the various forms of media in which you have participated, including print, TV, online, and radio.

- ◆ **MARKETING/PUBLICITY PLAN:** Do you have any special relationship to the market? Are there any special conferences, trade shows, or magazines for which your book would make an ideal fit? Is the timing of publication crucial to the sales of the book? Please indicate your speaking schedule, including past and future dates. Where do you see opportunities for media in all forms—online, radio, social media, TV, print—and what unique relationships do you have with the various media?

- ◆ **COMPETITION OR RELATED TITLES:** What other titles might this book relate to? Are there other titles published that discuss the same topic? How does your title offer a different approach? What information will the reader get from your book that isn't already out there? What are you providing that the current competition is not? Please include, author, title, publisher, page count, and publication date of the competitors' works.

- ◆ **BOOK SPECIFICATIONS:** How long will the book run? Are you interested in a special format? Are there any special design features anticipated, photographs, or maps?

- ◆ **SAMPLE CHAPTERS:** You will want to include three full sample chapters.

1. Understand the Agent's Role

You might be wondering whether you need an agent or even what they do. Whatever decision you make, it helps to remember that now that the industry has become exceedingly complicated, agents do a lot more than just sell manuscripts. So it's important to look at important considerations concerning today's market, as well as the different tasks agents handle, and why it might be to your benefit to have one.

Today, most of the major publishing houses take few, if any, unsolicited manuscripts. That means if you haven't been asked to submit your materials, they will be sent back to you or they may sit in a slush pile until (and if) someone notices it.

CHANGES IN THE INDUSTRY

- ◆ **INDUSTRY FLUIDITY:** The industry is constantly undergoing change. Historically, authors established relationships with editors and pretty much worked with those editors for most of their careers. Things have changed. Many editors now move from one house to the next. It's not rare to see editors work for as many as four to five different publishing houses during the span of their editorial careers. So the new anchor relationship involves the author and agent.

- ◆ **WHO WE KNOW COUNTS:** Agents devote considerable time to maintaining relationships with editors. I arrange at least two meetings a week with editors. If an editor changes houses, we make it our business to stay current about the types of books the editor is seeking. An editor's house might change, but that individual's standards and tastes generally remain fixed. It's difficult for individuals who are not following the business closely to remain current with editors.

- ◆ **AGENTS OPERATE ON EDITORS' TRUST:** Seasoned writers have said that securing an agent is just as difficult as finding an editor. Unfortunately, that can often be true. There's a reason for this. Agents and editors think alike. You'll find that many agents were editors first. Agents are keenly aware of a great story and what it takes to sell it to a house and then in the marketplace. It's not

surprising that editors trust agents. Securing an agent improves
your chances of getting your work published.

What an agent does:

- ◆ Reviews the client's work and offers advice on quality and
  marketability.

- ◆ Offers editorial advice.

- ◆ Offers advice on current trends and practices.

- ◆ Reviews and negotiates contracts on the client's behalf.

- ◆ Submits a client's work to appropriate editors.

- ◆ Acts as a representative to attract the interest of other business
  entities.

- ◆ Sells subrights, including movie options and merchandising.

- ◆ Advocates on behalf of a client in a publishing house, once a book
  is purchased.

- ◆ Strategizes with the author on how to improve her platform.

2. Find an Agent That Fits Your Needs

- ◆ **SOCIAL MEDIA:** The best possible way to find an agent is to have
  him or her approach you. That may sound impossible, but if you
  have followed many of the suggestions in this book—finding a
  niche, launching a blog, getting articles written about your writing,
  writing your own articles, writing a feature in highly circulated
  periodicals (print or online)—your strong platform will attract agents.

- ◆ **CONFERENCES:** Attend a writers' conference in which agents are
  scheduled to be in attendance. Read up on these agents before
  registering, to make sure they are interested in the memoir subgenre
  you've written.

- ◆ **REFERRALS:** Get a referral from a friend, classmate, or member of a writing group.

- ◆ **ACKNOWLEDGMENTS:** Read the acknowledgment pages of memoirs and find mentions of agents.

- ◆ **AGENT GUIDES:** Check with the Association of Authors' Representatives (www.aar-online.org); *The Guide to Literary Agents,* published annually by Writer's Digest Books; or *Jeff Herman's Guide to Book Publishers, Editors, and Literary Agents.*

- ◆ Read agent columns in *Writers Digest Online* (www.writersdigest .com).

- ◆ Check Publishers Marketplace and subscribe to publishers lunch (www.publishersmarketplace.com).

3. Research Agents and their Agencies

- ◆ Remember that not all agents are created equal.

- ◆ Narrow down your list after checking out agent Web sites, with an eye on authors and books the agent represents. You can also Google the agent's name.

- ◆ Pay attention to: how long the agent has been in business, location, commission structure, size of the agency, the number of listed clients, agent history, terms of representation—look for the qualities that serve you best.

- ◆ Remember that some new agents are hungry and will work harder to develop RUs, but they may not have as many connections.

As mentioned earlier, there's fluidity in the industry and that includes how agents are restructuring their business models. With new publishers emerging, such as Amazon, there's a paradigm shift. To match new market needs you will see agents starting a consulting business in conjunction with their agencies or as separate entities, to help authors develop their manuscripts. As a signed client of a literary agency you can still expect that an agent will do some minor tweaking of your manuscript and will offer advice on how to strengthen it. However, if it is determined that your work requires a more substantial revision the agent may suggest that you work with an outside editor or work with another part of their company to develop a proposal or receive more developmental attention.

Once controversial, fees were the mark of unregulated and potentially disreputable agencies and writers were told to steer clear. But reputable agencies are now expanding their offerings. And as we look to the future, agencies will continue to develop services to match market needs. You will find agencies that include publicity, social media, marketing, and the use of publishing tools such as Amazon's CreateSpace, Kindle Direct Publishing, Barnes & Noble's PubIt, Smashwords, and a host of others. In fact, some agents including me are becoming publishers as well.*

4. Prepare to Make Contact

- ◆ A query letter is the first piece of writing that an agent will see from you. If it's done well, it becomes the golden ticket and will open the door to you sending your full manuscript and proposal.

- ◆ Keep in mind that you will want to tailor query letters to each agent. You will probably have multiple agent names on your list. It is fine and even advisable that you approach numerous agents.

- ◆ Read submission guidelines. Most agents are very specific about how you should proceed—note which ones will accept e-mail or

---

*In 2010, I cofounded a new publishing venture called OPEN LENS, www.openlens.co, partnering with veteran literary agent Marie Brown and Marva Allen, owner of Hue-man Bookstore.

snail mail submissions. Many will discourage you from making multiple submissions, but most will understand the difficulty of finding an agent. Few expect you to short-circuit your process by insisting that you send queries out one at a time.

5. Understand the Components for a Query Letter

If the agency will allow you to send in snail mail submissions:

- Keep it at one page in length, to show you can write concisely.
- Use white or ivory paper.
- Use a twelve-point font, single line space, and black ink.
- Avoid fancy script, keep it simple and legible (Times New Roman is standard).
- Use a professional business-letter format.
- Avoid sending your query letter bound in a folder, binder, or any fancy wrapper.
- Pitch only one project per letter.
- Use a standard business envelope or mailer. Keep it simple and professional.
- Send your query via first-class mail unless you would like to track delivery with FedEx or UPS.

6. Compose a Query Letter

- Mention the person who has referred you—if you have been referred.
- Don't open with the fact that you are seeking representation.
- Include a one-sentence hook.
- Include no more than one paragraph that describes the book.

- Lead with a creative, catchy title.

- Make note of the manuscript's word count.

- Identify what you believe is the ideal audience for your work.

- If comparing your project to a popular work, make sure that your writing style, in addition to your topic, is similar.

- Describe your platform (blog, published articles, Twitter and Facebook followers, etc.) if you are concerned about the size of your platform refer to *Get Known Before the Book Deal: Use Your Personal Strengths to Grow an Author Platform,* by Christina Katz (Writers Digest Books: 2008).

- Describe your education, credentials, and writing experience as it pertains to the project.

- Be sure to include your contact information: if sending by snail mail include a self-addressed envelope with postage, include your e-mail address, as well as telephone number, physical address, Twitter handle, Facebook address, and Web site—if you have one.

- As a courtesy, indicate whether you are contacting multiple agents (no need to name the agents). You need only say this is a simultaneous submission.

7. Other Materials (Depending on Agent Submission Guidelines)

- Synopsis: In one page or less, briefly describe the book's subject and provide a sense of the structure.

- Sample pages or chapters: unless this is specifically discouraged in the submission requirements, include a couple of pages or an entire chapter.

- Avoid sending DVDs or suggesting that the agent download your project from a Web site. Agents typically do not want to download and print your materials. Many agents also use e-readers for submissions and prefer to review materials as a Microsoft Word document.

8. If You Get an Opportunity to Verbally Pitch Your Idea, Follow These Suggestions from Katherine Sands

- Don't begin your pitch with words such as "self-transformation" or "redemption" (they are overused) before others know the story.

- What sells the story is your personal journey.

- Remember: Your reader—or listener—has not yet read the book. While yours may be an intriguing premise, you need to use this as an opportunity to really bring the story to life, especially your own personal journey.

- Don't mention humor and satire if you aren't including any in your pitch.

- Live by the golden rule of pitching: Show, Don't Tell.

- You want to use the pitch to deliver enough of the flavor of the book to whet the agent's appetite for more.

- Make sure your pitch explains why the market needs this book, how that need can be satisfied, and why your project is unique.

- Other questions to consider, based on the Place, Person, Pivot approach (Where do you take the reader—what is the story's universe? Who do you introduce and why would anyone care about this person's story? At what point do you enter the story (at a lively and dramatic point)?

- Give a visual snapshot—fast.

- Don't open with the story's nadir—your story may start at a mind-numbing point, or you having hit rock bottom, but why choose these elements as the most interesting introduction?

- When you introduce any kind of information in a pitch, for example, your personal life, you must define it. Remember, you have lived these events, your readers haven't.

- Ask yourself whether you have introduced yourself and given reasons why the agent would want to spend time in your world.

- Your pitch will succeed if the agent can remember the three elements: Place, Person, and the Pivot Point (the point at which the tension is the highest and from that point on, things begins to change).

9. Learn to Play the Waiting Game

Refrain from phoning and e-mailing the agent after a few weeks, to ask about your submission. Follow up after five weeks, with a short e-mailed note. If the agent does not respond, move on. Not responding is rude, but keep in mind that most agents and their staff members read about two hundred queries a week, along with about four to six full manuscripts. This does not include authors on the agent's roster who are also sending new material.

Of course there are times when a manuscript gets regarded as worthy of an agent's immediate attentions, for reasons that include:

- The author has a great platform.

- The manuscript is extremely timely.

- The agent gets excited about the writing.

- The agent has met you at a conference and has made a commitment to read your manuscript right away. Conference-goers get priority because they have shown a commitment to developing themselves as writers, and in return, agents tend to give them priority.

10. Which Submissions Don't Get Read

◆ The author has not followed the required submission guidelines as indicated on the Web site. For example, at my agency, I no longer take snail mail submissions. I sometimes get calls from authors requesting to send me hard copy in the mail. My first reaction is to say no and to ask them to submit via e-mail. I've had people say they don't have access to the Internet or don't have an e-mail address. These are red flags for me. In today's Internet-driven marketplace it really is no longer acceptable to not be on the Internet. As discussed earlier, editors and agents think of social media as a requirement with authors, and participation is considered a benchmark for showing the sales viability of a work. Even if you have a thrilling story, once you signal that you can't promote it through technology, you will have lost the agent's attention.

If an agent asks you to submit your manuscript, be sure to follow the guidelines that the agent might suggest. If the agent does not provide guidelines, the following are standard specifications:

HEADER: 0.5 inch with the title of the memoir and your name on the left side and the page numbers on the right side.

MARGINS: 1 inch all around

LINE SPACING: Double or multiple for body text, single in long quotes

LINES PER PAGE: twenty-four or twenty-five

FONT: Times New Roman or Courier (not a mix, one or the other). Use a different font only if it is essential to the story (rare).

FONT SIZE: 12 point

RIGHT MARGIN: ragged

LEFT MARGIN: justified

Insert a page break instead of a series of returns at the end of a chapter or section.

PAGINATION: start chapter headings at the top of a new page.

Don't start a new chapter partway down the page.

PARAGRAPH INDENTS: five spaces, auto (don't type five blank spaces).

EXCLAMATION POINTS, COLONS, AND SEMICOLONS: Use sparingly, one or two per manuscript.

AFTERWORD

WE WROTE THIS BOOK TO BROADEN YOUR UNDERSTANDING about how to write, sell, and market a memoir. Our intent was to help you, but the work proved to be beneficial to us as well. After eighteen months of immersing ourselves in memoirs, our respect for this genre and memoirists only grew. Like William Deresiewicz, author of the highly praised *A Jane Austen Education: How Six Novels Taught Me About Love, Friendship, and the Things That Really Matter* (Penguin: 2011), our lives were enriched by the stories we read, our views of the world expanded.

Perhaps you are already familiar with Plato's Cave story, but it bears recounting here. In this cave, people are chained in place staring at a wall. Behind them, a fire blazes, and still farther beyond, a puppet show is occurring—and the shadows of these puppets are cast upon the wall.

The people believe that the shadows they're watching are real life. They know of no other reality. If they were to turn around and look at the light, it would at first seem abrasive and harsh, because they have lived in the shadows for such a long time.

Some of the harshest experiences in our reading required the protagonists to turn around, to take account of a world outside the confines of their lives. Riveted to the pages, we sometimes felt that we were turning around with them, growing and changing as they did. Our greatest hope for you is that you will write a story that turns readers around and encourages them to move toward the light. We hope to hear from you at www.youshouldreallywriteabook.com.

All the best,
Regina and Brenda

ENDNOTES

INTRODUCTION

3 The nontraditional route: David Streitfeld, "Amazon Signing Up Authors, Writing Publishers Out of Deal," *New York Times*, October 17, 2011, A1.

3 thirty authors of various genres: Alexandra Alter, "How I Became a Best-Selling Author," *Wall Street Journal*, December 9, 2011. http://online.wsj.com/article/SB10001424052970204770404577082303350815824.html.

4 as Robert Darnton explains: Robert Darnton, "5 Myths About the 'Information Age'," *Chronicle of Higher Education*, April 7, 2011. http://chronicle.com/article/5-Myths-About-the-Information/127105/.

4 133,000 self-published titles: Alter, "How I Became a Best-Selling Author."

4 an author can digitally format: Deirdre Donahue, "Self-published authors hit it big with e-books," *USA Today*, December 12, 2011. http://www.usatoday.com/life/usaedition/2011-12-13-cover-on-selfpublished-author-cv_u.htm.

8 U.S. publishing professionals often discuss: advertisement, *New York Times*, September 25, 2011, 34. (*Mediamark Research Incorporated*, Spring 2010).

10 A survey of the publishing landscape: Julie Bosman, "Publishing Gives Hints of Revival, Data Show," *New York Times*, August 9, 2011, C1.

11 opportunities for newspapers: Julie Bosman and Jeremy W. Peters, "In E-Books, Publishers Have Rivals: News Sites," *New York Times*, September 18, 2011. www.nytimes.com/2011/09/19/business/media/in-e-books-publishing-houses-have-a-rival-in-news-sites.html.

14 Critics so often denigrate: Neil Genzlinger, "The Problem With Memoirs," *New York Times*, January 28, 2011. www.nytimes.com/2011/01/30/books/review/Genzlinger-t.html.

16 Lee Gutkind, a professor: Lynn Neary, "One Family, Three Memoirs, Many Competing Truths," National Public Radio, May 25, 2011. http://m.npr.org/news/Books/136620260.

18 the paper's gravitational force: Jonah Berger, Alan T. Sorensen, and Scott J. Rasmussen, "Positive Effects of Negative Publicity: Can Negative Reviews Increase Sales?" *Marketing Science*, September/October 2010, vol. 29, no. 5815-827.

ONE: LEARNING FROM MEMOIR'S HISTORY

28 estimated one-third of U.S. newsrooms: Jean E. Herskowitz, *Editor and Publisher*, "Newspapers and Nonprofits Team Up for Investigative Journalism," July 26, 2011. www.editorandpublisher.com/Features/Article/Newspapers-and-Nonprofits-Team-Up-for-Investigative-Journalism.

28 the newspaper industry was half: David Carr, "Newspaper Barons Resurface," *New York Times*, April 9, 2012, B1.

29 the paper's popular Web site: Jack Shafer, "The Frank Rich Switch," *Slate*, March 1, 2011. www.slate.com/articles/news_and_politics/press_box/2011/03/the_frank_rich_switch.html.

32 *Narrative* sold 5,000 copies: Toni Morrison, in an essay, "The Site of Memory" from *Inventing the Truth: The Art and Craft of Memoir*, edited by William Zinsser (Houghton Mifflin: 1998), 188.

39 Mary Breasted, suggested that McCourt's: Bob Hoover, "Frank McCourt surprised naysayers," *Pittsburgh Post-Gazette*, July 26, 2009. www.post-gazette.com/pg/09207/985956-44.stm.

40 The author of *The Memoir Project*: "'Memoir Project' Gives Tips For Telling Your Story," National Public Radio, July 13, 2011. www.npr.org/2011/07/13/137822505/start-your-memoir-project-with-a-relatable-story.

41 She wrote in a diary that: Elizabeth Podnieks, *Daily Modernism: The Literary Diaries of Virginia Woolf, Antonia White, Elizabeth Smart, and Anaïs Nin* (McGill Queen's University: 2000), 142.

47 as far back as the Mesolithic period: Shelley Esaak, "Mesolithic Art—Art History 101 Basics," About.com Art History. http://arthistory.about.com/cs/arthistory10one/a/mesolithic.htm.

50 on CBS's *60 Minutes*: "Paul Allen and the birth of the PC, Microsoft," www.cbsnews.com/stories/2011/04/14/60minutes/main20086892.shtml.

55 Max told a *New York Times* interviewer: Dave Itzkoff, "Rude, Crude and Coming to a Theater Near You," *New York Times*, September 4, 2009. www.nytimes.com/2009/09/05/movies/05tucker.html.

55 In reviewing *Tiger, Tiger*: Kathryn Harrison, "The Man Who Molested Me," March 4, 2011, *New York Times Sunday Book Review*. www.nytimes.com/2011/03/06/books/review/Harrison-t.html?pagewanted=all.

56 "Is there anyone more likeable than Jon-Jon Gouilan?": Christopher Glazek, "Dude . . . Where'd You Get That Sarong? Jon-Jon Gouilan's 'Man in the Gray Flannel Skirt'" *New York Observer*, May 3, 2011. www.observer.com/2011/culture/dudedudewhered-you-get-sarong-0.

57 wrote in a National Public Radio review: Dan Kois, "A Party Boy Reflects On Life, Lip Gloss," National Public Radio, May 16, 2011. www.npr.org/2011/07/14/136242022/a-partyboy-reflects-on-life-lip-gloss.

57 According to the *New York Post*: "'Skirt' too small for the hype," *New York Post*, June 23, 2011. www.nypost.com/p/pagesix/skirt_too_small_for_the_hype_voThuea7vbVhF5EtQxONPK.

59 Stanford University offered a no-credit: John Markoff, "Virtual and Artificial, but 58,000 Want Course," *New York Times*, August 15, 2011. www.nytimes.com/2011/08/16/science/16stanford.html.

60 a cancer survival story: Dwight Garner, "Sex, Drugs and E Chords While Seeking Remission," *New York Times*, December 20, 2011. www.nytimes.com/2011/12/21/books/sic-a-memoir-by-joshua-cody-review.html.

62 President Obama contributed $100,000: Cary Stemle, "The Greg Mortenson Scandal: One University's Bitter Cup of Tea," *Time* magazine, April 20, 2011. www.time.com/time/nation/article/0,8599,2066239,00.html.

62 *60 Minutes* segment charged Mortensen: "Questions over Greg Mortenson's stories," CBS News, April 15, 2011. www.cbsnews.com/stories/2011/04/15/60minutes/main20054397.shtml.

63 Herman Rosenblat, a Jewish Holocaust survivor: Motoko Rich and Joseph Berger, "False Memoir of Holocaust Is Canceled," *New York Times*, December 28, 2008. www.nytimes.com/2008/12/29/books/29hoax.html?pagewanted=all.

63 incidents were not entirely verifiable: Geraldine Bedell, "Child abuse as entertainment," *Guardian*, September 2, 2001. www.guardian.co.uk/books/2001/sep/02/biography.features.

63 sued for defamation: "Turcotte Family Settles With Burroughs, St. Martin's in Running With Scissors Suit," *Poets & Writers*, August 30, 2007. www.pw.org/content/turcotte_family_settles_burroughs_st_martin039s_running_scissors_suit?cmnt_all=1.

63 their different perspectives served: Lynn Neary, "One Family, Three Memoirs, Many Competing Truths," National Public Radio, May 25, 2011. www.npr.org/2011/05/25/136620260/one-family-three-memoirs-many-competing-truths.

64 a journalist accused him of getting dates and other: "Neither Side Backing Down in Ishmael Beah Memoir Dispute," *Poets & Writers* (online only), January 24, 2008. www.pw.org/content/neither_side_backing_down_ishmael_beah_memoir_dispute?cmnt_all=1.

64 even Tolstoy's masterpiece: Mark Mazower, "'War and Peace': The Fact-Check," *New York Times Book Review*, June 18, 2010. www.nytimes.com/2010/06/20/books/review/Mazower-t.html.

64 a highly regarded writing teacher: Judith Barrington, *Writing the Memoir: A Practical Guide to the Craft, the Personal Challenges, and Ethical Dilemmas of Writing True Stories* (Eighth Mountain Press: 2004), 27.

64 addressed the slipperiness of truth: Touré, "Malcolm X: Criminal, Minister, Humanist, Martyr," *New York Times Book Review*, June 17, 2011. http://www.nytimes.com/2011/06/19/books/review/book-review-malcolm-x-by-manning-marable.html?pagewanted=all.

66 writer criticized the author: "Her Last Death: A Memoir," *Publishers Weekly*, October 8, 2007. www.publishersweekly.com/978-0-7432-9108-8.

67 Walter Mosley suggested: Walter Mosley, "In an L.A. Childhood, the First Mysteries," *New York Times*, November 2, 2011. www.nytimes.com/2011/11/03/garden/walter-mosley-in-an-la-childhood-the-first-mysteries.html?pagewanted=all.

THREE: COMING-OF-AGE MEMOIRS

75 how she wowed Simon Cowell: "Susan Boyle-Britans Got Talent 2009-The woman who shut Simon Cowell." www.youtube.com/watch?v=S9t8evolgzE.

76 Karr is a child, riding in a car: excerpt from Mary Karr, *The Liars' Club* (Viking: 1995), 90.

77 a rarity for poetry: Julie Bosman, "Poet Laureate's Book Sales Soar," *New York Times*, August 12, 2011, C2.

79 concerts at Versailles. Eire writes: excerpt from Carlos Eire, *Waiting for Snow in Havana: Confessions of a Cuban Boy* (Free Press: 2004), 4.

82 an NPR critic wrote: Rachel Syme, "What We're Reading," National Public Radio, April 12, 2011. www.npr.org/2011/07/14/135326866/what-were -reading-april-12-18.

84–85 Ebert said of the film's protagonists: Roger Ebert, "The Best Films of 2011," *Chicago Sun Times*, December 15, 2011. http://blogs.suntimes.com/ ebert/2011/12/the_best_films_of_2011.html.

94 driven by the question of: "Briefly Noted: Cocktail Hour Under the Tree of Forgetfulness," *The New Yorker*, September 5, 2011, 79. www.newyorker.com/ arts/reviews/brieflynoted/2011/09/05/110905crbn_brieflynoted3.

95 the reviewer praising the author: *Publishers Weekly*, "The Other Wes Moore: One Name and Two Fates—A Story of Tragedy and Hope," March 8, 2010. www.publishersweekly.com/978-0-385-52819-1.

95 also received a starred review: Vanessa Bush, "The Other Wes Moore: One Name, Two Fates," *Booklist* Online, May 1, 2010. www.booklistonline.com/ The-Other-Wes-Moore-One-Name-Two-Fates-Wes-Moore/pid=4055603.

96 74 percent of people in the U.S. have: "74% Have Favorable Opinion of U.S. Military," *Rasmussen Reports*, May 29, 2010. www.rasmussenreports.com/ public_content/lifestyle/holidays/may_2010/74_have_favorable_opinion_of _u_s_military.

FOUR: ADDICTION AND COMPULSION MEMOIRS

99 13 percent of the U.S. population. "Former Addict Helps Families Of The Afflicted," National Public Radio, March 17, 2010. www.npr.org/templates/ story/story.php?storyId=124775878.

99 Amy Winehouse: Associated Press "Coroner Rules Amy Winehouse Died From Alcohol Poisoning," ABC News, October 26, 2011. http://abcnews .go.com/blogs/health/2011/10/26/coroner-rules-amy-winehouse-died-from -alcohol-poisoning.

99 Lindsay Lohan: Associated Press, "Lindsay Lohan Arrested on Suspicion of DUI, Cocaine Possession After Car Chase," Fox News online, July 25, 2007. www.foxnews.com/story/0,2933,290544,00.html.

99 Charlie Sheen: Alex Crees, "Charlie Sheen: How Much Abuse Can He Take?" Fox News online, January 28, 2011. www.foxnews.com/health/2011/01/ 28/charlie-sheen-abuse.

99 Robert Downey Jr: Walter Kirn, "The Tao of Robert Downey Jr.," *Rolling Stone*, May 2010. http://www.rollingstone.com/movies/news/the-tao-of-robert-downey-jr-the-new-issue-of-rolling-stone-20100429.

99 Michael Jackson: Russell Goldman, "Michael Jackson Had 'Lethal Levels' of Propofol Before Death," ABC News, August 24, 2009. http://abcnews.go.com/Entertainment/MichaelJackson/story?id=8401979#.Ty_76hyQccM.

99 Kate Moss: "H&M drops Moss over drug claims," BBC News, September 20, 2005. http://news.bbc.co.uk/2/hi/4263792.stm.

99 Keith Richard: "Keith Richards Did Drugs and Other ~~Shocking~~ Obvious Facts From 'Life,'" *Atlantic*, October 28, 2010. www.theatlantic.com/entertainment/archive/2010/10/keith-richards-did-drugs-and-other-del-shocking-del-obvious-facts-from-life/65287.

99 Whitney Houston: Dahvi Shira and Anne Marie Cruz, "Whitney Houston in Rehab for Drug and Alcohol Treatment," *People*, May 09, 2011. www.people.com/people/article/0,,20488032,00.html.

99 Britney Spears: Ken Lee, "Judge: Britney a 'Habitual' User of Alcohol, Drugs," *People*, September 18, 2007. www.people.com/people/article/0,,20057621,00.html.

99 Kiefer Sutherland: Alex Tresniowski, "48 Days in Jail for DUI: Can Kiefer Stop Drinking?" *People*, October 29, 2007. www.people.com/people/archive/article/0,,20160869,00.html.

99 Aldous Huxley: David J. Linden, "Addictive Personality? You Might be a Leader," *New York Times*, July 23, 2011. www.nytimes.com/2011/07/24/opinion/sunday/24addicts.html.

99 William Faulkner: "Famous Literary Drunks and Addicts," *Life* magazine. http://life.time.com.

99 John Cheever: "Famous Literary Drunks and Addicts," *Life*.

99 Ernest Hemmingway: "Famous Literary Drunks and Addicts," *Life*.

99 F. Scott Fitzgerald: "Famous Literary Drunks and Addicts," *Life*.

99 James Baldwin: "Famous Literary Drunks and Addicts," *Life*.

99 Stephen King: Stephen King, *On Writing* (Scribner: 2000).

99 use of buzz-creating substances: Meredith F. Small, "Drug Addiction? Blame it on Evolution," *Cosmos*, Issue 4, September 2005. www.cosmosmagazine.com/features/print/3456/state-mind.

100 "vividly rendered": David Carr, "Crack Agent," *New York Times Book Review*, June 25, 2010. http://www.nytimes.com/2010/06/27/books/review/Carr-t.html.

100 "brutally specific and oddly poetic": Susan Juby, "A Crack in the Mirror," *Globe and Mail*, June 25, 2010. www.theglobeandmail.com/news/arts/books/article1617834.ece.

100 Clegg's agent is said: Denny Lee, "Tale of a Life, Unabridged," *New York Times*, May 28, 2010. www.nytimes.com/2010/05/30/fashion/30CLEGG.html ?src=mv.

102 Despite a wealth of evidence suggesting: Linden, "Addictive Personality? You Might be a Leader."

102 explained that this: Carr, "Crack Agent."

103 tried unsuccessfully to sell his: Evgenia Peretz, "James Frey's Morning After," *Vanity Fair*, June 2008. www.vanityfair.com/culture/features/2008/06/ frey200806.

104 excerpt of *Portrait* and photos of Clegg ran: Bill Clegg, "Flying," *New York Magazine*, May 23, 2010. http://nymag.com/arts/books/features/66183.

104 circulation of 405,000: Jack Shafer, "The Frank Rich Switch," *Slate*, March 1, 2011. http://www.slate.com/articles/news_and_politics/press_box/ 2011/03/the_frank_rich_switch.html.

104 "Sunday Styles" section: Denny Lee, "Tale of a Life, Unabridged," *New York Times*, May 28, 2010.

104 David Carr's review: Carr, "Crack Agent."

104 including one in *Vogue*: Jonathan Van Meter, "Portrait of an Addict as a Young Man," *Vogue*, May 25, 2010. http://www.vogue.com/culture/article/vd -books-portrait-of-an-addict-as-a-young-man.

105 His publisher reportedly contracted: Denny Lee, "Tale of a Life, Unabridged," *New York Times*, May 28, 2010. Odyl cofounder and CEO: Judith Rosen, "Odyl Launches Facebook Marketing Platform for Publishing," *Publishers Weekly*, September 12, 2011. http://www.publishersweekly.com/pw/by-topic/ industry-news/bookselling/article/48655-odyl-launches-facebook-marketing -platform-for-publishing.html.

110 a study on the palliative affect of music: David H. Bradshaw, Gary W. Donaldson, Robert C. Jacobson, Yoshio Nakamura, C. Richard Chapman, "Individual Differences in the Effects of Music Engagement on Responses to Painful Stimulation," *Journal of Pain*, vol. 12, issue 12, 1262–73. www.jpain.org/ article/S1526-5900(11)00745-0/abstract.

113 Julie Myerson described how: "The Julie Myerson Controversy," The Book Show, ABC Radio National, April 3, 2009. www.abc.net.au/radionational/ programs/bookshow/the-julie-myerson-controversy/3136042.

114 Dani Shapiro, the author: Dani Shapiro, "The Me My Child Mustn't Know," *New York Times Book Review*, July 14, 2011, BR27.

118 *Publishers Weekly* described: "Loose Girl: A Memoir of Promiscuity," *Publishers Weekly*, February 11, 2008.

119 A *Kirkus* reviewer wrote: "What's Left of Us," *Kirkus Reviews*, June 1, 2009. http://www.kirkusreviews.com/book-reviews/richard-farrell/whats-left-of-us.

120 Farrell's fans have reason to be hopeful: *Boston Globe*, "Richie Farrell's Heroin Addiction Nearly Killed Him, But He Lived to Write About It," August 18, 2009, 10.

FIVE: TRANSFORMATION MEMOIRS

125 echoing a similar sentiment: Maureen Corrigan, "The 'Unbroken' Spirit Of An Ordinary Hero," National Public Radio, December 1, 2010. http://www .npr.org/2010/12/01/131724901/the-unbroken-spirit-of-an-ordinary-hero.

140 the emotion of disgust: Josie Glausiusz, "The Biology of . . . Disgust," *Discover*, December 1, 2002. http://discovermagazine.com/2002/dec/featbiology.

140 Rachel Herz, a Brown University researcher: Robin Marantz Henig, "What We Find Gross and Why," *New York Times Book Review*, January 20, 2012, 12.

142 including the one that follows: excerpt from Ishmael Beah, *A Long Way Gone: Memoirs of a Boy Soldier* (Farrar, Straus and Giroux: 2007), 27.

147 more than five hundred public radio: This American Life Web Site, About Us. http://www.thisamericanlife.org/about.

148 praise heaped upon first-time author: Christopher Lehmann-Haupt, "Lucy Grealy, 39, Who Wrote a Memoir on Her Disfigurement," *New York Times* obituary, December 21, 2002. http://www.nytimes.com/2002/12/21/arts/lucy-grealy -39-who-wrote-a-memoir-on-her-disfigurement.html.

148 Alice Sebold was a graduate student: *The Encyclopedia of World Biography*, "Alice Seabold." http://www.notablebiographies.com/newsmakers2/2005 -Pu-Z/Sebold-Alice.html.

149 finishing his manuscript: Bob Hoover, "Frank McCourt Surprised Naysayers," *Pittsburgh Post-Gazette*, July 26, 2009. www.post-gazette.com/pg/09207/ 985956-44.stm#ixzz1itoEJQbM.

157 and the instructor intones: excerpt from Howard E. Wasdin and Stephen Templin, "A Veteran of SEAL Team Six Describes His Training," book excerpt of *SEAL Team Six: Memoirs of an Elite Navy SEAL Sniper* (St. Martin's: 2011), *Vanity Fair*, May 4, 2011. www.vanityfair.com/politics/features/2011/05/navy-seal-team -six-excerpt-201105.

158 "visceral and as active as": Michiko Kakutani, "Muscle Memory: The Training of Navy Seals Commandos," *New York Times*, May 8, 2011. www .nytimes.com/2011/05/09/books/seal-team-six-and-the-heart-and-the-fist-reviews .html?pagewanted=all.

SIX: TRAVEL AND FOOD MEMOIRS

161 He wrote of a group of female mill workers: excerpt from Charles Dickens, *American Notes for General Circulation* (Chapman & Hall: 1842), 77.

167 when she writes of Milan: excerpt from Barbara Grizzuti Harrison, *Italian Days* (Grove: 1989), 8.

168 Santa Maria del Calcinaio: excerpt from Frances Mayes, *Under the Tuscan Sun: At Home and in Italy* (Chronicle: 1996), 155.

168 A *Salon* reviewer: Scott Sutherland, "Passage to Juneau: A Sea and It's Meanings, by Jonathan Raban," *Salon*, October 26, 1999. Salon.com/1999/10/26/raban/.

175 *Chicago Tribune* praised *Cakewalk*: Jane Ciabattari, 'Cakewalk: A Memoir' by Kate Moses," *Chicago Tribune*. http://www.chicagotribune.com/entertainment/books/chi-books-cakewalk-a-memoir-moses,0,5707901.story.

177 she was praised with a starred review: "Climbing the Mango Trees: A Memoir of Childhood in India," *Publishers Weekly*, August 14, 2006. www.publishers weekly.com/1978-1-4000-4295-1.

177 can be felt also in: Don George, "Trip Lit: Maman's Homesick Pie, by Donia Bijan," *National Geographic Traveler*, October 2011. http://travel.nationalgeographic.com/travel/traveler-magazine/trip-lit/mamans-homesick-pie.

185 a starred review: "Daughter of Heaven: A Memoir of Earthly Recipes," *Publishers Weekly*, March 3, 2005. http://www.publishersweekly.com/978-1-55970-768-8.

187 she would enjoy. She writes: excerpt from Julia Alvarez, "Picky Eater," from *We Are What We Eat: 24 Memories of Food*, edited by Mark Winegardner (Harcourt Brace: 2008), 19.

SEVEN: RELIGION AND SPIRITUALITY MEMOIRS

190 More than 90 percent of: Frank Newport, "More Than 9 in 10 Americans Continue to Believe in God," Gallup Poll, June 3, 2011. www.gallup.com/poll/147887/americans-continue-believe-god.aspx.

190 Back in 1997 Meredith McGuire's essay: Meredith McGuire, "Mapping Contemporary American Spirituality: A Sociological Perspective," *Christian Spirituality Bulletin* 5 (Spring 1997), 4. 3.

191 A February 17, 2010, Pew Research study: "Religion Among the Millennials," The Pew Forum on Religion & Public Life, February 17, 2010. www.pewforum.org/Age/Religion-Among-the-Millennials.aspx.

192 Gallup Survey of December 23, 2011: "Poll: 78 percent in U.S. are Christians," UPI, December 23, 2011. www.upi.com/Top_News/US/2011/12/23/Poll78-percent-in-US-are-Christians/UPI-94171324668702.

192 Mark Kuyper, chief executive: Jeffrey A. Trachtenberg, "HarperCollins Acquires Religion-Book Publisher," *Wall Street Journal*, November 1, 2011.

192 In 1998, HarperCollins: Julie Bosman, "HarperCollins Acquires Religious

Book Publisher," *New York Times*, October 31, 2011. mediadecoder.blogs.nytimes.com/2011/10/31/harpercollins-acquires-religious-book-publisher.

193 According to a December 2009 Pew: "Many Americans Mix Multiple Faiths," The Pew Forum on Religion & Public Life, December 9, 2009. www.pewforum.org/other-beliefs-and-practices/many-americans-mix-multiple-faiths.aspx.

194 Leonard Riggio, the chairman: Julie Bosman, "Unusual Benefactor Finances Book Tour" *New York Times*, September 16, 2011. www.nytimes.com/2011/09/17/books/barnes-noble-chief-finances-book-tour.html.

195 and its Christian roots: Philip Sheldrake, *A Brief History of Spirituality* (Blackwell: 2007), 1–2.

195 gratitude can lead people to feel: Robert A. Emmons and Michael E. McCullough, *The Psychology of Gratitude* (Oxford USA: 2004).

198 Genesis, writes: [quotation from] Bruce Feiler, "Walking the Bible Reading Guide," http://brucefeiler.com/books/walking-the-bible/readers-guide/.

199 in the story in uppercase: [quotation from] Rebecca Nichols Alonzo with Bob DeMoss, *The Devil in Pew Number Seven* (Tyndale: 2011).

201 editor Robert Giroux: Robert Giroux, "Thomas Merton's Durable Mountain," *New York Times*, October 11, 1998. http://www.nytimes.com/books/98/10/11/bookend/bookend.html.

203 Elmore Leonard, whose bestselling: Nick Paumgarten, "Detroit Valentine," *New Yorker*, December 12, 2011. www.newyorker.com/talk/2011/12/12/111212ta_talk_paumgarten#ixzz1izen1ml9.

206 A *Publishers Weekly* starred review: "The Bread of Angels: A Memoir of Love and Faith in Damascus," January 11, 2010. www.publishersweekly.com/978-0-385-52200-7.

206 *O* magazine described: Cathleen Medwick, "Children of Dust," *O* magazine, November 2009. www.oprah.com/omagazine/Os-Fall-Reading-Guide-Book-Reviews/4.

210 Pew Research Center, told: Jennifer Preston, "Media Decoder; Top Social Topics in '11: Bin Laden and Mubarak," *New York Times*, January 2, 2012. http://query.nytimes.com/gst/fullpage.html?res=9D04E1DD1E3CF931A35752C0A9649D8B6.

210 According to Beliefnet: Sharon Kirk, "Beliefnet Announces Web Channel with Jesus Daily," August 31, 2011. www.beliefnet.com/About-Us/Press-Releases/Jesus-Daily-Partnership.aspx.

211 Sexless in the City blog: Heidi Benson, "Anna Broadway, SWF, seeks wild celibate time," *San Francisco Chronicle*, May 4, 2008. www.sfgate.com/cgi-bin/article.cgi?f=/c/a/2008/05/02/LV1H106PVI.DTL.

211 "spicy and funny Gen-X memoir": "Sexless in the City: A Memoir of Re-

luctant Chastity," *Publishers Weekly*, February 25, 2008. www.publishersweekly
.com/978-0-385-51839-0.

213 an O magazine reviewer wrote: Cathleen Medwick, "Take This Bread," *O*
magazine, March 2007. www.oprah.com/book/Take-This-Bread-by-Sara-Miles.

EIGHT: OUTLIER SUBGENRES

216 her ability to celebrate: Donna Seaman, "The Possessed: Adventures
with Russian Books and the People Who Read Them," *Booklist*, February 15,
2010. http://www.booklistonline.com/The-Possessed-Adventures-with-Russian
-Books-and-the-People-Who-Read-Them-Elif-Batuman/pid=3794656.

221 Kate Pickert pointed out: Kate Pickert, "Our Puppies Ourselves, *Time*,
January 17, 2011. http://www.time.com/time/magazine/article/0,9171,2041093
,00.html.

227 described it as "a quiet, fierce work": "Let's Take the Long Way Home: A
Memoir of Friendship," *Publishers Weekly*, May 24, 2010. http://www.publishers
weekly.com/978-1-4000-6738-1.

227 the author had created: "Lives Other Than Our Own," *New Yorker*, December 12, 2011, 89.

228 The inmate memoirist should be aware of the Son of Sam law that was
designed to prevent convicted criminals from profiting financially from the publicity of their crime. For details refer to http://www.freedomforum.org/packages/
first/SonOfSam/index.htm.

228 with convicted murderer: *Variety*, "Jack Henry Abbott," February 12,
2002, http://www.variety.com/article/VR1117860666?refCatId=25.

228 former journalist and Black Panther: Timothy Williams, "Execution Case
Dropped Against Abu-Jamal," *New York Times*, December 7, 2011. http://www
.nytimes.com/2011/12/08/us/execution-case-dropped-against-convicted-cop
-killer.html.

NINE: RUS WORKING WITH COLLABORATORS

241 An O magazine reviewer: Peter Cameron, "Trouble in Bedford," *O* magazine, October 2009. http://www.oprah.com/omagazine/The-Kids-Are-All-Right
-by-Diana-Liz-Amanda-and-Dan-Welch-Review.

INDEX